Reassessing Political Ideologies

!

'A volume of first class essays by top class contributors, all of whom are acknowledged experts in their field.' *Jeremy Jennings, University of Birmingham*

'The editor opens and closes the volume with conceptual and methodological considerations, and each essay in between offers an insightful and readable reassessment of a particular ideology. This book is "must" reading for any student of the subject.' *Terence Ball, Arizona State University*

'It is often said that we live in a post-ideological age. This important new collection of essays by leading scholars dispels that notion by revealing the subtlety, vitality and complexity of ideological argument in contemporary political thought.' *Andrew Gamble, University of Sheffield*

Reassessing Political Ideologies brings together expert analyses of the development – and current state – of the major political ideologies of the twentieth century. Ideologies, despite recent political upheavals and crucial transformations throughout the past century, are still very much with us. This book offers both a framework for understanding the nature of ideology today and a re-evaluation of the dominant Western political belief systems, with particular regard to their evolution and the differences between them.

The following ideologies are discussed: liberalism, Marxism and post-Marxism, socialism, conservatism, Christian democracy, fascism, the radical right, nationalism, feminism and green political thought. The introductory and concluding chapters by Michael Freeden offer new tools for understanding ideologies that take account of recent ideological fragmentation and recombination, and advance the micro-analysis of ideologies. These studies reveal significant changes in both the presentation of ideologies and their substance.

The renowned specialist political theorists and historians, who engage with ideologies from a number of methodological perspectives, demonstrate to sceptics that ideologies are an ineliminable dimension in thinking about politics. Through their combination of continuity and malleability, ideologies remain central resources for political systems.

Michael Freeden is Professor of Politics at the University of Oxford and Professorial Fellow, Mansfield College, Oxford. He is the author of a number of books including *The New Liberalism*, *Liberalism Divided*, *Rights*, and *Ideologies and Political Theory*. He is the founding editor of the *Journal of Political Ideologies*, published by Taylor & Francis Ltd under the Routledge imprint.

Reassessing Political Ideologies

The durability of dissent

Edited by Michael Freeden

London and New York

This book is based on a series of articles that originally appeared in the *Journal of Political Ideologies*. Chapters 3, 9, 11 and 12 were written especially for the volume. I would like to thank Craig Fowlie of Routledge for his support and efficiency, and the contributors for their whole-hearted collaboration on the project.

First published 2001
by Routledge
11 New Fetter Lane, London EC4P 4EE

Simultaneously published in the USA and Canada
by Routledge
29 West 35th Street, New York, NY 10001

Routledge is an imprint of the Taylor & Francis Group

© 2001 Michael Freeden for selection and editorial matter;
individual chapters, the contributors

Typeset in 10/12pt Baskerville by
The Running Head Limited, Cambridge
Printed and bound in Great Britain by
The Cromwell Press, Trowbridge, Wiltshire

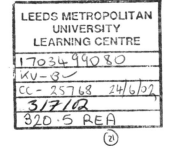
British Library Cataloguing in Publication Data
A catalogue record for this book is available
from the British Library

Library of Congress Cataloging in Publication Data
Reassessing political ideologies: the durability of dissent/edited by Michael Freeden.
   p. cm.
Includes bibliographical references and index.
   1. Ideology—History—20th century 2. Political science—History—20th century.
I. Freeden, Michael.
 JA83   R43 2001
 320.5'09'04—dc21   2001019501

ISBN 0–415–25573–2
ISBN 0–415–25572–4 (pbk)

Contents

Contributors

Terrell Carver is Professor of Political Theory at the University of Bristol. He has degrees from Columbia University and the University of Oxford, and has published widely on Marx and Engels. His most recent book is *The Postmodern Marx* (Manchester University Press, 1998), and he has also done the new translations of *Marx's Later Political Writings* (Cambridge University Press, 1996).

Diana Coole is Professor of Political Theory and head of department at Queen Mary and Westfield College, University of London. She is the author *of Women in Political Theory*, Harvester-Wheatsheaf, second edition 1993, and *Negativity and Politics*, Routledge, 2000. She is currently writing a book for Routledge on Merleau-Ponty and the Political.

Robert Eccleshall is Professor of Politics at the School of Politics of the Queen's University of Belfast, and Head of the School. He is the author of *English Conservatism Since the Restoration* (1990) and the co-author of *Political Ideologies* (second edition, 1994; third edition, forthcoming). He is also co-editor of *Western Political Thought: A Bibliographical Guide to Post-War Research* (1995), *Biographical Dictionary of British Prime Ministers* (1998) and *Political Discourse in Seventeenth and Eighteenth Century Ireland* (2001).

Michael Freeden is Professor of Politics at Oxford University and Professorial Fellow of Mansfield College, Oxford. Among his books are *The New Liberalism: An Ideology of Social Reform*, Clarendon Press, 1978; *Liberalism Divided: A Study in British Political Thought 1914–1939*, Clarendon Press, 1986; *Reappraising J.A. Hobson* (ed.), Unwin Hyman, 1990; *Rights*, Open University Press, 1991; *Ideologies and Political Theory: A Conceptual Approach*, Clarendon Press, 1996. He is the founder-editor of the *Journal of Political Ideologies*.

Gerald F. Gaus is Professor of Philosophy and Political Science at Tulane University, New Orleans. He has been Research Fellow at the Australian National University and Visiting Scholar at the Social Philosophy and Policy Center, Bowling Green State University. He is the author of *The Modern Liberal Theory of Man* (1983), *Value and Justification* (1990), *Justificatory Liberalism* (1996), *Social Philosophy* (1999) and *Political Theories and Political Concepts* (2000). He is co-editor of *Public and Private in Social Life* (1983) and *Public Reason* (1998), and of Bernard Bosanquet's *The Philosophical Theory of the State and Related Essays* (2000). Professor Gaus is an editor of the *Australasian Journal of Philosophy*.

Roger Griffin is Professor of History of Ideas at Oxford Brookes University. He is the author of *The Nature of Fascism* (1991, 1993), and editor of *Fascism* (1995) and *International Fascism: Theories, Causes, and the New Consensus* (1998). In addition he has published widely articles and chapters on comparative aspects of interwar fascism as well as neo-fascism and new forms of the radical right, nationalism, racism, modernity and globalization. He is at present working on a major study of the relationship between modernity, modernism and fascism.

James Meadowcroft is a Reader in the Department of Politics at the University of Sheffield. His research interests are focused on political ideologies and environmental politics. His publications include *Conceptualizing the State: Innovation and Dispute in British Political Thought 1880–1914*, Oxford University Press, 1995; *Democracy and the Environment* (ed., with William Lafferty), Edward Elgar, 1997 and *Planning Sustainability* (ed., with Michael Kenny), Routledge, 1999.

Paolo Pombeni is Professor of European History at the Faculty of Political Sciences, University of Bologna. Editor of the journal *Ricerche di Storia Politica*. Main works: *Demagogia e tirannide. Uno studio sulla forma partito del fascismo*, Il Mulino, 1984; *Partiti e sistemi politici nella storia contemporanea*, Il Mulino, 1994, third revised edition; French translation, PUF, 1992; *Autorità sociale e potere politico nell'Italia contemporanea*, Marsilio, 1993; *Lo stato e la politica*, Il Mulino, 1997. At present he is completing a volume about *The Democracy of Affluence. Politics in Europe 1945–1969* and has started a new study: *The People and Its Leaders. The Backbone of Western Constitutionalism*.

Donald Sassoon is Professor of Comparative European History at Queen Mary and Westfield College, University of London. He is the author of numerous books, essays and articles on twentieth-century European history and politics (especially Italy). His *One Hundred Years of Socialism*, Fontana, won the Deutscher Prize 1997 and is being translated in several languages. He is completing a book on the construction of the popularity of Leonardo's *Mona Lisa* and has embarked on a history of cultural markets in Europe since 1800.

Zeev Sternhell is an historian of ideas working on the nineteenth and twentieth centuries. He holds the Léon Blum chair of Political Science at the Hebrew University in Jerusalem. He is the author, among works in several languages, of *Neither Right nor Left: Fascist Ideology in France* (1986); *The Birth of Fascist Ideology: From Cultural Rebellion to Political Revolution* (1994) and most recently, *The Founding Myths of Israel: Nationalism, Socialism and the Making of the Jewish State* (1997). The three books have been published by Princeton University Press.

Andrew Vincent is Professor of Political Theory, University of Sheffield (formerly Professor of Political Theory, University of Cardiff), life member of the Collingwood Society, and Senior Fellow in Humanities, Research Center, Australian National University. He is author of *Modern Political Ideologies* (1992 and second edition 1995); and co-author of *A Radical Hegelian: The Social and Political Philosophy of Henry Jones* (1993) and most recently *British Idealism and Political Theory* (2000). He is also co-editor of *G.W.F. Hegel's Philosophical Propaedeutic* (1986), and *Political Theory: Tradition and Diversity* (1997).

1 Political ideologies in substance and method

Appraising a transformation

Michael Freeden

Developments and disputes

The advent of a new millennium has been a good excuse for much taking of stock, and this volume takes advantage of that opportunity to direct a retrospective, and a tentatively prospective, eye at some of the major ideological currents of the past century, and to assess them in line with current scholarly understandings. In this introduction I have not followed the conventional practice of commenting on the subsequent chapters. That commentary is proffered at the end of the book, in the form of several second-order thoughts. Readers may quite properly prefer to permit the various contributors to speak first for themselves, savouring their multifarious and reflective arguments to which no commentary can do justice. The basic approach shared by all of the contributors is to locate ideologies at the heart of the political process, constituting as they do a mainstay of the art of politics, and to recognize that their colossal impact on the course of past and present events requires their detailed analysis from a viewpoint that is fundamentally sympathetic rather than hostile to their natures and roles. As vehicles of dissent ideologies are an indispensable resource for the intelligent conducting and re-inventing of politics in its variegated forms. As families of political thought displaying clear consensual patterns and continuities, ideologies are a vital and energizing ingredient in the fashioning of group identities and policies. In both these forms they are scarcely a flash in the pan but a durable and ineliminable facet of social life, at once creative and consolidating.

Some years ago, Karl Dietrich Bracher wrote a book about twentieth-century political thought entitled *The Age of Ideologies*.[1] That title summons up a couple of diverse questions: to what extent has that been the case and, alternatively, can we now imagine an age without ideologies? Bracher had a particular conception of ideologies in mind: grandiose, abstract and threatening. Undoubtedly, the century has experienced clashes of such titans, with the emergence of mass politics and sophisticated modes of recruiting popular support and activism. Undoubtedly, it has also seen the rapid rise and fall of an ideology such as fascism and a rather more protracted process with regard to communism, though to proclaim their death would still be premature. It has been fascinated by the power of totalitarian ideologies, sweeping all impediments and opposition in their paths like an avalanche. But these very ideologies have provoked enormous resistance and abhorrence. Those reactions have created in the Western world a coalition of convenience with Marxist critics of ideology – a coalition eager to assume a world immune to, and transcending, the noxious distortions of ideology. But take away the menace of ideology, both as practice and as word, and you no longer require the protection, either. If ideologies are normal and extensive forms of thought rather than aberrations, and if they occur in more modest – though by no means less influential – forms, we might as well begin to search for some of the benefits they bestow on their host societies. We need to take them seriously; we may even have to treat them with respect.

So where do we stand in the new century? That question needs to run on two parallel, though interrelated, axes: what is the state of concrete ideologies, and what is the state of the study of ideologies? Twice, in the mid-twentieth century and towards its end, we have been informed that the age of ideologies is over. Twice this has proved to be incorrect. But here the students of ideology have been at fault, for failing to identify as ideologies certain phenomena placed right under their eyes, and for mistaking ideological convergence for ideological invisibility, while concurrently predicting with confidence the end of radical ideational dissent. However, the end of ideology would be – to put it simply – no less than the end of politics, a cause to which Saint-Simon and Engels were deeply committed, and to which some contemporary philosophical liberals seem curiously attracted. Yet we may dismiss that option and still argue that politics has changed significantly over the century, and that such change is reflected in its symbiotic relationship with ideology. Conversely, we cannot ignore the truism that, although the forms of structuring, presenting and disseminating ideologies may have varied over time, some of those variations do not reflect an altered reality. They are rather a function of different questions, and novel perspectives, focused on by students of ideologies.

Looking back, what can we say of twentieth-century ideologies? Did they creep up on us, from their misty and sometimes mystical eighteenth- and nineteenth-century origins in central Europe, all those populist, even vulgar, socialisms, fascisms and religious conservatisms, to be met by a proud English (and later American) liberalism, whose banner was held high by the wise guardians of a moderate civilization? Were those older ideological families further adopted by third-world movements, whose added local flavour transformed them into tools both of modernization and of oppression? Were all these ructions the temporary price of introducing 'the people' into positions of power and authority, of the gradual percolation of democracy from centre to periphery inside each society and across the globe? Certainly, there have been vocal advocates for all these views, but those narratives are culpable in their simplifications and misconceptions.

At the beginning of the twentieth century, the major ideologies – conservatism, liberalism and socialism – were all at a point of transformation. Conservatism was adapting, with considerable success, to the rise of powerful forces to its left, while at the same time it was collecting the disaffected from among the liberal camp and reaching beyond its traditional class and religious bases. Liberalism and socialism were experiencing dramatic growth, but of different kinds. As a political movement, liberalism was under pressure; while as an ideology it was innovative and dynamic, unearthing its communal principles and embarking upon the project of reformulating utilitarianism that culminated in the welfare state. Socialism, to the contrary, was fast expanding as a political movement, but was beset from its infancy with centrifugal tendencies and ideological factionalism – Marxist, evolutionary, syndicalist, as well as contention within each of these categories – which weakened its effectiveness and attraction. Nevertheless, it was an era that witnessed strong public competition of these ideological groupings over the formation of public policy, and in which political argument and debate were markedly salient; indeed, comprising a significant part of the intellectual pursuits of the educated and the socially aware. It is no accident that the prestigious Home University Library commissioned three books, published in 1911–12, titled *Liberalism*, *Conservatism*, and *The Socialist Movement* – the first penned by L.T. Hobhouse becoming a highly influential twentieth-century classic, while the last illustrated the amalgamation of theory and practice, typical of ideological thinking,[2] through the person of its author, J. Ramsay MacDonald, Britain's first Labour prime minister. The preferred words to describe those sets of ideas may have been doctrines, programmes or simply ideas but, at least on the progressive side of the spectrum, few might have objected to their designation as ideologies, had that term in its non-Marxist sense been in common circulation.

The interwar years saw the advent of the totalitarianisms of left and right, a ferocious new political weapon as yet unknown on such a scale, in which rigid and binding dogmas, promulgated by authoritarian dictatorships, were employed as mobilizing instruments not only to coerce but to enthuse mass publics to conduct unbecoming of people in full command of their rational and moral properties. Their political opponents were quick to excoriate these phenomena as ideologies *qua* manipulative and pervasive ideas, purveyors of cataclysmic change, more powerful and efficient than guns or tanks, that overruled the natural divergence of human thought. In their anxiety to curb this epidemic of thought-control, its detractors confused the power of superimposed idea-systems with the necessary production of political ideas as a communal resource, and even resisted the efforts made by reforming democratic states to ally themselves to alternative visions of collectively beneficial futures. Ideologies were firmly put beyond the pale of acceptable politics.

But of course ideologies had been there all the time, and not just in abstract and systemic garb. Karl Mannheim had taken an important step in that direction when he identified ideologies as systems that endorsed the *status quo*, in the face of *status quo* defenders who objected to the labelling of what they alleged was a pragmatic and *ad hoc* approach as an ideology.[3] In so doing, Mannheim had adapted the Marxist understanding of ideology as reflecting the social and class bases of particular groups, and had designated all such known constructs as ideologies. However, Mannheim continued to endorse the Marxian-Engelsian notion of ideology as falsehood, deliberate or not, in his category of the partial concept of ideology. He accompanied that with a total concept that was akin to a *Weltanschauung*, but which suffered from the stigma of relativism – a label which certain philosophical purists have habitually used to denigrate contextual analysis. In his haste to escape the relativist constrictions of ideology, Mannheim endowed intellectuals with the supra-social capacity to transcend its group-perspectives, thus perpetuating the Marxist relegation of ideologies to temporal ephemerality, to rational inferiority, and to interest-serving group-egoism.

Mannheim nevertheless left the road to overcoming ideologies open, but already their presentation to the world of social understanding was of a peculiar kind. Ideologies continued to be seen as dissimulations, at worst patently false and at best the indispensable accoutrement of political ambition in the shape of a non-binding rhetoric, increasingly necessary to pick up new voters as fast as the political system could endow them with full citizenship. Ideologies were also assumed to be block edifices, massive and encompassing in their range, markedly monolithic in their internal structure (with the above-noted exception of socialism, split into socialism-cum-social-democracy and communism), and perceived as few in number: the big three at century's advent plus the two interwar totalitarianisms, despite lesser instances such as anarchism. Implicit was a view of plugging into an entire package, and of clearly defined and sealed boundaries that separated all five. Implicit, too, was a view that liberalism and conservatism were rather different kinds of packages, accompanied by their own resistance to be termed ideologies. The former appeared to be too flexible and open-ended to insist on rigid and total ideational solutions to political problems; while the latter deftly side-stepped the issue by claiming to purge its contents of political ideas altogether and to engage instead in piecemeal and unplanned institutional reactions to historical contingencies. If liberalism was not an ideology, it was through the definitional fiat of ideology as closed and doctrinaire; if conservatism was not one, it was through the definitional fiat of ideology as abstract and non-empirical. No wonder that the end of ideology could become a message of hope, if not of scholarly accuracy.

In the meantime, however, American political scientists were directing the cold eye of empiricism at a recently discovered, or recently appreciated, social phenomenon and employing the term 'ideology' to denote it. Political attitudes, opinions and evaluations were what constituted ideology and, crucially, they were not dissimulative. No attempt was made to argue for their underlying truth in the sense of being morally right or rationally valid. Rather, their truth was deemed to lie in their being a reliable vehicle and representation of what their bearers actually thought and preferred. Truth became a question of empirical accuracy. Robert Lane and Philip Converse were among the pioneers who applied behavioural positivism to these 'grassroots' positions of individuals and attempted to aggregate them into functional instruments of political participation, support or disapproval. Lane wished to expand ideology to signify not only articulated political arguments but also 'loosely structured, unreflective statements' of the common people,[4] breaking away from the cohesion many philosophers expect of political thinking, as well as from the association of ideology with the interests of a ruling class. Converse refined the study of mass publics by seeking regularities, compatibilities and constraints in their ideologies, and exploring their relationship to élite belief systems.[5] Thus began the process of unpacking ideologies and looking at their internal components, often in a way that ill-matched the parts with the wholes they purportedly constituted.

One major outcome of these approaches was to present ideologies as demo-cratically produced, a process whose embryonic origins emanated from the writ-ings of Antonio Gramsci. Gramsci had repositioned ideology within the normal thought processes of individuals located in social groups. But these popular faiths, he argued, were still rudimentary and inchoate and had to be led by élites offering cohesion, direction and refinement to a thought-structure that was ultim-ately a homogeneous tool for revolution. Ideology, he held, could then trans-mogrify into truth.[6] By contrast, the individualist conception of ideology offered by mid-century American political scientists exalted ideological fragmentation by permeating ideology with an atomized, person-centred, and pluralist value system. This was only one facet of changes in concrete Western ideologies which, through their formative fashioning by political parties or crucial interest groups, including the press and television, still presented hegemonic features of the kind identified by Gramsci. But political discourse, and the production and dissemin-ation of ideologies, were certainly broadening out, with the major ideological families becoming more internally complex and variable due to the more diverse input upon which they could draw.

As a consequence, ideology was consciously reintroduced into liberalism, but only by renaming ideology – not as a total system of ideas installed from an unassailable 'rationalist' or political stratosphere, but as a manifestation of a pluralist multitude of views acting on a replaceable élite, emerging out of methodological individualism and subsumed within the insights of cognitive psychology. A counter-strategy was necessary in order to reinject theoretical cohesion and analytical power into a branch of political studies no longer able to rely on the Marxisant usages of ideology, irrelevant as they appeared to the understanding of Western political thought manifestations. Here anthropology and linguistics came to the rescue, with their notions of mapping, myths and symbols, all heavily dependent on interpretative frameworks through which to decode forms of thought-behaviour that were to a considerable degree non-transparent. Through a transition, mediated also via hermeneutics, to a focus on constructed and invented realities as necessary forms of reproducing knowledge and understanding, the concept of ideology regained both scholarly purchase and intellectual gravitas. In particular, the permanence of ideology could be asserted as against its evanescence in the Marxist approaches.

Rediscovering commonalities

Surely, though, people were not talking about the same thing? Surely the end of total and false systems was entirely separate from the semantic and cultural recapturing of diverse patterns of social meaning and communication across societies? This 'two concepts of ideology' view is to a large extent misleading. What has taken place, rather, is a refinement and cross-fertilization of a sub-discipline which still shares in the broadest sense the common objective of accounting for and assessing the political thinking that aims to direct – or simply directs – the public activities of a society.

Far from witnessing the end of ideology, a plethora of new ideologies has continued to emerge (green ideology is one such instance), while older ideologies have been undergoing continuous processes of breaking-up and regrouping (as attested to by developments on the radical right, for example). Our sensitivity to these ideational births and rebirths has been considerably enhanced not only because of the vocal presence of political movements acting in the name of these ideologies, but because we are seeing a veritable explosion in the usages of ideology, which at the same time involves significant modifications in its con-ceptualizations. Shifts have occurred and are still occurring from an analytical concentration on macro-ideologies to an exploration of their micro-ingredients by political theorists and conceptual historians; from the detection of grand, full ideologies to thin, partial, or eclectic ones; from the study of overtly proclama-tory ideologies employing conventional political language to psychoanalytical and symbolic modes of interpretation; and from an emphasis on the political values of ideology to a focus on the medium of language, the forms of human communication, and the ubiquity of style. The problem is that many of these developments are moving along different axes, apparently segregated from each other. But that is not equivalent to contending that they lack common denominators from which to assemble, perhaps even consolidate, a rich body of theory which serves, among others, as a subtle detector of undiscovered but already existing, as well as nascent, ideological phenomena.

Now that the dust has begun to settle, we can appreciate one remarkable legacy of the emergence of totalitarian ideologies, namely, that many of their attributes were simply exaggerated and contorted forms of features evident in all ideologies. By means of the critique of totalitarianism – and despite the contrary assertions of their promoters – ideologies were exposed as inconsistent, dishar-monious, irrational, and inflexible, whereas 'decent' sets of political ideas put to public use aspired to logical consistency, to ethical harmony, to intellectual rationality, and to political flexibility. But that critique should have revealed not the untenability of ideology but its real complexity. Characteristics first emerging through a dismissive approach to extreme and inhumane ideologies were now perceived as widespread in all ideologies, though of course they were not always as preponderant or as weighty. In particular, irrationality had not previously been conceived of as the property of major political doctrines. So rather than separate the pure world of political theories and doctrines from these ideological abominations, inconsistency, disharmony, irrationality and inflexibility were – methodologically speaking – drawn into the former. An umbilical cord con-nected, for instance, liberalism with fascism – not in the sharing of core values, nor in their moral codes, but in the eclectic regularities that political thinking displayed in its actual usages and manifestations, as part of a social and linguistic culture. Not the least part of that was the existence within liberalism of a non-negotiable core set of beliefs, one instance of which echoed Rousseau's famous injunction with regard to his civil religion: 'As for the negative dogmas, I would limit them to a single one: no intolerance'.[7] As a result, political ideologies are now perceived to be centrally concerned with new themes: the management of inconsistency and indeterminacy (a consequence of the essential contestability of concepts and of the elusiveness of their signified subject matter); the recognition of emotion as a motive force in the construction of political argument (witness the resurgence of interest in the beneficial formation of group identity through nationalism, side by side with rational hybrids such as constitutional patriotism); the navigation through internal disharmony (pure unadulterated harmony is now assumed to be both impossible and undesirable within ideologies based, as they are, on multiple internal configurations in which dissonance and consonance jockey continuously for position); and the decontestation and closure of meaning and argument (at the very least with regard to core concepts) for variously limited stretches of time and space.

However, the developments of concrete ideologies over the century cannot be captured as a sequence of successive historical stages, as most of the forms and understandings noted above still exist as parallel or cumulative phenomena. What is, from a postmodern perspective, a process of fragmentation may well be one of differentiation from the standpoint of political ideas. That differentiation is closely linked to the rise of mass politics and its accompaniment, the mass media, but it is also a simple reflection of the entrance of new members into the often charmless circle of modernity. African socialisms, Indonesian guided democracy and South American liberation theology are examples of new political ideologies of the 1960s and 1970s which were spawned following on more intense contacts of the third world with the first, or of old worlds with new, and they belied the supposed stagnation that had befallen ideological expression. In Europe (and to a lesser extent the USA), though, new social movements were epitomizing the increasing detachment, initiated by socialists, of ideology formation and dissemination from political establishments. Conservatism, liberalism, communism and fascism had all been meticulously constructed and controlled by political, cultural and intellectual élites. Now, however, the opening up, if not extensive democratization, of manifold group discourse permitted a new range of forces to compete over the legitimization of public language and values: ecologists, feminists, the new left, neo-fascists. To begin with, the first three of these new ideational products were created by disaffected intellectuals, but they were rapidly taken over by wider social circles not as mere consumers but as opinion formers, programmatic entrepreneurs and originators of new political messages. The fate of green ideology in Germany is a case in point, based as it has been on diverse groups pulling in a number of disparate directions from an eclectic base of core beliefs.[8]

Eventually, the increasing mass-politicization of ideology caused a decline in its articulateness, as its public production no longer remained a monopoly of the so-called intelligentsia, many of whom retreated to semi-private – because highly specialized and technical – political languages. It also caused a rupture in the public face of ideology, its modes of expression and loose unity, as a result of the centrifugal movement away from family membership of the grand ideologies. While on the one hand the style of the mass media was constraining the message, and ideological intricacies were reduced to oversimplified and consumer-friendly (or consumer-patronizing) sound-bites, on the other hand ideological arguments, and their second-order analysis, became increasingly complex. Intellectual ideological producers – both post-Marxists and Rawlsians spring to mind – removed themselves from the practice and language of politics and engaged in private discourses. They forsook the contest over the public meaning of words, and aspired instead to legitimate their interpretation through professional acclaim. The peregrinations of the term 'liberal' in the USA amply illustrate this rift between popular senses and the technical formulations of intellectual élites. Indeed, most members of such élites have lost confidence in their ability to act as an ideological vanguard in the more assertive and egalitarian democratic cultures that have developed in the course of the century.

Recent refinements

It is not uncommon to hear liberalism now described as history's winner, without much consideration of the variant of liberalism that has supposedly won, of the widespread disaffection in the industrial world with the costs of liberal capitalism (an old-new theme), of the other kinds of ideology predominant in much of Asia or sweeping across the Muslim world or, perforce, of the criteria for 'winning' the ideological competition. Does this fly in the face of the emergence of Czech 'Thatcherism' and of new brands of American conservatism, as well as of contemporary nationalisms and feminisms? For a winner one has to have a finishing post and none of these contestants has yet collapsed exhausted in mid-course. Indeed, the current state of play suggests to the contrary that ideologies have, over the past decade or so, undergone further disintegration and re-formation. This perception is reinforced by the development of powerful (and occasionally esoteric) theoretical tools by which to analyse ideology.

Foremost among those is the emergence of postmodernism and post-structuralism at whose centre lies – as far as ideology is concerned – an extension of the Marxist project of ideological critique, but without those crucial elements of the Marxist conceptual framework that enable ideology to be transcended. For many scholars of that persuasion, ideology is a modernist remnant which requires exposure in order to identify the fictions produced by a social order bent on self-preservation or, as with the Lacanians, papering over the voids which belie the existence of such an order.[9] It is a device that retains the hegemonic function of articulating meaning by constructing the unity of society out of its absence, out of antagonisms and dislocation.[10] This view of ideology is post-Marxist in the sense that undistorted reality can no longer be discovered, because it may not exist. Thus ideology does not have a falsifying role and the aim of the critique of ideology is not to supply truth but to underscore what has become, in effect, an inescapable ephemerality and contingency, which themselves assume the features of permanence. It is at odds with modernism because its notion of ideology does not appeal to rationality but regards ideology as surviving on the concealment of social chaos, and hence on non-transparency as the foundation of social order.

That undercurrent of irrational unintentionality coalesces, from a very different and more rational starting point, with the hermeneutic insistence on the multiplicity of meanings embedded in speech acts and texts. According to this school, intentionality is overtaken by the polysemy of thought and utterance as understood by readers and audiences. The language through which ideas are expressed requires constant interpretation and reinterpretation in order to accommodate changing temporal and spatial perspectives. This hermeneutic understanding of ideology combines the identification of empirical thought-practices with an emphasis on their consumption. Because of the constant variability in the group consumption of ideologies, a dynamism is introduced that secures the continuous durability of ideological life.

The effect of postmodernist standpoints has been to expand the signifier ideology to cover myriad types of cultural conduct and practice, and consequently to remove it from an exclusively political sphere while – which may be much the same thing – extending the sphere of the political to encompass an ultimately doomed struggle for control over words and language and what they signify. The relation of such analyses to the concrete world of political ideologies is thus multifold: they relegate them not to insignificance (for ideologies are obviously vital to preserve a semblance of order, even of comfort, in a fissiparous world) but to superficiality, to a veneer for an unfathomable reality, necessary but inherently fragile. They also present the world of political ideas as infinitely reconstitutable and hence bereft of moral anchorage: epic struggle among grand ideologies is replaced with a liquidity of ephemeral ideological combinations, a continuous patchwork on a quilt that is forever tearing apart at the seams. Internally, ideologies are proffered as structurally suspect, because structure itself is construed as an artefact, whether conscious or unconscious, and traditions of political thinking are interpreted as contingent stop-gaps, incidental historical continua. And as all ideologies are perceived as dancing to the same tune, their minutiae and differentiae become the object of soft focus, rather than of the meticulous analysis that political theorists apply to the details and units of their subject-matter.

Viewed, though, as a configuration of political thought, it is not always the most useful strategy to deny, or side-step, the importance of ideological structure. The problem is that it is unnecessary to have to choose between the permanent and the fortuitous, or between the true and the symbolic. Neither dichotomy is sustainable on its own. Ideologies construct fleeting, temporary and strictly circumscribed consistencies out of more fundamental, abstract and purist inconsistencies. The fleeting, however, can be held together in a number of combinations which, although impermanent, may be long-standing. The temporary is bounded by particularities of circumstance, but cultural constraints may reproduce these particularities across space and in different societies, creating discernible patterns. And the circumscribed is an especially intriguing contrivance. Unlike the methodological and substantive aspirations of some political philosophers, it abjures the attempt to attain cascading chains of consistency from core postulates to peripheral conclusions, so that basic premises lead to secondary and tertiary ones in a logically flawless system. Rather, ideologies operate by cutting off the full range of internal reasoning at the point of political relevance, the point required for political action and for what is necessary to optimize, not to maximize, given values. To illustrate, the logical maximization of liberty is socially destructive; its constrained optimization, in whatever ideational context, is necessary for its social taming. Beyond the point of optimization conceptual haziness and uncontainable contradictions may lie, but they are irrelevant to the argument at hand. The essential contestability thesis suggests that extensive internal coherence is always chimerical. Ideologies offer the only coherence that stands a chance of realization in practice, a curtailed and manufactured coherence, which is why they are such central products of the political arena and such a valuable resource for politics. Oakeshott recognized this function of abridgement as part of the technique of ideology, but for him this was the falsification of political activity.[11] There is no need to take that bleak view of ideology as a limited and artificial device. Any discourse becomes intelligible only by means of 'artificial' checks on its significatory potential. If a constructed ideological harmony with the capacity for cultural survival emerges, it becomes an asset for any society, enhancing its communicative capacity, adumbrating boundaries among alternative ideological patterns and thus offering the ideological choices that eschew the post-structural approach. Indeed, through the insights of hermeneutics one may endow the phenomenon of ideology with the stimulating function of introducing unceasing ideational richness and vitality into the political thinking of groups and societies.

So if knowledge and identification of phenomena are a reflection not only of new facts in the field but of conceptual sensitivity to what we have hitherto been impervious to, where do concrete ideologies stand today? First, disillusionment with the state (domestically with the welfare state, and externally through the rise of the twin adversaries, environmentalism and global capitalism) indicates the possible detachment of ideologies from the nation-state. This is by no means at odds with the re-emergence of nationalisms, and sub-nationalisms of various kinds, to reclaim their place within the world of respectable ideologies. Second, on a theoretical level, we are more attuned to the difference between full and thin ideologies, the former still offering the customary range of putative solutions to the central issues of redistribution, the boundaries between private and public, and the status and goods conferred by political membership; whereas the latter – nationalism itself is an example – sever themselves from a wider ideational agenda, by the deliberate removal and replacement of concepts. Alternatively, they are often to be found as part of a broader host ideology, from whose ideas and arguments they need to borrow.[12]

Third, we have obtained from postmodernism a sense of the fragmentary and elusive nature of political ideologies, and from the notion of essential contestability an inkling of the way decontested concepts are reconfigured by ideologies into new, if impermanent, wholes. But it is at the same time impossible for us to conceive of a world without political ideologies, given the current theories at our disposal. We are now conceptually prepared for a world of ideologies in which recombinations are normal and frequent, and in which boundaries are there to be traversed. The recent movement of libertarianism, in the guise of the 'new right', back and forth between the established families of liberalism and conservatism, not to mention its links with older versions of anarchism, illustrates that pliability. The very obsession of 'New Labour' with modernism and millennarianism has indicated its precarious dependence on the time dimension, while its internal components display hybrid features from a number of major ideological families.[13] New variants and cross-fertilizations have always existed, but the apparatus for recognizing them as significant ideological permutations, rather than as deviant aberrations from a stable ideological family, is now available. Whether this is a deplorable fragmentation or a desirable pluralism, is itself an ideological question. At any rate, ideological phenomena over the past decade appear more fragile. Indeed, the implosion of some of the larger ideological families cannot rule out future totalizing constructs, though social differentiation lives uneasily with totalisms.

Fourth, we now realize that ideologies may assume many diverse cultural forms, in literature, film, advertising and everyday speech; hence our understanding of the range of political thinking and its symbolization is more generous than in the past. And we may glean from hermeneutics that new understandings do not necessarily entail new ideological families but new decodings of those families, and that patterns of argument may recur in modified but not transformed shape. Indeed, the old forms of ideology are, contra some postmodernists, far from being superseded by other forms of messaging, because questions of justice, of liberty, of rights, of political obligation, and of sovereignty will still be at the heart of political debate for the foreseeable future, so that political morality has not yet become a field open to all comers. Were we to rest content with ideology's characterization as power we would reduce it merely to one of its components, and overlook its role in shaping the contours of morality. Nor can we abandon logic and reason as features of ideological discourse and communication, both as means of persuasion and as criteria for the assessment of its validity, as befits a crucial form of political thought. We have, nonetheless, to push beyond those constraints, for tests of logic and reason fail to come to grips with ideology as a ubiquitous form of political argument and meaning-endowing thought-practice, or with the multi-dimensionality of its content. Though the dawning century may no longer be an age of ideologies in Bracher's doctrinaire sense, an age of ideologies it nevertheless is and will continue to be.

Notes and references

1 K.D. Bracher, *The Age of Ideologies*, London, Methuen & Co., 1985.
2 On some of the distinctive theory–practice issues pertinent to ideology see M. Freeden, 'Practising ideology and ideological practices', *Political Studies*, 2000, Vol. 48, pp. 302–22.
3 K. Mannheim, *Ideology and Utopia*, London, Routledge & Kegan Paul, 1936.
4 R.E. Lane, *Political Ideology: Why the American Common Man Believes What He Does*, New York, Free Press, 1962, p. 16.
5 P.E. Converse, 'The nature of belief systems in mass publics', in D.A. Apter (ed.), *Ideology and Discontent*, New York, Free Press, 1964, pp. 206–61.
6 A. Gramsci, *Selections from Prison Notebooks*, London, Lawrence and Wishart, 1971.
7 J.J. Rousseau, *The Social Contract*, Harmondsworth, Penguin Books, 1968, p. 186.
8 See G. Talshir, 'Modular ideology: the implications of Green theory for a reconceptualization of "ideology"', *Journal of Political Ideologies*, 1998, Vol. 3, pp. 169–92.
9 S. Žižek, 'The spectre of ideology', in S. Žižek (ed.) *Mapping Ideology*, London, Verso, 1994.
10 E. Laclau and C. Mouffe, *Hegemony and Socialist Strategy*, London, Verso, 1985.
11 M. Oakeshott, *Rationalism in Politics*, Methuen & Co., London, 1962, p. 125.
12 For the difference between full and thin ideologies see M. Freeden, 'Is nationalism a distinct ideology?', *Political Studies*, 1998, Vol. 46, pp. 748–65.
13 See M. Freeden, 'The ideology of New Labour', *Political Quarterly*, 1999, Vol. 70, pp. 42–51.

2 Ideological dominance through philosophical confusion

Liberalism in the twentieth century

Gerald F. Gaus

A surprisingly liberal century

In evaluating liberalism's success in this century, it would do well to recall briefly the prospects for liberalism a hundred years ago. At the turn of the twentieth century a number of thoughtful observers, from both the right and left wings of liberalism, feared that its days were numbered. In 1891 Herbert Spencer warned that hard-won liberal freedoms were being undermined by socialists and communists, who were leading civilization back to bondage.[1] To L.T. Hobhouse, the nineteenth century was the 'age of Liberalism, yet its close saw the fortunes of that great movement brought to their lowest ebb'.[2]

> Whether at home or abroad those who represented Liberal ideas had suffered crushing defeats. But this was the least considerable of the causes of anxiety. If Liberals had been defeated, something much worse seems about to befall Liberalism. Its faith in itself was waxing cold. It seemed to have done its work. It had the air of a creed that is becoming fossilized as an extinct form, a fossil that occupied, moreover, an awkward position between two very active and energetically moving grindstones – the upper grindstone of plutocratic imperialism, and the nether grindstone of social democracy.[3]

Writing in 1911, Hobhouse held out hope that a revised liberalism, which had learned from socialism, might not only survive, but grow along with democracy, though he also thought it was possible that liberalism could 'gradually sink'.[4] And the prospects of liberalism did not quickly improve. Writing in 1927 Guido de Ruggiero analysed the 'crisis of liberalism'.[5] During the 1930s it was widely held that liberalism was besieged by fascism from the right and socialism and communism from the left. In 1935 John Dewey observed that liberalism 'has long been accustomed to onslaughts' from the right, but such attacks were mild compared to the new assaults from the left. In the minds of many people, said Dewey, 'liberalism has fallen between two stools, so that it is conceived as the refuge of those unwilling to take a decided stand in the social conflicts going on'.[6] Dewey too saw a 'crisis in liberalism' and believed that liberalism was in 'eclipse'.[7] Indeed, it seems that Dewey was convinced that socialism, not liberalism, was the wave of the future: 'we are in for some kind of socialism, call it by whatever name you please, and no matter what it will be called when it is realized'.[8] In 1958 one commentator still thought the prospects for liberalism had dimmed: while in his view 'at the beginning of the twentieth century the outlook for liberalism appeared bright', the 1930s and 1940s constituted an attack on liberalism, while Russian communism posed the most powerful and implacable enemy liberalism had ever faced.[9]

In light of the alarm – indeed dismay – of liberals throughout much of the first part of the twentieth century, liberals at the advent of the next century may understandably feel entitled to celebrate. The twentieth century was a surprisingly liberal century. Liberalism has apparently vanquished socialism, the rival that so attracted but also worried Hobhouse and Dewey. Consensus on the pre-eminence of the liberal ideals of liberty and markets appears well-nigh universal. To a large extent what is today called 'socialism' is a sort of left-wing liberalism. Today's democratic socialists, arguing for a generous welfare state and a healthy democratic life within an essentially private-property market society are much closer to the new liberalisms of Hobhouse and J.A. Hobson than to the socialism of Karl Marx or even that of G.D.H. Cole. Indeed, so dominant is liberal thought that many socialists adopt some version of John Rawls's liberal theory of social justice. The difference between 'egalitarian liberal' and socialist theories of justice is often impossible to discern.[10]

Liberalism's victory over conservatism is not so clear-cut or complete. Conservatism remains the main alternative to liberalism, and it has been powerfully argued that some versions of classical liberalism, such as F.A. Hayek's, are themselves deeply influenced by conservative thought.[11] Nevertheless, the conservative alternative has moved far in the direction of liberalism: 'plutocratic imperialism' is no longer a contender, nor is the rejection of a pluralistic, market society. A recent conservative critic of liberalism speaks in a distinctly liberal voice when he reassures us that conservatism 'does not presuppose agreement about conceptions of the good life'.[12]

Of course criticisms of the liberal project – or, more accurately, projects – not only still occur, but are almost the staple of contemporary political philosophy. Feminists, communitarians, greens and various 'liberationists' join conservatives, social democrats, critical theorists and a host of others in constantly criticizing almost every aspect of liberal theory and politics. As Stephen Holmes has argued, disparaging liberalism is a recurring activity in western culture, and one which thrives today.[13] Unlike at the beginning of the previous century, however, at the commencement of this one such criticisms appear not as the final assaults on a fossil that is being overtaken by history, but as attacks on the dominant political doctrine by those who would challenge its pre-eminence.

The lack of progress of liberal theory in the twentieth century

My aim in this chapter is not to celebrate the apparent victory of liberalism, or even to sigh a breath of relief that it survived the twentieth century in what must be seen, given the prognostications of a hundred years ago, as surprisingly good shape. Quite the opposite. I wish to suggest that, whatever cause for celebration liberals might derive from their political victories over traditional rivals, in an important respect the twentieth century has been a disappointment for liberal theory. Writing in the midst of the Great Depression, Dewey noted 'that liberals are divided in outlook and endeavor . . . is well-nigh commonplace'.[14] In the first part of the century liberalism was divided on a host of fundamental issues: it was split between staunch advocates of private property and those who wished to embrace some form of socialism, between individualists and collectivists, and between those who sought to plan society and those who insisted on the impossibility of social planning. Dewey hoped that these cleavages could be overcome, and a 'renascent liberalism' would arise, characterized by an 'organized unity of action attended by consensus of belief'.[15] No such unified liberal theory has arisen. In fact, to a surprising extent, the cleavages that characterized liberalism at the end of the nineteenth century continue to haunt it today.

In this essay I wish, first, to explain more fully and defend this controversial claim – that in many ways liberal theory has not notably advanced in the century now brought to a close. Let me stress that I have no intention of belittling the important and innovative contributions to liberalism by, among others, T.H. Green, Hobhouse, Bernard Bosanquet, Dewey, Hayek, Rawls, Robert Nozick and Isaiah Berlin. My point is that despite the flurry of liberal theorizing over the last century, liberalism today is characterized by essentially the same antinomies or tensions that marked it at the close of the nineteenth century. The cleavage between individualists and communitarians, rights and the general welfare, rationalists and anti-rationalists, social evolutionists and constructivists, are no more or less of a feature of current liberalism than they were at its outset. As a political theory liberalism has left the century very much as it entered it – unable to resolve enduring tensions between rival formulations. While we have witnessed new and sophisticated statements of the rival formulations, the debate has not appreciably moved forward. Having tried to establish this claim, I shall turn in the last part of the essay to several analyses of its importance, or lack of it, and what it might tell us about the nature of liberalism and political theory.

Three enduring antinomies of liberalism[16]

Individualism versus collectivism

Throughout the last century, liberalism was beset by controversies between, on the one hand, those broadly identified as 'individualists' and, on the other, 'collectivists', 'communitarians' or 'organicists'. These vague and sweeping designations have been applied to a wide array of disputes. I focus here on controversies concerning (1) the nature of society; (2) the nature of the self; and (3) the relative weight of the rights and claims of the individual and society.

The nature of society

Liberalism is often associated with individualist analyses of society. Jeremy Bentham's view is well known: '[t]he community is a fictitious *body*, composed of the individual persons who are considered as constituting as it were its *members*'.[17] For an individualist such as Bentham, 'community' is simply a name we use to describe the actions, traits and interactions of individuals, who alone are real. Social properties are ultimately reducible to real, individual, properties. Spencer agreed: 'the properties of the mass are dependent upon the attributes of its component parts'.[18] In the last years of the nineteenth century this individualist view was increasingly subject to attack, especially by those who were influenced by idealist philosophy. D.G. Ritchie, criticizing Spencer's philosophy in 1891, explicitly rejected the idea that society is simply a 'heap' of individuals, insisting that it is more akin to an organism, with a complex internal life.[19] This anti-individualist conception of society reached its purest form in Bosanquet's liberalism. 'If we consider my unity with myself at different times as the limiting case,' wrote Bosanquet, 'we shall find it very hard to establish a difference of principle between the unity of what we call one mind and that of all the "minds" which enter into a single social experience'.[20] The unity of the individual is, in principle, no different than the unity between individuals that forms the social mind. Indeed, in Bosanquet's idealism, what is more coherent and complete is more real, and thus society, because it is more complete and coherent than any individual person, is more real than its constituent persons.[21] Liberals such as Hobhouse and Dewey refused to adopt such a radically collectivist view,[22] but they also rejected the radical individualism of Bentham and Spencer.[23] Throughout most of the first half of the twentieth century 'organic' analyses of society held sway in liberal theory, including much of economics. A.F. Mummery and J.A. Hobson insisted that the 'view, that a community means nothing more than addition of a number of individual units, and that the interest of Society can be obtained by adding together the interests of individual members, has led to as grave errors in Economics as in other branches of Sociology'.[24] Even John Maynard Keynes, in his critique of *laissez-faire* individualism, stressed the importance of the 'organized society as a whole'.[25]

Despite the dominance in early twentieth-century liberalism of collectivist analyses of society, individualist views persisted. During and after the Second World War they challenged, and it seemed for a time eclipsed, collectivist accounts. Karl Popper's *The Open Society and its Enemies* presented a sustained critique of Hegelian and Marxist theory and its collectivist and historicist, and to Popper inherently illiberal, understanding of society.[26] The re-emergence of economic analysis in liberal theory brought to the fore a thoroughgoing methodological individualism. Writing in the early 1960s, James Buchanan and Gordon Tullock adamantly defended the 'individualistic postulate' against all forms of 'organicism'.

> The organic State has an existence, a value pattern, and a motivation independent of those individual human beings claiming membership. Indeed,

the very term 'individual' has little place in the genuinely organic conception; the single human being becomes an integral part of a larger, and more
meaningful, organism . . .

> This approach or theory of the collectivity . . . is, however, essentially
opposed to the Western philosophical tradition in which the human individual is the primary philosophical entity.[27]

Buchanan and Tullock went on to argue that, 'having rejected the organic
conception of the State', 'we are left with a purely individualist conception of the
collectivity'. Human beings are the only real choosers and decision-makers, and
their preferences determine both public and private actions.[28] The renascent
individualism of late-twentieth-century liberalism was closely bound up with the
induction of Hobbes as a member of the liberal pantheon. Hobbes's relentlessly
individualistic account of society, and the manner in which his analysis of the
state of nature lent itself to game-theoretical modelling, yielded a highly individualist, formal analysis of the liberal state and liberal morality.[29]

The nature of the self

Of course, as is widely known, the last years have witnessed a renewed interest in
collectivist analyses of liberal society – though the term 'collectivist' is abjured in
favour of 'communitarian'. Writing in 1985, Amy Gutmann observed that '[w]e
are witnessing a revival of communitarian criticisms of liberal political theory.
Like the critics of the 1960s, those of the 1980s fault liberalism for being mistakenly and irreparably individualistic'.[30] Starting with Michael Sandel's famous
criticism of Rawls, a number of critics charged that liberalism was premised on
an abstract conception of individual selves as pure choosers, whose commitments, values and concerns are possessions of the self, but never constitute the
self.[31] Although the now famous, not to say infamous, 'liberal–communitarian'
debate ultimately involved wide ranging moral, political and sociological disputes about the nature of communities, and the rights and responsibilities of
their members,[32] the heart of the dispute was competing views of selfhood. For
Sandel the flaw at the heart of Rawls's liberalism was its implausibly abstract
theory of the self, the pure autonomous chooser. Rawls, he charged, ultimately
assumes that it makes sense to identify us with a pure capacity for choice, and
that such pure choosers might reject any or all of their attachments and values
and yet retain their identity. Will Kymlicka, in the spirit of these new communitarians, sought to reintroduce into liberal theory elements of Green's,
Hobhouse's and Dewey's 'new liberalism', arguing once again that core liberal
values are consistent with, indeed can only thrive in, communities characterized
by cultural commonalities: 'membership in a cultural structure is what enables
individual freedom, what enables meaningful choices about how to live one's
life'.[33] Throughout the 1990s various liberals sought to show how liberalism may
consistently advocate a theory of the self which finds room for cultural membership
and other non-chosen attachments and commitments which at least partially

constitute the self. Much of liberal theory has become focused on the issue as to how we can be social creatures, members of cultures and raised in various traditions, while also being autonomous choosers who employ our liberty to construct lives of our own.[34]

Gutmann believed that this new wave of communitarian criticism of liberal individualism was 'not a mere repetition of the old. Whereas the earlier critics were inspired by Marx, the recent critics are inspired by Aristotle and Hegel'.[35] By 'older', however, Gutmann had in mind the 'new left' criticisms of the 1960s. Closer examination reveals that throughout the outgoing century liberal theory grappled with problems posed by Hegel's and Aristotle's philosophies: in many cases the earlier liberal theories were much more sophisticated in this regard than more recent formulations.[36] A starting point for Green's idealism was a criticism of the associationist theories of the self advocated by individualist liberals of the nineteenth century such as Bentham and John Stuart Mill; rather than seeing the 'self' as an abstract pure ego – as Sandel charges of Rawls – Green charged that these Humean-inspired theories had no real account of the self at all. They sought to analyse the self as simply a series of desires, feelings or thoughts connected by the laws of association (such as similarity, continuity, and so on). Although, Green argued, the self is 'not something apart from feelings, desires and thoughts', it is not to be identified with them – it is 'that which unites them'.[37] This may look as if Green is advocating the so-called 'pure ego' but, drawing on Aristotle and especially Hegel, Green insists that the self is also a system of content. As Bosanquet was later to stress, the self is a system of organized content; it supposes both content – constituent commitments, values, beliefs and so on – as well as an organizing capacity.[38] Just how these two aspects of the self – the substantive commitment and the organizing ego – are to be combined has perplexed liberals throughout the twentieth century.

The rights and claims of the individual and society

The ongoing debate between individualists and collectivists about self and society has been intractable not simply because it involves such complex philosophical issues, but because it is seen as relevant to determining the relative weights of the moral claims of individuals and society. To be sure, Buchanan and Tullock took care to distinguish their individualist analysis of society from 'individualism' – 'an organizational norm that involves the explicit acceptance of certain value criteria.'[39] However, despite their attempt to render their analysis free of such value commitments, it seems uncontroversial that the theory of constitutional democracy that arises out of their work provides a strong defence of individual rights against collective decision-making. This follows the tradition of liberal individualism; Spencer, for example, saw his individualist analysis of society as bound up with a strong defence of individual moral rights.

> [E]very social phenomenon must have its origins in some property of the individual. And just as the attractions and affinities which are latent in

separate atoms become visible when those atoms are approximated, so the forces that are dormant in the isolated man are rendered active by juxtaposition with his fellows.

This consideration . . . points out the path we must pursue in our search for a true social philosophy. It suggests that the idea of a *moral* law of society, like its other laws, originates in the attribute of the human being. It warns us against adopting any fundamental doctrine which, like that of 'the greatest happiness of the greatest number', cannot be expressed without presupposing a state of aggregation. On the other hand, it hints that the first principle of a code for the right ruling of humanity in its state of *multitude* is to be found in humanity in its state of *unitude*; that the moral forces upon which social equilibrium depends are resident in the social atom – man.[40]

Thus to Spencer 'there exists in man what may be called an *instinct of personal rights* – a feeling that leads him to claim as great a share of natural privilege as is claimed by others'.[41]

Of course it was not only liberal individualists who saw a tie between their analysis of selves-in-society and morality. Bosanquet's idealism and organic conception of society led him to be critical of 'moral individualism' – what he saw as a 'materialistic or Epicurean view of life' – favouring instead 'moral socialism' – 'which makes Society the moral essence of the individual'.[42] However, though liberal political theorists of all persuasions have supposed that (a) individualist (or collectivist) accounts of society and self somehow undergird (b) an individualist (or collectivist) morality, the nature of the tie between them is often obscure, and is anything but certain. Recall that Spencer rejected Benthamite utilitarianism just because a principle such as 'the greatest happiness of the greatest number' inherently presupposes 'a state of aggregation'. Classical utilitarianism was thus morally collectivistic despite Bentham's radically individualistic view of society. This charge, of course, was levelled by later moral individualists, who claimed, for instance, that the utilitarian moral viewpoint saw society as a 'sort of single great person'.[43]

A history of twentieth-century liberal theory would have much to say about the various defences of moral individualism, criticisms by more collective or communal liberals, as well as attempts to reconcile the two. Green and Hobhouse are perhaps the most significant of the reconcilers; for them, the common good necessarily included the good of the individuals. Wrote Green:

Now the self of which a man thus forecasts the fulfillment, is not an abstract or empty self. It is a self affected by manifold interests, among which is an interest in other persons. These are not merely interests dependent on other persons for the means to their gratification, but interests in the good of those persons, interests which cannot be satisfied without the consciousness that those other persons are satisfied. The man cannot contemplate himself as in a better state, or on the way to the best, without contemplating others, not merely as a means to that better state, but as sharing it with him.[44]

Green thus presents an analysis of rights which, while aimed at providing the conditions for the development of personality, also can be said to derive from the common good. To say that 'a right is a power claimed and recognized as contributory to the common good'[45] is not to deny that it is crucial to an individual's development; rather it is to call attention to the fact that 'the perfection of human character' is 'also that of society'.[46] Green's and his followers' attempt to reconcile moral individualism with the morality of the collective good, though pre-eminent for a time in Britain, gave way in the latter part of the twentieth century to a renewed, indeed intensified, dispute between proponents of individual rights and those who insist that liberalism can only be grounded on appeals to collective welfare.

Constructivism versus anti-constructivism

Liberalism has a core commitment to rationality. 'All that man is and all that raises him above animals', said Ludwig von Mises, 'he owes to his reason. Why should he forgo the use of his reason . . . in the sphere of social policy and trust to vague and obscure feelings and impulses?'[47] As Holmes has pointed out, liberalism's critics often associate it with 'hyperrationalism'. Writes Holmes:

> Rationalists are said to believe that human reason is powerful enough to construct a workable blueprint for the best possible social order and that people can be led by rational argument to accept this blueprint. The critics of such hyperrationalism argue that reason is too feeble for such a task, given the complexity of social life.[48]

As Holmes recognizes, liberals are not committed to hyperrationalism. Liberalism, while drawing on the Enlightenment's faith in reason, also is informed by a scepticism about – or at least a cautious attitude towards – the powers of human reason.[49] Von Mises not only asserted the importance of being guided by reason, but drew our attention to its limits: 'our powers of comprehension are limited. We cannot hope ever to discover the ultimate and most profound secrets of the universe'.[50] Indeed, Popper's *The Open Society and its Enemies* is not simply a criticism of collectivism, but a criticism of the highly rationalistic philosophies of, among others, Plato and Marx. Although liberalism is certainly more rationalistic than conservatism,[51] it falls far short of the near hyperrationalism of many socialisms. In the words of a contemporary socialist,

> The human race, rationalism maintains, has now grown up and at last has freed itself from the age-old yokes of ignorance and superstition. We have in our possession 'science', the rational, ordered knowledge of the laws of nature: we can progressively domesticate, mould nature as to make it serve our own ends, and we can apply this knowledge to human society. Since it is primarily material wealth (objects gained through the process of subjugating nature) that conduces to our happiness, we should organize our lives,

our relationships, as to secure the maximum technical, economic and administrative efficiency in all our social activities. The rationalistic critique of capitalism, therefore, decries most of the *chaos* and *waste* involved in capitalist production, and its continued enthronement of ignorance and superstition . . . Socialism, the rational organization of society . . . [is] the self-evident crowning of the values and aspirations of the Enlightenment: it needs only common sense and the right kind of education to make people accept it and work towards its realization.[52]

Few liberals have been so convinced of the ability of reason not only to understand, but to shape and control nature and society according to human plans. Dewey, whom we have seen believed that some sort of socialism awaited us, came as close as any liberal to this extreme rationalism. His call for 'social control of economic forces' exemplified a deep faith in the ability of human intelligence to arrive at workable social and economic plans.[53] Dewey and his pragmatist followers in America had had enough of 'drift with attendant improvizations to meet special emergencies'.[54] Intelligence and experimental control were necessary. In a similar vein, Keynes wrote that 'the transition from economic anarchy to a regime which deliberately aims at controlling and directing economic forces in the interests of social justice and social stability, will present enormous difficulties both technical and political. I suggest, nevertheless, that the true destiny of New Liberalism is to seek their solution.'[55]

Admittedly, faith in conscious and relatively detailed control of the economy, which was 'winning recognition everywhere'[56] in the 1930s, has been abandoned by today's liberals. This is perhaps the chief development in liberal political theory over the past century: all liberalism is now market liberalism. Nevertheless, liberalism still vacillates between approaches to a version of socialist rationalism and an anti-rationalism that moves it closer to conservatism. Throughout the outgoing century liberals defended two opposing views of the nature of liberal order one stressing the spontaneous, unplanned order of a market society, the other stressing the crucial role for intentional design. The former has been of fundamental importance to classical liberalism. As Lord Robbins observed:

> The essence of Classical Liberalism was the belief that, within a suitable system of general rules and institutions, there will arise spontaneous relationships also deserving the name 'order' but which are self-sustaining and, within the limits prescribed by the rules, need no detailed and specific regulation.[57]

The most sophisticated articulation of this conception of liberal society and institutions is, of course, to be found in the work of Hayek. 'It would', says Hayek, 'be no exaggeration to say that social theory begins with – and has an object of study only because of – the discovery that there exist orderly structures which are the product of the action of many men but are not the result of human design'.[58] In contrast to a constructed or designed social order, the complexity of a spontaneous order 'is not limited to what a human mind can master . . . And not having been made it *cannot* legitimately be said to have a particular purpose'.[59] Because such orders can be highly complex Hayek is deeply sceptical of the ability of human reason to understand and control them. For Hayek this does not mean that they are either static or, as Dewey thought, adrift. As with Spencer before him, Hayek appeals to an evolutionary explanation of spontaneous adjustment, for evolution is the model of how individual decisions can generate overall changes and adaptations that were not intended by anyone.

Although Hayek's conception of a spontaneous order can be traced at least as far back as Adam Smith's analysis of the market in *The Wealth of Nations*,[60] it is wrong to see this conception of liberal order as necessarily individualistic. Strikingly, Bosanquet, writing at the close of the nineteenth century, develops a very similar understanding of social order. In ways remarkably akin to Hayek, Bosanquet insists that because of the complexity of social life, 'no one, not the greatest statesmen or historical philosopher, has in his mind, even in theory, much less as a practical object, the real development in which his community is moving'.[61] The very complexity and systemic character of society and its will thus precludes comprehensive economic planning. Bosanquet explicitly criticizes 'Economic Socialism' for failing to grasp that the social whole is composed of complex interactions of highly differentiated parts rather than essentially identical modules that can be arranged according to a plan. 'If you want to treat your social units as bricks in a wall or wheels in a machine, you cannot also and at the same time treat them as elements of an organism . . . Economic Socialism need not presuppose the social organism. It is, in appearance, a *substitute for* the life of that organism'.[62] Thus, Bosanquet concludes, socialism arises out of a 'blindness to the essential elements of the social organism, which can only exist as a structure of free individual wills, each entertaining the social purpose in an individual form appropriate to its structural position and organic functions'.[63] Bosanquet sums up his spontaneous, non-designed conception of society in telling us that

> on the whole, we are to the structure of legal, political, and economic organization like coral insects to a coral reef. All these things, and the body of science itself, are on one side natural products – that is to say, that, although conscious purpose works in them, the effect it produces is always part of a system which is more than any particular agent intended.[64]

Interestingly, Bosanquet, like Spencer and Hayek, identifies evolutionary competition as the path to social improvement. In social animals, Bosanquet argues, 'the struggle for existence has, in short, become a struggle for a place in the community; and these places are reserved for the individuals which in the highest degree possess the co-operative qualities demanded by the circumstances'.[65] Social progress, it seems, occurs mainly through this competition to produce successful social co-operators.

Opposing this long-standing liberal view is what Hayek describes as the 'constructivist' conception of society, which 'holds that human institutions will serve human purposes only if they have been deliberately designed for these purposes, often also that the fact that an institution exists is evidence of its having been created for a purpose, and always that we should so re-design society and its institutions that all our actions will be wholly guided by known purposes'.[66] Bentham was surely a constructivist in this sense, putting tremendous faith in the powers of reason to design rational and humane social institutions. Contemporary constructivists are apt to be more cautious than either Bentham or Dewey, acknowledging that social institutions cannot be redesigned *en masse* by a master designer. According to R.E. Goodin, a contemporary utilitarian:

> The Myth of the Intentional Designer (still less the Myth of the Intentional Design) is greatly to be avoided in theories of institutional design. Typically, there is no single design or designer. There are lots of localized attempts at partial design cutting across one another, and any sensible scheme for institutional design has to take account of that fact. Thus, even within the realm of our intentional intervention what we should be aiming at is not design of institutions directly. Rather, we should be aiming at designing schemes for designing institutions – schemes which will pay due regard to the multiplicity of designers and to the inevitably cross-cutting nature of their intentional interventions in the design process.[67]

Goodin's caution notwithstanding, we witness here a fundamentally different attitude to the nature of the liberal social order and the power of reason to understand, to design and redesign, to shape and reshape, social institutions to achieve human purposes. Thus, even though almost two centuries separate Bentham and Goodin – and in these centuries the hopes for an all-powerful social science that would allow us to consciously control society have dimmed – Goodin reasserts Bentham's understanding of governments as 'centralized co-ordinating agencies issuing orders . . . to maximize social utility'.[68]

Rationalism versus scepticism about values

Throughout the past hundred years liberalism has been torn between, on the one hand, varieties of value subjectivism and pluralism and, on the other, objectivist and monistic understandings of what is valuable. In contrast to the antinomy between advocates of the spontaneous order and constructivists, this cleavage partakes less of a debate between two well-defined positions than a multitude of theories that tend to group themselves into two loose camps. The 'sceptical' camp includes all those liberalisms premised on the supposition that the powers of human reason are insufficient to provide public, definitive, answers to the enduring questions concerning what makes life worth living, and to what ends we should devote ourselves. The sceptical camp can trace itself back to Hobbes and Locke. According to Locke:

The Mind has a different relish, as well as the Palate; and you will as fruitlessly endeavour to delight all Men with Riches or Glory, (which yet some Men place their Happiness in,) as you would satisfy all Men's Hunger with Cheese or Lobsters; which, though very agreeable and delicious fare to some, are to others extremely nauseous and offensive: And many People would with Reason prefer the griping of a hungry Belly, to those Dishes, which are a feast to others. Hence it was, I think that the Philosophers of old did in vain enquire, whether the *Summum bonum* consisted in Riches, or bodily delights, or Virtue, or Contemplation: And they might have as reasonably disputed, whether the best relish were to be found in Apples, Plumbs or Nuts; and have divided themselves into Sects upon it.[69]

Such subjectivist theories of value – which equate values with tastes or preference – have a prominent place in twentieth-century liberal theory. A subjective conception of value was integral to the Austrian school; Carl Menger and his followers such as von Mises explicitly endeavoured to integrate a subjectivist theory of value into economics.[70] Of course insofar as economic liberalism is based on the supposition that the satisfaction of preferences alone determines value, then it too is subjectivist. Subjectivist accounts of value have been defended by philosophers as well as economists: indeed it may well be that some form of subjectivism – that locates value either in the desires or feelings of agents – is the dominant account of value in twentieth-century philosophy.[71] The upshot of these subjective accounts is that, by relativizing value to the desires, feelings or preferences of the individual agent, they undermine the proposal that the state should devote itself to pursuing the *summum bonum*. Liberal politics, on this view, cannot be reasonably grounded on pursuit of what is truly valuable, for value is a matter of taste, and our tastes differ. Thus understood, the liberal state must, to use a controversial term, be *neutral* in the sense that (1) it cannot justify its policies by appeal to the correct value and (2) the liberal state necessarily tolerates diverse values. This idea is by no means the invention of late-twentieth-century thought. It was implied in Edward Westermarck's idea that the recognition of the subjective nature of value judgements quite properly leads to tolerance of the different values of others.[72]

Understood thus, the pluralism of Berlin, as well as the supposition of 'reasonable pluralism' by 'political liberals' such as Rawls and Charles Larmore, advocates a similar position: human reason does not unambiguously tell us what is truly of value, so a liberal state does not identify itself with the promotion of any of these controversial values. For Berlin, reason does not tell us what values to choose because values are ultimately plural and conflicting, and there simply is no correct choice to be made; for Rawls and Larmore questions of value are so complex and contentious that, even should there be a uniquely correct answer, our reason does not unambiguously tell us what it is.[73] The upshot of all these views is that a shared public rational discourse about the proper functioning of the liberal state cannot appeal to our controversial values. 'Agonistic liberals' [74] such as Rawls and Larmore have become especially concerned with the idea of 'public reason' – of articulating a shared basis for political reasoning in a society in which appeal to what is truly good or valuable is precluded.[75] Again, though, while recent political thought has been more self-conscious in exploring the idea of public reason, it has been an enduring problem, stemming back through Kant to Hobbes.[76] For Hobbes, who advocated a subjectivist theory of value which explicated goodness simply in terms of what a person desires, the core political problem was arriving at some notion of public reason. For Hobbes the conflict in the state of nature arises from conflicting private judgements; people's private reasoning yields conflicting judgements of good and bad, right and wrong, as well as about matters of fact, and this leads to the less intellectual conflict that characterizes the state of nature. Hobbes's solution is to appoint an 'arbitrator'. This 'judge', says Hobbes, provides 'public reason' to which private reason 'must submit'. The arbitrator proclaims what each has reason to do, and so defines a single, coherent conception of reason. And because, on Hobbes's view, we have authorized the judge (i.e., sovereign) to define public reason for us, the sovereign's pronouncements constitute a shared public reason on which there is consensus.[77]

The opposing camp has long insisted that a vibrant liberalism cannot be built on such sceptical foundations. 'No form of political life', proclaims William Galston, 'can be justified without some view of what is good for individuals'.[78] Scepticism and subjectivism have recently been attacked; as one recent critic of contemporary liberalism has put it, 'For some important reason – I am not sure why – many liberals have concluded that reason's scope is drastically limited'.[79] Neither liberal scepticism about value, nor a liberalism based on a robust theory of what is good for individuals – often called 'perfectionism' – is a late-twentieth-century innovation. Green's *Prolegomena to Ethics* was built on a theory of human self-realization or perfection, a theory that gave rise to his account of positive liberty.[80] Indeed, John Stuart Mill, Hobhouse, Bosanquet and Dewey all advocated theories of human development, and, as they saw it, the task of the legitimate liberal state was to promote human growth.[81] 'The foundation of liberty', said Hobhouse, 'is the idea of growth'.[82]

Why antinomies?

I have sketched three fundamental antinomies of twentieth-century liberalism: individualism–communitarianism, constructivism–anti-constructivism, rationalism–scepticism about values. Of course there are other, more familiar, antinomies such as that between classical and welfare liberalism, between liberty and equality, and between negative and positive liberty. My aim has been both to demonstrate that these antinomies do indeed mark liberal theory, and that they have done so throughout the twentieth century and even earlier. Although many contemporary political philosophers see the 'communitarian critique of individualism', the constructivist–anti-constructivist debate about institutional design, and the 'perfectionist critique of scepticism and neutrality' as distinctive features of late-twentieth-century liberal thinking, this is surely wrong. All were crucial debates in the first, as well as the last, decades of the century.

But *why* is liberalism characterized by these enduring antinomies? Why is it the case that so many of the debates of the last few years are in fundamental – though obviously not in all – respects re-enactments of debates of a century ago? Critics of liberalism insist that these enduring antinomies demonstrate the psychological, logical and political impossibility of the liberal project.[83] I wish to briefly comment on three other possible explanations of the antinomous nature of liberalism.

Liberalism as the political theory of compromise

In an earlier work, I remarked that 'one of the remarkable characteristics of liberal theory as it has evolved in the last two centuries has been its ability to integrate new ideologies, albeit in a greatly modified form, within a revised liberal outlook. Although the founders of liberal theory were not feminists, socialists or environmentalists, all these emerging ideologies are now part of the public morality of liberal society'.[84] At the time, it seemed to me that the unique, and appealing, feature of liberal theory was precisely that it was characterized by enduring antinomies, for this was an indication of its ability to justify itself to individualists and communitarians, subjectivists and objectivists, proponents of the market and socialists. To be sure, I argued that those favouring the radical proposals would be committed to compromising with others in a liberal regime, but I nevertheless saw it as a unique strength of liberal theory that it was marked by these antinomies. So given my own earlier analysis, the previous section identified a strength, not a weakness, of liberal theory.

We must distinguish, however, (1) liberalism as a political doctrine that can accommodate diverse and conflicting values or preferences and (2) liberalism as a doctrine with incompatible theoretical commitments. It is a virtue of liberalism that it can accommodate those whose values clash; some seek individuality while others strive after community, some believe that values are objective while others insist they are subjective, some are egalitarians while others insist that liberty must come first. Moreover, on at least some contentious political issues liberals may well advocate a compromise that benefits all parties. But all of this is quite different from saying that, according to liberalism, society is both simply a system of individuals moved by their subjective values, and an organic collectivity in which shared values define the nature of the individual selves. Embracing *that* type of antinomy can hardly be a virtue of a political theory, if we understand political theories as reasoned attempts to understand the social and political world. For the social world cannot be both as the individualist sees it and as the collectivist sees it. To provide a framework accommodating conflicting values and goals is catholic; to advocate a theory that embraces contradictory views of individuals, values and society is confused.

Reason, plurality and ambivalence

Liberalism, we have seen, seems torn between polar opposites. If we understand these antinomies to be basic to liberal theory, we seem driven to conclude that liberalism is inconsistent. As a movement, it is both individualist and communitarian, both constructivist and anti-constructivist, both rationalistic and sceptical. Yet, insofar as political theory is rational, it aims to construct a coherent view of humans and their social and political world. John W. Chapman has conjectured that our reason, understood as a drive to construct a coherent experience, may be in tension with our ambivalent nature.[85] Berlin repeatedly insists that values are plural and irreconcilable. To commit to individuality, for example, is to preclude intense forms of community.[86] If however, we are deeply attracted to both individuality and community, or attracted to pluralism and the choice it offers us while also longing for what Berlin calls 'the final solution' of an ultimate reconciliation of values, we may well find any consistent political theory to be unacceptable, as it precludes some aspects of value and human existence that we cherish. The lessons of opportunity costs come hard, and may not be appealing; if we are to be consistent, to endorse some view entails the cost of abandoning those positions that are inconsistent with it. But if Chapman is correct that our nature is ambivalent, and Berlin is correct that all the enduring values cannot be harmoniously integrated, then it seems inevitable that any widely appealing view – in order to be widely appealing – must be inconsistent. Interestingly, a recent survey of Americans' attitudes is consistent with this analysis: Americans seem simultaneously drawn to both individualist self-interest and community-oriented sacrifice and duty. 'Americans like to lament their individualistic bent, all the while pursuing it.'[87]

Let us distinguish a political theory from a political ideology.[88] A political theory aims at a coherent and justified account of humans, society and the political. A hallmark of political theory is its reasoning and consistency; an inconsistent political theory is necessarily flawed. In contrast, we can understand an ideology as an action-guiding set of beliefs that is both widely appealing and helps make sense of the main features of social and political experience to those who embrace it. From the philosophical point of view, of course, an inconsistent doctrine cannot help make sense of the world. But if we understand 'making sense' as accounting for the main values and having a place for all the things to which we are attracted, then a successful ideology will almost inevitably be contradictory. Anything so stark as a well reasoned and fully consistent view of the world will not be widely appealing, for it will seem to most of us to leave out too much of human experience. Although we crave consistency, we also crave to have our longings met, even when these longings are themselves contradictory. This conception of ideology does not see it as 'intensely theoretical' and systematic;[89] indeed, its core trait is lack of true system. Ideologies seek an emotionally and psychologically compelling package of beliefs, commitments and values; it is dubious indeed that any philosophical theory can be so accommodating.

This explanation of the antinomies of liberalism makes sense of both the success and failure of liberalism in the last century. As a political ideology it has been immensely successful; it has found room for individualism and communitarianism, for planners and free marketeers, for value sceptics and perfectionists. But this success as an ideology is the root of the failure of liberalism as a political theory to resolve its antinomies; the very scope of its appeal ensures that no fully consistent liberal theory will emerge vindicated over its rivals.

Liberal political theory versus liberal ideology

The foregoing suggests that, given our inherently ambivalent nature and the plurality of values, any successful ideology will necessarily appeal to contradictory views so as to be satisfying. An alternative account – to which, I shall confess, I am attracted – takes over much of this idea, but abjures strong claims about our human nature or the inherent plurality of values. On this more modest – though somewhat pessimistic – account, liberalism as a reasoned and consistent political theory is inevitably in conflict with liberalism as a ruling ideology because, although liberal political theory is in many ways highly attractive, it is too principled and severe a doctrine to have widespread political appeal.

It is plausible, though of course contentious, to identify core liberal political theory with something like classical liberalism, in particular what might be called 'economic liberalism'. Although, of course, the liberal tradition in politics goes back far beyond *The Wealth of Nations*, Smith's work may plausibly be understood as commencing a line of thinking that transformed liberalism from a loose set of Whiggish commitments concerning the importance of consent, liberty of conscience, property and toleration into a systematic view of individual purposes, social relations and the role of the state. This theory, of course, does not arise full-blown from Smith, but develops, over two centuries, out of his work.[90] The resulting theory is in most senses resolutely and radically individualistic; it understands societies as unintended systems of individuals, created by individuals pursuing their subjective values and tastes. To be sure, limited possibilities for intentional intervention have long been justified; but the analysis of the virtues of the market, conjoined with the theory of 'government failure', does not leave room for extensive intentional planning and interventions by government.[91] The only consistently non-individualistic element of this theory is utilitarian moral collectivism, but even that is greatly modified and individualized. According to Samuel Brittan's restatement of economic liberalism, '[t]he traditional economist's case for a form of market economy has been based on what might be called *liberal utilitarianism*. This is a belief that individual desires should normally be satisfied to the maximum degree possible without interfering with the desires of others. The utilitarianism involved is a highly qualified one.'[92] Moreover, insofar as the Paretean criterion[93] replaces classical utilitarianism as the measure of social improvement, society is no longer viewed as 'one big person'.

My suggestion – it is clearly nothing so grand as an argument – is that classical liberalism presents a unique, consistent and systematic view of individuals, values, society and government. Because it endorses individualism, anti-constructivism and value scepticism it is a consistent doctrine, and is responsible for most of the innovations that are uniquely liberal. In some respects it is an appealing doctrine; it liberates humans to act on their own subjective values or preferences, and dethrones élites who would claim special insight into the nature of the good life, and how it should be pursued. And it has provided the rationale for the market economy, which has generated a phenomenal growth in wealth over the last 150 years. Yet, while it is appealing in many ways, it is also deeply unattractive to many. Most people see it as too limited a view of the social order. Classical liberalism does not attribute shared purposes, or great and noble projects to civil society as such, nor does it provide its citizens with assurances that their lives will go as well as possible. People must pursue their own visions of greatness and nobility within their own lives and voluntary associations, for there simply is no correct or communal understanding of what is good, great and noble. There are no objective values that all must serve, no communal projects in which we all can participate and experience solidarity. While its individualism liberates each to pursue his own preferences most people want more from society and politics. Even Nozick, so long the *bête noire* of anti-libertarians, now *wants* more:

> Within the operation of democratic institutions . . . we want expressions of the values that concern us and bind us together. The libertarian position I once propounded now seems to me seriously inadequate, in part because it did not fully knit the humane considerations and joint cooperative activities it left room for more closely into the social fabric . . . There are some things we choose to do together through government in solemn marking of our human solidarity.[94]

Relatively few find the pure classical liberal theory a comfortable or exciting vision of individuals, society and politics. As one advocate has admitted, it has 'failed to capture the popular imagination as an acceptable form of civil society'.[95] Ludwig von Mises noted that although parts of the classical liberal programme have been adopted widely, nowhere has it been fully embraced. 'Liberalism was never permitted to come to its full fruition.'[96] If liberalism is to be a success as a political ideology – if it is to gain widespread allegiance, from policy-makers and citizens alike – it must be more inclusive, embracing forms of community, value objectivity and rational planning and institutional design. Recall Hobhouse's remark that if liberalism was to survive it must learn from socialism. He seemed to be entirely right; it did, and it survived and flourished as an ideology.

Conclusion: liberal theory and liberal ideology

I began this essay with a puzzle. At the outset of the twentieth century liberals were pessimistic about the prospects of liberalism, yet by its close liberalism had apparently defeated, or had certainly got the upper hand on, its traditional rivals. Yet liberal political theorists finished the century arguing about most of the things they were disputing at its outset. I first tried to defend this unflattering evaluation of liberal theory, showing how three antinomies (individualism–collectivism, constructivism–anti-constructivism, value rationalism–scepticism) characterized liberal debates throughout most of the last century. I was especially concerned to dispel the idea that these are all debates of recent origin. I then turned to three possible explanations of this paradox of political success and theoretical stalemate. Having considered and rejected the possibility that the presence of these tensions or antinomies is actually a strength rather than weakness of liberal theory, I explored two related proposals. First, I considered the hypothesis that our ambivalent nature ensures that any doctrine to which we form real allegiance is itself ambivalent and contradictory; thus the success of liberalism in engendering allegiance is accounted for by the persisting antinomies that block theoretical advance. I then considered a somewhat different, and probably more controversial, proposal, that the heart of liberalism is the classical view – a consistent theory that is highly individualistic, sceptical about value and anti-constructivist, or at least extremely cautious about the idea of 'institutional design'. I realize, of course, that others advance contrary views of liberalism, which marginalize the classical and economic tradition. I certainly have not refuted such analyses.[97] I have suggested, however, that if the classical view is understood as the heart of liberalism – containing its truly distinctive claims and insights – its failure to capture the popular imagination accounts for the enduring tensions of liberal ideology. Only by blending classical liberalism with inconsistent doctrines could liberalism become a ruling ideology.

Notes and references

1 Herbert Spencer, 'From freedom to bondage', in H. Spencer, *The Man Versus the State, with Six Essays on Government, Society and Freedom*, Indianapolis IN, Liberty Fund, 1982, pp. 487–518.
2 L.T. Hobhouse, *Liberalism*, London, Williams and Norgate, 1911, p. 214.
3 Ibid.
4 Ibid., p. 226.
5 Guido de Ruggiero, *The History of European Liberalism*, translated by R.G. Collingwood, Boston MA, Beacon Press, 1959, Part II, Chapter 6.
6 John Dewey, *Liberalism and Social Action*, New York, G.P. Putnam's Sons, 1980 [1935], pp. 1–2.
7 Ibid., Chapter 2, p. 90.
8 John Dewey, *Individualism, Old and New*, London, George Allen and Unwin, 1931, pp. 111–12.
9 J. Salwyn Schapiro, *Liberalism: Its Meaning and History*, Princeton NJ, D. Van Nostrand, 1958, pp. 88–9.
10 I argue for this claim in my *Political Concepts and Political Theories*, Boulder CO, Westview Press, 2000, Chapter 8.
11 See Michael Freeden, *Ideologies and Political Theory: A Conceptual Approach*, Oxford, Clarendon Press, 1996, Chapter 7.
12 John Kekes, *A Case for Conservatism*, Ithaca NY, Cornell University Press, 1998, p. 19.
13 Stephen Holmes, *The Anatomy of Antiliberalism*, Cambridge MA, Harvard University Press, 1993, p. xi.
14 Dewey, *Liberalism and Social Action*, p. 91.
15 Ibid.
16 I draw here on Edward Shils, 'The antinomies of liberalism', in Zbigniew Brzezinski *et al.* (eds), *The Relevance of Liberalism*, Boulder CO, Westview Press, 1978, pp. 135–200.
17 Jeremy Bentham, *Introduction to the Principles of Morals and Legislation*, edited by J.H. Burns and H.L.A. Hart, London, Athlone Press, 1970, Chapter 1, section 4. Compare J.S. Mill, *A System of Logic: Ratiocinative and Inductive*: 'Human beings in society have no properties but those which are derived from, and which may be resolved into, the laws of the nature of individual men'. *The Collected Works of John Stuart Mill*, edited by J.M. Robson, Toronto, University of Toronto Press, 1963, Vol. VIII, p. 879.

18 Herbert Spencer, *Social Statics*, New York, Robert Schalkenback Foundation, 1995 [1851], p. 1. See also his *First Principles*, London, Williams and Norgate, 1862, Chapter 10, section 85.

19 D.G. Ritchie, *The Principles of State Interference: Four Essays on the Political Philosophy of Herbert Spencer, J.S. Mill, and T.H. Green*, London, George Allen and Unwin, 1902, p. 13. This view is closer to Spencer than it may first appear. Spencer criticized Bentham for failing to appreciate the 'complexity of the social organism', though Spencer's understanding of the social organism was distinctly individualist: Spencer, *Social Statics*, p. 12.

20 Bernard Bosanquet, *The Philosophical Theory of the State and Related Essays*, edited by Gerald F. Gaus and William Sweet, Indianapolis IN, St Augustine Press, 2001, p. 175.

21 See Gerald F. Gaus, 'Green, Bosanquet and the philosophy of coherence', in C.L. Ten (ed.), *The Routledge History of Philosophy*, Vol. 7, *The Nineteenth Century*, general editors S.G. Shanker and G.H.R. Parkinson, London, Routledge, 1994, pp. 408–36.

22 See L.T. Hobhouse, *The Metaphysical Theory of the State*, London, Allen & Unwin, 1926, pp. 61ff.; John Dewey, 'Time and individuality', in *John Dewey: The Essential Writings*, edited by David Sidorsky, New York, Harper and Row, 1977, p. 137.

23 On Hobhouse, see Michael Freeden, *The New Liberalism: An Ideology of Social Reform*, Oxford, Clarendon Press, 1978; on Dewey, see Alfonso J. Damico, *Individuality and Community: The Social and Political Thought of John Dewey*, Gainesville FL, University Press of Florida, 1978.

24 A.F. Mummery and J.A. Hobson, *The Physiology of Industry*, New York, Kelly and Millman, 1956, p. 106.

25 John Maynard Keynes, 'The end of *laissez-faire*', in his *Essays in Persuasion*, London, Macmillan, 1972, p. 275.

26 Karl Popper, *The Open Society and its Enemies*, Vol. 2, London, Routledge, 1945.

27 James M. Buchanan and Gordon Tullock, *The Calculus of Consent: Logical Foundations of Constitutional Democracy*, Ann Arbor MI, The University of Michigan Press, 1965, pp. 11–12.

28 Ibid., pp. 13 and vi.

29 Buchanan himself develops a Hobbesian individualist liberalism in *The Limits of Liberty: Between Anarchy and Leviathan*, Chicago, University of Chicago Press, 1975. Jean Hampton's *Hobbes and the Social Contract Tradition*, Cambridge, Cambridge University Press, 1986, was also influential in this regard, as was Gregory S. Kavka's *Hobbesian Moral and Political Theory*, Princeton NJ, Princeton University Press, 1986. For a critical evaluation, see Jody S. Kraus, *The Limits of Hobbesian Contractarianism*, Cambridge, Cambridge University Press, 1993.

30 Amy Gutmann, 'Communitarian critics of liberalism', *Philosophy and Public Affairs*, 1985, Vol. 14, p. 308.

31 See Michael Sandel, *Liberalism and the Limits of Justice*, Cambridge, Cambridge University Press, 1982.

32 This aspect of the 'communitarian critique' is more evident in Robert N. Bellah, Richard Madsen, William M. Sullivan, Ann Swidler and Steven M. Tipton, *Habits of the Heart: Individualism and Commitment in American Life*, Berkeley CA, University of California Press, 1985.

33 Will Kymlicka, *Liberalism, Community and Culture*, Oxford, Clarendon Press, 1991, p. 208.

34 The most sophisticated recent attempt is S.I. Benn, *A Theory of Freedom*, Cambridge, Cambridge University Press, 1988.

35 Gutmann, 'Communitarian critics of liberalism', p. 308.

36 On the relevance of earlier twentieth-century liberal theory to the recent 'communitarian critiques', see Alan Ryan, 'The liberal community', in John W. Chapman and Ian Shapiro (eds), *NOMOS XXXV: Democratic Community*, New York, New York University Press, 1993, pp. 91–114; Avital Simhony and David Weinstein (eds), *The New Liberals*, Cambridge, Cambridge University Press, forthcoming.

37 See T.H. Green, *Prolegomena to Ethics*, edited by A.C. Bradley, Oxford, Clarendon Press, 1890, p. 104; *Works of Thomas Hill Green*, edited by R.L. Nettleship, London: Longmans, 1893, Vol. I, pp. 339–41. For a more complete analysis of Green's and Bosanquet's theories of the self, see my 'Green, Bosanquet and the philosophy of coherence', pp. 414–16.
38 See especially Bosanquet's *Psychology of the Moral Self*, London, Macmillan, 1904.
39 Buchanan and Tullock, *The Calculus of Consent*, p. vii.
40 Spencer, *Social Statics*, p. 18.
41 Ibid., p. 87.
42 See Bosanquet, 'The antithesis between individualism and socialism philosophically considered', in *The Philosophical Theory of the State and Related Essays*, pp. 324–46.
43 John W. Chapman, 'Justice and fairness', in Carl J. Friedrich and John W. Chapman (eds), *NOMOS VI: Justice*, New York, Atherton, 1964, p. 153.
44 Green, *Prolegomena to Ethics*, p. 210. For Hobhouse, see his *The Rational Good*, London, Watts, 1947 [1921].
45 T.H. Green, *Lectures on the Principles of Political Obligation and Other Writings*, edited by Paul Harris and John Morrow, Cambridge, Cambridge University Press, 1986, p. 79.
46 Green, *Prolegomena to Ethics*, p. 429.
47 Ludwig von Mises, *Liberalism in the Classical Tradition*, San Francisco, Cobden Press, 1985, p. 7.
48 Holmes, *The Anatomy of Antiliberalism*, p. 247.
49 This aspect of the liberal tradition is stressed by D. Manning, *Liberalism*, London, Dent, 1976, pp. 43–50. Cf. J. Roland Pennock, *Liberal Democracy: Its Merits and Prospects*, New York, Rinehart and Co., 1950, pp. 24–32.
50 Von Mises, *Liberalism in the Classical Tradition*, p. 7.
51 See Michael Oakeshott, *Rationalism in Politics*, expanded edition, Indianapolis MI, Liberty Press, 1991, pp. 5–42. For an excellent summary of Oakeshott's anti-rationalism, see Kirk F. Koerner, *Liberalism and its Critics*, London, Croom Helm, 1985, p. 272.
52 R.N. Berki, *Socialism*, London, Dent, 1975, pp. 27–8.
53 Dewey, *Liberalism and Social Action*, pp. 87ff.
54 Ibid., p. 87.
55 Keynes, 'Am I a liberal?', in his *Essays in Persuasion*, p. 305.
56 J.A. Hobson, *The Science of Wealth*, fourth edition, revised by R.F. Harrod, London, Oxford University Press, 1950, p. 200.
57 Lord Robbins, *Political Economy: Past and Present*, London, Macmillan, 1977, p. 9.
58 F.A. Hayek, *Law, Legislation and Liberty*, Vol. I: *Rules and Order*, London, Routledge & Kegan Paul, 1973, p. 37.
59 Ibid., p. 38.
60 See my 'Public and private interests in liberal political economy, old and new', in S.I. Benn and G.F. Gaus (eds), *Public and Private in Social Life*, London, Croom Helm, 1983, pp. 186ff.
61 Bernard Bosanquet, 'The reality of the general will', in his *Aspects Of The Social Problem*, London, Macmillan, 1895, pp. 319–32. I explore the relation of Bosanquet's and Hayek's conceptions of society and economy in my 'Bosanquet's communitarian defence of economic individualism', in Simhony and Weinstein (eds), *The New Liberals*.
62 Bosanquet, 'The antithesis between individualism and socialism', p. 330.
63 Ibid., p. 334.
64 Bosanquet, 'The reality of the general will', pp. 328–9.
65 Bosanquet, 'Socialism and natural selection', in *Aspects Of The Social Problem*, p. 294.
66 Hayek, *Law, Legislation and Liberty*, pp. 8–9.
67 R.E. Goodin, 'Institutions and their design', in R.E. Goodin (ed.), *The Theory of Institutional Design*, Cambridge, Cambridge University Press, 1996, p. 28.
68 R.E. Goodin, *Utilitarianism as a Public Philosophy*, Cambridge, Cambridge University Press, 1996, pp. 62 and 76. For a criticism, see my 'Why all welfare states (including

laissez-faire ones) are unreasonable', in Ellen Frankel Paul, Fred D. Miller and Jeffrey Paul (eds), *Problems of Market Liberalism*, Cambridge, Cambridge University Press, 1998, pp. 1–33.

69 John Locke, *An Essay Concerning Human Understanding*, edited by Peter H. Nidditch, Oxford, Clarendon Press, 1975, p. 269 (Book II, Chapter XXI, section 55). For Hobbes, see *Leviathan*, edited by Michael Oakeshott, Oxford, Blackwell, 1948, Chapter 6.

70 See Carl Menger, *Principles of Economics*, translated by James Dingwall and Bert F. Hoselitz, Grove City PA, Libertarian Press, 1994, Chapter III; *Subjectivism, Intelligibility and Economic Understanding*, edited by Israel M. Kirzner, New York, New York University Press, 1986; Ludwig von Mises, *Human Action: A Treatise on Economics*, third edition, Chicago, Contemporary Books, 1966.

71 See G. Gaus, *Value and Justification: The Foundations of Liberal Theory*, Cambridge, Cambridge University Press, 1990, Chapter 3.

72 See Edward Westermarck, *Ethical Relativity*, London, Kegan Paul, 1932, pp. 59–60.

73 See, e.g., Isaiah Berlin, 'Two concepts of liberty', in his *Four Essays on Liberty*, New York, Oxford University Press, 1969; John Rawls, *Political Liberalism*, New York, Columbia University Press, 1993, p. 57; Charles Larmore, *The Morals of Modernity*, Cambridge, Cambridge University Press, 1996, Chapters 6 and 7.

74 I borrow this term from John Gray, *Berlin*, London, Fontana, 1995, p. 8. Jon Riley has argued that Berlin's account straddles the rationalist–agnostic divide. See his forthcoming essay on Berlin's agnostic liberal rationalism in the *American Political Science Review*.

75 For an overview, see my entry on 'Public reason', in *The International Encyclopedia of the Social and Behavioural Sciences*, Oxford, Elsevier Scientific Publishers, forthcoming.

76 On Kant's understanding of public reason, see Fred D'Agostino and Gerald F. Gaus, 'Public reason: why, what and can (and should) it be?', in Fred D'Agostino and Gerald F. Gaus, (eds) *Public Reason*, Aldershot, Ashgate, 1998, pp. xi–xxiii.

77 See Hobbes, *Leviathan*, p. 291 (Chapter 37). See also Lawrence B. Solum, 'Constructing an ideal of public reason', *San Diego Law Review*, Fall 1993, Vol. 30, p. 754; David Gauthier, 'Public reason', *Social Philosophy and Policy*, Winter 1995, Vol. 12, pp. 25–6.

78 William Galston, *Liberal Purposes: Goods, Virtues and Diversity in the Liberal State*, Cambridge, Cambridge University Press, 1991, p. 79.

79 George Sher, *Beyond Neutrality: Perfectionism in Politics*, Princeton, NJ, Princeton University Press, 1997, p. ix.

80 Recall that for Green, a person is in the positive sense unfree when 'the objects to which his actions are directed are objects in which, according to the law of his own being, satisfaction of himself is not to be found. His will to arrive at self-satisfaction not being adjusted to the law which determines where this self-satisfaction is to be found, he may be considered in the condition of a bondsman who is carrying out the will of another, not his own.' Green, 'On the different senses of freedom', in *Lectures on the Principles of Political Obligation and Other Writings*, p. 228.

81 As I argued in my *Modern Liberal Theory of Man*, London, Croom Helm, 1983. I also argued there that Rawls's *A Theory of Justice*, Cambridge MA, Harvard University Press, 1971 advanced such a conception of 'perfection'. In this respect his later *Political Liberalism* is distinctly more agonistic.

82 Hobhouse, *Liberalism*, p. 122.

83 See Roberto Mangabeira Unger, *Knowledge and Politics*, New York, Basic Books, 1975. For liberal replies to Unger, see Holmes, *The Anatomy of Antiliberalism*, pp. 141–75; Gerald F. Gaus and John W. Chapman, 'Anarchism and political philosophy: an introduction', in J. Roland Pennock and John W. Chapman (eds), *NOMOS XIX: Anarchism*, New York, New York University Press, 1978, pp. xxii–xl.

84 Gaus, *Value and Justification*, p. 465.

85 See John W. Chapman, 'Toward a general theory of human nature and dynamics', in J. Roland Pennock and John W. Chapman (eds), *NOMOS XVII: Human Nature in Politics*, New York, New York University Press, 1977, pp. 292–319. See also J. Roland Pennock, *Democratic Political Theory*, Princeton NJ, Princeton University Press, 1979, Chapter 3.

86 I have argued this in *The Modern Liberal Theory of Man*. See also my *Social Philosophy*, New York, M.E. Sharpe, 1999, pp. 39–46. For an excellent analysis, see S.I. Benn, 'Individuality, autonomy and community', in Eugene Kamenka (ed.), *Community as a Social Ideal*, London, Edward Arnold, 1982, Chapter 3.

87 Andrew J. Cherlin, 'I'm OK, you're selfish', *New York Times Magazine*, 17 October 1999, p. 50.

88 I have dealt with this contrast in depth in *Political Concepts and Political Theories*, Chapter 2. The critical contemporary work on this subject is Freeden, *Ideologies and Political Theory*.

89 Cf. Kenneth Minogue, *Alien Powers: The Pure Theory of Ideology*, London, Weidenfeld and Nicholson, 1985, pp. 3 and 15.

90 In particular, it should be stressed that Smith himself, especially when *The Wealth of Nations* is read in the light of his other works, may depart from this view in many ways. For an overview of Smith's philosophy, see Stephen Darwall, 'Sympathetic liberalism: recent work on Adam Smith', *Philosophy and Public Affairs*, Spring 1999, Vol. 28, pp. 139–64.

91 The idea of 'government failure' is not the invention of recent public choice theorists. For the views of classical liberal economists on government failure, see my 'Public and private interests in liberal political economy, old and new'. See also Alan Peacock, *Public Choice Analysis in Historical Perspective*, Cambridge, Cambridge University Press, 1992.

92 Samuel Brittan, *A Restatement of Economic Liberalism*, Atlantic Highlands NJ, Humanities Press, 1988, p. 43.

93 Roughly, social condition S2 is Pareto superior to S1 if and only if everyone is at least as well off in S2 as in S1 and at least one person is better off than in S1.

94 Robert Nozick, *The Examined Life*, New York, Simon and Schuster, 1989, pp. 286–7.

95 See Jonathan R. Macey, 'On the failure of libertarianism to capture the popular imagination', in Paul, Miller and Paul (eds), *Problems of Market Liberalism*, pp. 372–411. See also Loren Lomasky's essay in the same volume, 'Libertarianism as if (the other 99 per cent) people mattered', pp. 350–71.

96 Von Mises, *Liberalism in the Classical Tradition*, p. 1.

97 But see von Mises (*Liberalism in the Classical Tradition*, pp. 198ff.) on what is unique to liberalism, and what distinguishes it from other doctrines.

3   Did ideology fall with 'the wall'?

Marx, Marxism, post-Marxism

Terrell Carver

Marxism is not only variable as an ideology, it also incorporates variable views as to what an ideology is in the first place. Some of the views within the ideology, and within Marxist theories about ideology itself, are actually not just different from each other, but contradictory. This makes the exposition of 'Marxism' quite complicated and difficult to comprehend.[1] How can an ideology, supposedly an identifiable unity, contain contradictions, and yet still inspire intellectuals and practitioners in politics?

The answer is that this variability within Marxism has arisen over 150 years of theoretical and practical input by different people in different circumstances. Marxism is thus an unusually productive political and intellectual resource, and has taken adaptation and innovation past even logical limits. Within its protean conceptual framework, there are a number of specifiable approaches to political action, and to the relationship between ideas and action, which have survived very stringent intellectual and historical tests. In a sense any failures are marks of success. Marxism has thus captured numerous positions on theory and practice in politics, or is at least compatible with them. The Marxist tradition is so well developed that these debts are readily acknowledged in the literature, whether pro or con, and can be easily traced whenever ideology as such is discussed. Marxism is thus an enduring and foundational system of ideas. Even Post-Marxism is not really 'after Marxism', but rather Marxism reinterpreted yet again.

During the twentieth century Marxism was viewed as an ideology. What it was thought to be, and to say, was profoundly influenced by this conceptual framing. That is, your view of Marxism was at least somewhat determined by your view of ideology; knowing that Marxism was supposed to be an ideology told you what to look for, and what kinds of things you were looking at. Thus a view of ideology as a dogmatic system linked to totalitarian politics yielded variants of Marxism that, self-confessedly or not, approached this syndrome (e.g., Stalinism or Maoism). A view of ideology, by contrast, as merely action-oriented ideas found a rather different Marxism (e.g., Trotskyite or Gramscian thought). And a view of ideology as a theory of knowledge gave rather a different Marxism again (e.g., dialectical materialism or critical realism).

While it may seem at times that Marxism involves a rather pedantic exegesis of texts, it must also be remembered that much of the publicity and controversy surrounding Marxism has come from hostile or unsympathetic accounts. Self-defined Marxists have replied to these, invoking foundational ideas and figures, and have therefore constructed the rather variable and politically attuned Marxisms mentioned above in response to criticism and persecution. Any account of Marxism is not only framed by an understanding of ideology as such but also by the political circumstances and views of the writers involved.[2]

Perhaps the most synoptic way to view Marxism conceptually and historically is to see it as a way of linking liberalism and economics explicitly and critically, that is, linking ideas of individual rights and democratic decision-making with the competitive individualism based on private property and capitalist relations of production and exchange. While liberals acknowledge this linkage historically, they diverge among themselves on the extent to which either liberalism or capitalism implies and validates the other. Some liberals argue that democratic politics requires a 'free' market in capital, goods and services; others take a more restrictive line, seeing the inequalities and uncertainties of capitalist economies as avoidable precisely because liberal political systems allow for a necessary minimum of collective management. Any form of Marxism makes this ambivalence amongst liberals much more problematic.

The subsequent ability of liberals to manage such economies and to deliver on their constitutive rights and freedoms is very severely questioned by Marxists, and sometimes flatly denied, presenting liberals as dupes, or worse, of the great economic interests that constitute national and global capital. The ability of such economies to deliver defensible standards of living over time, rather than worsening crises and class warfare, is roundly contested by Marxists, arguing that what passes for freedom is in fact exploitation. On this synoptic view there is going to be an area of overlap intellectually and politically between 'left' liberals, socialists and 'gradualist' Marxists. Either this does not matter very much in practice, or Marxists can be distinguished by a reverence for foundational texts (as could 'left' liberals and socialists, too, albeit for different writers).

Unlike liberals and socialists, Marxists made the concept of ideology their own. Even in a weak sense of ideology ('action-oriented ideas') many liberals and socialists would fight shy of using the term, and there have been many polemics and philosophies erected by liberals and socialists precisely to deny the truth and efficacy of a strong sense of the term ('a master science of ideas').[3] Karl Marx occupied a critical position with respect to ideology as a concept, employing it as a pejorative term in his manuscript work (co-authored with Friedrich Engels) *The German Ideology*. While largely unpublished as such in Marx's lifetime, the ideas in this polemical work circulated around the time of writing (1845–6) and reappeared in later works up to his death in 1883.[4] Ideologists, on this view, were intellectuals who promulgated illusions, dogma, dreams and distortions. Politically they were said to be a problem because, wittingly or no, these illusions often served the interests of classes or interests in society, whilst pretending rather hypocritically to promulgate descriptive truths and prescriptive norms. Thus class position for Marx often explained why such illusions were promulgated and why they were perceived as truths.

The specific writers attacked by Marx and Engels as 'German ideologists' were also, as it happens, philosophical idealists (or at least Marx and Engels portrayed them as such). Philosophical idealists reckon that ideas are the only reality, or the only effective reality, and that existence, and any change in it, is predominantly a matter of ideas and thoughts, or at least that the linkage between ideas and action is direct and unproblematic. Thus the complaint in *The German Ideology* was that a certain school of writers ('critical critics') were not only unwitting servants of middle-class interests (as opposed to the interests of an impoverished working class) but that they underplayed or denied the importance of economic interests in life, and the need for effective change in the production and distribution of wealth.

Whether or not these allegations were true or important is of course debatable, and was so at the time. Historically it was an important episode in giving currency to 'ideology' as a term of critique, and to a particular line of criticism, namely that discourse about social change should be angled towards an explicit engagement with class politics, economic interests, and radical economic as well as political change. Moreover *The German Ideology* offered a sociological thesis as well, distinguishing between 'active' ideologists and those who passively reproduce it in the course of their ordinary activities and working lives:

> [W]ithin this class one segment steps forth as the thinkers of the class (its active, conceptive ideologues, whose living derives mainly from cultivation of this class's illusion about itself), while the other segment relates more passively and receptively to these ideas and illusions, because in actuality they are the active members of this class and have less time to formulate these illusions and ideas about themselves.[5]

The association between influential intellectuals and ideologists was a natural one, in that the concept, as formulated by Destutt de Tracy in the 1790s, had started out with that presumption, albeit presented in a favourable light. Marx's notion of democratic politics by contrast was non-élitist in its rhetoric, and almost non-existent in his own practice as an intellectual. He seemed content to advocate class struggle at the level of nearly spontaneous class action, rather than at any level of leadership beyond the merely advisory. Even the concept of a political party was problematic in his writing, as was any leading role for intellectuals in working-class politics.[6]

Marx was thus doubly hostile to ideology, even as action-oriented ideas, in that he had two problems with 'ideas'. Firstly, 'ideas' were propounded by intellectuals, whereas class politics for Marx was portrayed, perhaps rather naively, as action coincident with class interests, rather than the fulfilment of any truth or system, as intellectuals often had it. Secondly, 'ideas' for Marx had an air of philosophical idealism, a view that obscured the realities of politics and revolutionary change in endless rhetoric and wars of words, again an intellectual and generally nugatory pursuit. Marx was, of course, an intellectual giving voice to ideas (often very complex ones about both philosophy and economics) that were intended to serve the interests of working-class people, or ultimately anyone disadvantaged by modern economic relations. In so far as he looked at his own ideas and their dissemination, he referred to them as a critique or an outlook, and characterized them as *wissenschaftlich*, scientific or systematic in the broadest sense of valid knowledge about anything concrete or abstract, and certainly not limited to, nor based upon, the physical sciences.

While superficially Marx's views about the dissolution of capitalism and the inevitability of working-class revolution might seem to qualify formally as an ideology on his own terms (an intellectual system serving the interests of a class), it is clear that in his own mind he drew a sharp line between helping a movement which he said was already under way, and propounding an ideology, which for him was by definition élitist and illusory. Quite how Marx would have distinguished his thought as both non-élitist and non-illusory from the thought of ideologists and the thoughts in the ideologies that he criticized is something of an unknown. His arguments have the air of assertion, rather than more conventional philosophical demonstration.

Marx's ontology and epistemology have been hypothetically constructed by others in a number of different ways, with the presumption that this would distinguish his work from mere ideology and demonstrate its truth. Marx did not do this himself, but it is clear that he assumed that there was a distinguishing line of this kind between his own views and critiques and the self-serving and class-serving systems propounded by ideologists. Part of the problem here is that writing up this kind of philosophical prolegomenon would have somewhat contradicted the political thrust of his writing. This was towards the seamless merger of his thought and action into the spontaneous working-class politics that he seems to have envisaged.

From 1859 Engels took on the job of introducing his friend Marx, and Marx's newly published critical study of modern political economy, to the world. He presented Marx as a great systematic thinker in the manner of Hegel, but, unlike Hegel, propounding ideas that were in line with, and indeed explanatory of, the developments in physical science that had occurred since the 1840s. Engels identified Marx with philosophical materialism, the view that existence is comprised only within, and is explicable only by, matter in motion. Marx's thought was thus presented as a coherent and comprehensive whole, aligned with the evident successes of the latest natural science. While Marx was interested in modern physical science, this interest was generally directed towards the function of science-driven technologies in economic development, rather than philosophical systems claiming to be 'materialist' and therefore congruent with physics and chemistry as understood at the time. Perhaps it would not be unjust, nor unduly anachronistic, to characterize Engels's presentation of Marx and his work in this particular way as 'spin'.[7]

Marx's work has thus been read in the light of Engels's view of him as the author of a systematic science ('scientific socialism', a phrase not used by Marx) incorporating a universal methodology ('laws of dialectics', another phrase Marx never used). In Engels's view Marx's works offered incontrovertible truths about history as a succession of economic epochs, about the nature and future of global capitalism, and about the certainty of working-class victory in worldwide political struggle. In Engels's terms Marx was thus the originator of 'the materialist interpretation of history' or 'historical materialism', the thinker who 'inverted' Hegel's idealism in order to produce a 'materialist dialectics' (or 'dialectical materialism' as later Marxists termed it), and the theorist who formulated the 'special law of motion' applicable to capitalist society (the 'theory of surplus value'). Engels's gloss on Marx's work was the origin of Marxism.[8]

Engels also argued a distinction between science, with which Marx was firmly identified in Engels's mind, and ideology, which he (Engels) famously dismissed in a widely circulated correspondence as 'false consciousness' (Marx never used the phrase).[9] The concept of falsity in opposition to science fitted with Engels's view of science as truth, but rather poorly with Marx's view of ideology as illusion, indeed illusion that served class interest. If a set of ideas functioned in society to validate and preserve important interests for particular classes, then in what sense could that set of ideas be dismissed as false? What force did 'consciousness' add to a claim about ideas? Did it imply that there are levels of consciousness such that a move from falsity to truth involved something more than reason? If so, what? A change of circumstances? of personality? Or perhaps consciousness once formed could not be changed? What processes were involved in changing 'consciousness' from false to true?

The phrase is rather typical of Engels, poorly thought through and productive of muddle. The implied individualism (Engels said 'false consciousness' not 'false social consciousness') is rather at odds with Marx's more general level of theorization anyway. The concept of falsity, while superficially sharp and specific, is of less use in a critical conceptualization of social phenomena than one might expect. Illusion is actually rather more powerful analytically and true to life. Nonetheless 'the Marxist view of ideology' has been firmly aligned with Engels's phrase since the late nineteenth century.

It was a small step for Marxists, such as V.I. Lenin, to map the functional definition of ideology as Marx saw it (systems of ideas promoting class interests) onto the characterization of Marx's work as comprehensive science that Engels had promoted. Given that Marxism, as Engels presented it, necessarily explained the role of the industrial working classes in history, proved the validity of their political struggle, and guaranteed the inevitability of their victory, it followed that Marxism was a systematic body of thought serving working-class interests. Hence it was like an ideology in this functionalism, and so – in an elision – it became an ideology as such. This elision seemed to remove the distinction between ideology and science that Engels had argued, and the distinction between ideological illusion and factual truth that Marx had employed. Or did it? In an obvious move to avoid an abyss of relativism (in which ideologies are merely functional for particular classes and there are no criteria of truth distinguishing one from another), Lenin and others identified 'Marxist ideology' with 'scientific knowledge'. Thus 'scientific ideology' arose as a Marxist concept. This was in clear contradiction with an earlier distinction between the two as argued in their different ways by both Marx and Engels.

There is no doubt that Marxism, understood in this way as a 'scientific ideology', was a twentieth-century political force of incomparable magnitude, playing an evident role in socialist, nationalist and anti-colonialist revolutionary politics from around 1900 through to the present. While conforming to fairly loose notions of ideology that even liberals could accept (action-oriented ideas promoting interest group politics), Marxism in this vein often made totalizing claims to truth, universality and effectiveness that inspired ordinary people and their leaders to brave acts of liberation and also to mindless acts of inhumanity. Not all the politics of this kind can be viewed or summarized in terms of self-identified Marxist regimes, though the former Soviet Union and its satellites, China, the former North Vietnam, North Korea and Cuba should be mentioned. Marxist politics in local variants is a worldwide feature, and that it does not always issue in a Marxist regime should not make it invisible.[10] Politics is always about struggle, even if history is written by victors.

In terms of the way that Marxism has been represented as an intellectual and political movement it should be clear that the relationship between Marxism as a 'scientific ideology' and the regimes listed above is problematic in two ways. First, individually or collectively their various brands of Marxism do not sum up, even in formal terms, the 'basics' of Marxism, and certainly not of Marx's thoughts themselves, not least because the historical, political and philosophical contexts were all so different. Thus attempts to work from the 'scientific ideologies' of these regimes back through the history of Marxism and ultimately to Marx himself are flawed exercises resting on the assumption that there is some feature or quality of totalitarian or ideological thought that can be isolated, that is typically or even peculiarly associated with Marxism, and that is best attacked through intellectual critique. This type of intellectual activity was in some ways complicit with the worst aspects of the regimes in question. This kind of Cold-War critique was most powerful when focused on the most narrow-minded, dogmatic and implausible aspects of Marxism as a 'scientific ideology'.[11] If there were more to Marxism than that, the critique began to lose its bite, but it did not follow that less stringent critics of Marxism were very interested in it as a flexible and successful mode of social transformation.

Second, it is very unclear what Marxist politics is supposed to be like. Marx operated within a framework of revolutionary liberalism (in both the political and the economic senses) in the 1830s and 1840s. His own political activity suggested a contingent and ancillary role for intellectuals in this movement, and he made no authoritarian claims for their ideas or for their role in interpreting them. This is quite the reverse of the revolutionary cadres required for national liberation, and the bureaucrats and soldiers required to implement large-scale economic and political transformations. Marxism as a 'scientific ideology' played a huge role in politics of this kind, but whether this had any relationship with Marx's own theory and practice, even at some rarefied level of conceptual logic, is very questionable. Marx, Engels and others in the Marxist tradition had an unwitting personal role in these political developments as icons, 'founding fathers' whose images evoked certainty and inevitability. In his later years Engels himself became somewhat iconic in the socialist international, making such an appearance at an international conference before his death (in 1895), but Marx was never more than a 'Red Terror Doctor' demonized in the public eye at the time of the Paris Commune (1871).

The 'fall of the wall' in 1989 not only removed much of Marxism as a 'scientific ideology', it also removed much of the Cold-War critique by default. It is not particularly clear that the critique had played any crucial part in the succeeding events that have changed the major world power-blocs so dramatically. Indeed the question as to whether liberalism is itself an ideology in some sense has recently arisen, or whether the new era post-1989 is one in which there has been an end to history as produced by ideological politics.[12] It now seems implausible to view any system of ideas as totalizing in quite the way that Stalinism and fascism operated in the mid-twentieth century.

Unsurprisingly the concept of ideology has migrated away from this narrow and historically specific phenomenon towards a more relaxed view of ideas that are political, systematic and action-oriented. In that way liberalism would qualify, and most liberals would have little difficulty in seeing their own politics in that light, particularly those liberals committed to human rights activism and the authoritative enforcement of universal norms on governments. Liberals are rather unlikely to argue either that their outlook is valid because it is scientific in some specific way or that the opposition (e.g., 'fundamentalism', especially in 'non-Western' religions) is illusory and hence ephemeral. Liberal views tend to arise instead from philosophical arguments presenting an ethical individualism, and liberals tend to accommodate opposing views within doctrines of toleration and personal freedoms balanced against the rights of others.

What then of contemporary Marxists? The intellectual and practical critiques of ideology as 'false consciousness' and of 'scientific ideology' as an infallible guide to class politics have been largely convincing and effective, though only after an engagement in the 1960s and 1970s with the rarefied abstractions of Louis Althusser's work and his 'Althusserian' disciples.[13] Rejecting the Leninist view of Marxism as a 'scientific ideology', Althusser argued for a critical re-reading of Marx as a scientist. Famously this necessitated a division of his work across a 'break' between a pre-scientific outlook (influenced by Hegel, in Althusser's view emphatically not a scientist), and a scientific outlook, a system in which social 'apparatuses', with their own practical logics, hold individuals in a defining grip. Given the rarefied level of social and political analysis involved, it was hard to see this exercise as either scientific in the sense of formulating empirical propositions or as political in the sense of encouraging or validating individual choice and action. In a sense the 'Althusserian moment' marked a last gasp of Engels's orthodoxy with respect to economism and determinism.

'Critical realism', its philosophical successor, has effectively reformulated Althusser's rather ill-supported claims about science and reality as an almost neo-Kantian exercise in specifying what must be the case in thought in order to make statements about society and social development true in principle and efficacious in practice.[14] In other words orthodoxies concerning economic primacy have been detached from any crude grounding in the supposed 'material' truths of natural science, as Engels had it, and instead have been deflected into a realm of presupposition supported by historical and evidential argument and inference. Provided that a commitment to truth is kept intact in this way, it follows that ideology also maintains a position as an expression in ideas of both falsehood and illusion.

While there are those who maintain an outlook that is pre-1989 (or pre-1956, or pre-1939, or pre-1923) in philosophical and political terms, however well updated, the major developmental aspect of Marxist theory since the 1970s has been a re-reading of Marx through the works of Antonio Gramsci.[15] As this reading has developed, the tenets of Marxist orthodoxy have relaxed, particularly those related to the materialism of natural science, the formulaic and causal account of the historical succession of technological progress and forms of class rule, and the role of élites discerning when and where class struggle should and should not take place. Rather, Gramsci's commentary on anti-fascist Italian politics was taken to accommodate a more complex account of political behaviour, one more related to culture and tradition and less determined by class position.

Gramsci's firm political commitment to working-class politics thus licensed a reconceptualization of Marxist ideology that was less relentlessly scientific and economic and much more flexibly oriented towards popular consciousness and national struggles. Taking this view of Marxism ultimately leaves little distance between liberals and Marxists except the latter's insistence on the class dimension of progressive politics. Ideology at this point had become ideas oriented to working-class activism in producing large-scale political change. However, it was rather unclear exactly what kind of claim was being made here in support of working-class politics, other than a merely existential one deriving from the circumstances of individual choice. The historical, philosophical and scientific apparatus that had previously been taken to produce this as a conclusion had largely been discredited, but there was no developed account supporting working-class politics as some kind of premise that would make individual choices rational or inevitable.

Ernesto Laclau and Chantal Mouffe forced the issue by reconceptualizing class as a discursive rather than 'material' or objective phenomenon, as previous Marxisms had seen it.[16] With this the remnants of Marxist ideology (class as a 'material' or foundational phenomenon) disappeared, and notions of action-oriented ideas (about national or ethnic groups, sex or sexuality groups, class or any other kind of group) no longer seemed to count as ideology but rather merely as culture. This was treated as a derivative of Gramsci's concept of 'hegemony', descriptive of structures of upper-class domination and lower-class complicity. Following the 'linguistic turn' in philosophy, Laclau and Mouffe maintained that primacy or priority for 'class' or 'the economy' or 'means of production' or any other set of concepts, supposedly reflective of the 'primary' or 'constitutive' phenomena of history and social existence, could not be sustained, because all such arguments are reflective, not of some extra-linguistic reality, but of historically and culturally contingent 'language games' that people play.[17]

Thus it seems that without some view of extra-linguistic validation there is little scope for ideology to be a useful concept, or rather that attempts to deploy traditional concepts of ideology to persuade people to political action will increasingly fall prey to this kind of scepticism, as indeed will liberal universalist ethics. Laclau and Mouffe are thus self-consciously aligned with post-modern uncertainty and contingency in their philosophical views, and at odds with the foundationalism of both Marxism (in 'matter' and the economy) and liberalism (in individual worth and universalizable human rights). Politically Laclau and Mouffe have advocated a Gramscian focus on the need to work through and within culturally constructed political views and 'moments' of struggle, while also defending the apparatus of liberal rights, freedoms and participatory politics, albeit without the universalizing ethics. Having opened an era of contestation about ideology, and contestation between ideologies, it would seem that Marxists, in the sense of advocates of some version of class struggle as politically privileged, have now closed down ideological struggle, and any theory of ideology as politically efficacious.

On the other hand, there are areas of the world where scientific ideology in the Marxist sense, and ideological politics, both hold sway. China, Cuba, Vietnam and North Korea, at the time of writing, still have systems that resemble mid-twentieth-century, 'pre-fall-of-the-wall' political forms much more than they do the liberalizing successor regimes of Eastern Europe and Central Asia. While authoritarian nationalisms are of considerable importance in successor regimes, and while nationalisms are effectively ideologies as action-oriented systems of thought (stretching this to include potent symbols and histories), successor regimes tend to distinguish themselves from the communist ideologies that preceded them. By contrast the remaining 'orthodox' Marxist regimes do not, since the communist élites are still in power.

Thus the Cold War has not finished in East Asia and Cuba, and local sensibilities there on both sides of the East/West political divide are highly critical of political tendencies elsewhere to erase this fact. China is of course the major power in the region, historically and at present, and North Korea has played an especially significant and aggressive role in the area. Vietnam and Cuba are rather different cases economically and strategically, both being very poor and subject at times to sanctions. None of these countries could claim to be a model for other nationalist and anti-colonialist regimes in quite the same way as was the case fifty years ago, and it seems apparent that inertia, gerontocracy and pariah-status have a great deal to do with the maintenance of regimes embodying the old-style orthodoxies of Marxist ideologies.

The theoretical and practical relationship between the ideas and practice of Marx and Engels, on the one hand, and the ideas and practice of the revolutionary nationalist parties in these and other countries, on the other hand, has been highly problematic since the beginning. As indicated above, the basic philosophical premises of Marx and Engels have been distinguished from each other within Marxism by minority opinion since around 1900, and consequently defended as a unity by Marxist mainstream writers with considerable vehemence. Defence of these positions became a matter of practical politics in revolutionary nationalist movements and regimes when 'correct theory' was linked definitionally to correct practice, and correct practice to party discipline. These concepts and difficulties are not unknown in non-Marxist politics, and at times liberals taking a 'broad church' or even naïve approach to the force of ideas in politics have lost ground to more determined opponents willing to enforce party disciplines by invoking philosophical certainties.

Marxism, taken as a 'scientific socialism' based on doctrines of historical and dialectical materialism, has been hugely (though hardly uniquely) influential in twentieth-century politics, civil war, world war, Cold War, and nation-building. Even at the level of Marxist orthodoxy, however, the connections between particular situations, leaders, policies and some notion of what is and is not 'Marxist' are quite tenuous. While Marx and Engels (both) certainly looked forward to collective ownership of the means of production by the working class, and to an end to the disadvantages of 'the countryside' in comparison with the civilization and services of 'the town', it hardly follows that they were somehow authors of Stalin's forced collectivization policies in the Soviet Union, or that they would have agreed with it, or that it would never have happened without their ideas (or that alternatively capitalist modernization was accomplished with full respect for human rights and individual welfare and with due process and consent).

The drift in the Bolshevik party in Russia from internationalism and workers' democracy to nationalism and authoritarian rule has been very clearly traced, but given that neither Marx nor Engels ever seemed to envisage the political and economic processes of socialist transition with any clarity, nor were ever themselves anywhere near contemplating the immense practical difficulties faced by, say, Lenin, Stalin, Mao or Fidel Castro, it is hard to escape the conclusion that Marxism as a world-changing political force was largely extrapolated from a few phrases to suit the needs and policies of national liberation, at least as one man, or a small group of men, conceived it.

The internal coherence of any of these ideologies, never mind their coherence with one another, rose and fell with the exigencies of world politics, the turmoil of domestic politics, and the ire of internal and external opponents. Great power politics played a terrific role in this history in that variants of Marxism adopted within (or excoriated outside) empire-building regimes like Russia and China have received much more notice than anti-imperialist small-scale variants practised in Cuba and Vietnam. North Korea is perhaps a *reductio* and epitome of all these contradictions, and Eastern Europe is very largely a special case related both to empire-building and buffer-zone defence for the Soviet Union. While Marxist parties had considerable strengths in Eastern Europe before and after the Second World War, it is hard to imagine that one-party rule, and Soviet-style policies, would have been so thoroughly instituted there without Russian intervention. When it became evident that such intervention was no longer forthcoming, the collapse of these satellite regimes was breathtakingly swift.

Nonetheless there are certain commonalities amongst all these regimes that make them seem Marxist in some identifiable sense. These commonalities, however, are based on what is assumed without much reflection to be non-Marxist, so any judgement needs careful examination. Rapid industrialization, even if sometimes small-scale and in the countryside, central planning and abolition of capital markets, one-party rule and totalitarian disrespect for human rights, were common features that were moreover defined and defended inside and outside these countries as correct Marxist practice. But as mentioned above, the record of even liberal democratic regimes (or what seemed to pass as such in the nineteenth century) has seldom been questioned, rather than sanitized as victors' history, and there are many non-Marxist regimes that have been repressive and totalitarian, but yet have not produced the modernization that some of the major Marxist powers have generated. Almost all of the world's poorest countries today have never been Marxist nor have Marxists been the only or even the chief proponents of debilitating civil wars there. If there is some endemic and systemic problem there, it must be something else.

None of the 'actually existing' Marxist regimes ever really got to grips with the abolition of money (announced by Marx and Engels in the *Communist Manifesto* of 1848), nor with building the grassroots democracy that Marx sketched in his comments on the unfulfilled potential of the Paris Commune (*The Civil War in France* of 1871). In so far as Marxist regimes did not deliver a classically communist economy, and thus distribute goods according to needs (and work according to abilities), they actually laid the groundwork for a kind of social democracy that Marx and Engels were sometimes willing to endorse *pro tem*. As revolutionary socialists of the 1840s, both worked in conjunction with revolutionary liberals, fighting authoritarianism, supporting the process through which representative government was instituted and democratized, and advocating an internationalism of 'peoples' within and amongst nation-states. Perhaps naively neither got down to the harsh party politics involved in actually doing these things in practice, even when the revolutionary failures of 1849 loomed large. Perhaps this is the dividing line, not between liberals and Marxists, but between practical politicians, willing to turn an idea into a doctrine in order to seize the time, and theoretical writers, willing to wait for another time when more people will somehow seize an idea.

The Gramscian and post-structuralist Marxisms described above have been associated with 'new social movements' both in liberal democracies worldwide and in some of the 'fall of the wall' struggles in Eastern Europe, where civil protest was instrumental in instituting and maintaining successor regimes. These movements are variously grouped as egalitarian or liberation movements aligning popular forces around race, ethnicity, language, religion, sexuality or other minority status, and around women as a majority but disadvantaged group. What stands out here is the extent to which these movements are constituted as 'new' against the background of 'old style' class politics which was, of course, the

raison d'être of Marxism as a movement and of Marx's own direct political in-
volvements in the 1840s. There is a common thread here with Marx and Marxism, as introduced at the beginning of this chapter, namely the link between
liberalism and economics, in that movements to ameliorate disadvantage have to
measure disadvantage against something, and economic indicators have played a
role in that effort. However, these movements have also been concerned with
establishing identities and commanding respect in social and political contexts,
often in ways that cannot be readily measured in economic terms but rather in
arguments and evidence concerning dignity and recognition in social relations
and representations.

New social movements share a concern with forcing liberals to deliver on their
constitutive rights in practice much more broadly than many of them envisaged,
even redefining or obliterating certain supposedly agreed boundary lines (e.g.,
public/private, political relations/personal relations, majority predilections/per-
sonal desires, etc.). Like Marxists, new social movements have sometimes moved
beyond liberal goals altogether into more comprehensive and tenuous schemes
of social and personal liberation. For Marxists liberation and the realm of freedom were built up from an economic basis into a rather nebulous realm of social
co-operation and rational planning of production and distribution of material
goods and services. 'New' social movements have tended to develop other notions of liberation less tied to material things and more closely linked to personal
experiences and intersubjective evaluations.

Thus the line between Marxists and post-Marxists can be drawn in this way:
how crucial are economic issues in understanding social and personal liberation?
How fundamental is class politics? Marxists have engaged in vigorous debate
with post-Marxists, insisting that the latter have abandoned class politics and
hence any systematic account of the 'action-oriented ideas' that Marxism has
handed down for contemporary adaptation.[18] Post-Marxists have treated class as
a 'social imaginary' like any other 'new' social movement, with the potential for
developing ideas and practices that would be politically persuasive in mass
action. An acknowledgement that 'new' social movements and identity politics as
practised in the contemporary world are not based on class and do not pursue
issues recognizable as class politics in the economic sense, merely states the
problem that post-Marxists wish to address in theory and in practice. Their
politics often consists of drawing attention to the economic threads of class
analysis that could bring 'new' social movements together in coalitions, and thus
re-enact the characteristically Marxist project of tackling liberals where it hurts,
namely in their own ambivalence about the competitive individualism of capitalist economic systems. In those very systems the effects of the competitive economy
bear down on individuals who have rights, but whose human rights are insufficient armour against economic disadvantage, powerlessness and oppression.

As is well known the politics of individual rights and competitive elections can
easily succumb to large-scale economic interests in symbiotic private and public
sector economies. Post-Marxists have found inspiration in Marx's own accounts

of ideology as a realm of illusion serving the interests of the classes and 'class fractions' deriving power and advantage from liberal democracies and capitalist economies. While it is easy to suggest that Post-Marxist politics is ineffectual precisely because it is not systematic and universalizing, as ideological politics is, it might also be argued that the rhythm of global change in political ideas and effective action takes a very long time to move from one kind of politics to another. On that view it will be some decades yet before ideological politics dissolves and more diffident grounds of persuasion take hold.

The claim that liberalism itself marks an 'end' to ideology has not stood up well to scrutiny. There are too many universalizing claims in liberalism, and too much evidence of liberal blindness to local and personal 'difference' in their political practice, which was for many years complicit with imperialism and Cold-War *Realpolitik*. Post-Marxists are in the curious position of abandoning ideology as represented within both the liberal and the Marxist positions, and yet claiming to want to influence politics in significant ways. They also claim to want liberals to deliver on their constitutive values, and Marxists to deliver on their post-capitalist economics. Possibly this Post-Marxist politics is all critique in theory and no action in practice, but in any case the lines of critique are clear. In that sense – in relation to both liberals and Marxists – Post-Marxists can claim to be post-ideological.

Notes and references

1 For an exposition of the concept of ideology since the 1790s, see my 'Ideology: the career of a concept', in Terence Ball and Richard Dagger (eds), *Ideals and Ideologies: A Reader*, second edition, New York, HarperCollins, 1995, pp. 4–11.

2 For an encyclopaedic approach to Marxism, see Tom Bottomore (ed.), *A Dictionary of Marxist Thought*, second edition, Oxford, Blackwell, 1991. For a selection of writings by major Marxist thinkers worldwide, see David McLellan (ed.), *Marxism: Essential Writings*, Oxford, Oxford University Press, 1988.

3 For a notable example, see Karl Popper, *The Open Society and its Enemies*, two vols, fifth edition, London, Routledge & Kegan Paul, 1966.

4 For relevant extracts, see 'From "The German Ideology": Chapter One, "Feuerbach" ', in Karl Marx, *Early Political Writings*, edited and translated by Joseph O'Malley and Richard A. Davis, Cambridge, Cambridge University Press, 1994, pp. 119–81.

5 Ibid., pp. 145–6.

6 For an exploration of Marx's political attitudes and activities, see Alan Gilbert, *Marx's Politics: Communists and Citizens*, Oxford, Martin Robertson, 1981.

7 These issues are introduced and discussed in my *Engels*, Oxford, Oxford University Press, 1981, reprinted 1991, Chapters 5–7.

8 These issues are discussed in my *Marx and Engels: The Intellectual Relationship*, Brighton, Harvester/Wheatsheaf, 1983.

9 Engels's letter to Franz Mehring 14 July 1893, in Karl Marx and Friedrich Engels, *Selected Correspondence*, edited by S. Ryazanskaya, Moscow, Progress Publishers, 1965, p. 459.

10 Some idea of the breadth of Marxism as a 'family' of worldwide political movements can be gained from Robert A. Gorman (ed.), *Biographical Dictionary of Marxism*, London, Mansell, 1986, and Robert A. Gorman (ed.), *Biographical Dictionary of Neo-Marxism*, London, Mansell, 1985.

11 At times Leszek Kolakowski's three-volume study *Main Currents of Marxism*, translated by P.S. Falla, Oxford, Oxford University Press, 1978, falls into this trap. Bertram D. Wolfe, *Marxism: 100 Years in the Life of a Doctrine*, New York, Dial Press, 1965, and Alfred G. Meyer, *Marxism: The Unity of Theory and Practice*, Cambridge MA, Harvard University Press, 1954, reflect the relentlessly and reductively critical Cold-War view.

12 Francis Fukuyama's article sparked off a considerable controversy on these points: 'The end of history', *The National Interest*, Summer 1989, No. 16, pp. 3–18.

13 See Louis Althusser, *For Marx*, London, Allen Lane, 1969 (first published in French 1965).

14 See Roy Bhaskar, *A Realist Theory of Science*, Leeds, Leeds Books, 1975, reprinted 1978, and *The Possibility of Naturalism: A Philosophical Critique of the Contemporary Human Sciences*, Brighton, Harvester, 1979, reprinted 1989.

15 For an introductory treatment of Gramsci's career and thought, see James Martin, *Gramsci's Political Analysis: A Critical Introduction*, Basingstoke, Macmillan, 1998.

16 See Ernesto Laclau and Chantal Mouffe, *Hegemony and Socialist Strategy: Towards a Radical Democratic Politics*, London, Verso, 1985.

17 For a brief and very clear sketch of this outlook, see Richard Rorty, *Contingency, Irony, and Solidarity*, Cambridge, Cambridge University Press, 1995, Chapter 1.

18 See the exchanges involving Ellen Meiksins Woods and Norman Geras, on the one hand, and Ernesto Laclau and Chantal Mouffe, on the other, in *New Left Review*, from 1985 to the present.

4 Socialism in the twentieth century

An historical reflection

Donald Sassoon

Introduction

Those who venture to discuss the meaning of socialism confront two distinct but not incompatible strategies: the essentialist and the historical. The essentialist strategy proceeds in conventional Weberian fashion. Socialism is an ideal type, empirically deduced from the activities or ideas of those commonly regarded as socialists. Once the concept is constructed, it can be used historically to assess concrete political organizations, their activists and thinkers, and measure the extent to which they fit the ideal type, why and when they diverge from each other, and account for exceptional behaviour. This procedure, of great heuristic value, is still broadly accepted and widely used, even though its theoretical rigour is highly dubious as the analysis rests on a somewhat arbitrary selection of the 'socialist' organizations and individuals used to produce the ideal-type concept of socialism.

This procedure has the added disadvantage that, if strictly adhered to, it does not allow for historical change. Once the ideal-type is defined, novel elements cannot easily be integrated into it. However, life must go on, even in sociology. So when something new turns up, such as a revisionist interpretation, all that is required is to hoist the ideal-type onto the operating table, remove – if necessary – the bits which no longer fit, and insert the new ones. Thus rejuvenated, the concept of socialism can march on, rich with new meanings; social scientists, armed with a neatly repackaged ideal-type, acquire a new lease on life, produce more books on the new socialism, and make academic publishers happy. Alternatively, sociologists may defend the old ideal-type, pronounce the new revisions incompatible with it, and declare socialism dead. They can then write more books on the death of socialism and make academic publishers happier still.

Activists, unconsciously Weberian, proceed in the same essentialist fashion, either exalting the new revisionism and its intelligent adaptation to the realities of an ever-changing world, or bitterly recriminating the changes which have occurred, evidence of yet another dastardly betrayal of the old faith. In so doing they keep 'socialism' (i.e., their idea of socialism) alive, its body on a life-support machine, waiting for better times. Such a clash between modernizers and fundamentalists is a regular fixture of political movements, especially where ideologies and values are of central importance – as is the case in socialist and religious movements.

It is evident from the tone of the above remarks that I favour the second strategy, the historical one, though this has problems too. Its opening move is the same as that of the essentialists: one selects the organizations and thinkers which self-identify as socialists, and tells their stories in a conventional empirical fashion, highlighting similarities and differences. However, no definition of socialism is required: socialism becomes what socialists do. No prediction can be made: the death of socialism – like that of feudalism – can only be declared when it is universally acknowledged and no longer a matter of dispute; that is, when there are no socialists left except for the usual cranks, who, along with flat-earthers, may have some remaining anthropological interest.

While the essentialist strategy is overwhelmingly concerned with the question of definition, the historical one is obsessed with change and causality – why do socialists behave as they do? – and hence with the context within which organizations and thinkers act as they do. This method, far from discounting the importance of ideology, regards it as an integral part of the history of the movement. What is of interest here is the connection between the particular ethical view of the world championed by socialists and their action in the domain of practical politics. How such theory and such practice are modified over time is thus the central preoccupation of the historical approach.

This procedure, with its emphasis on the inevitability of historical change, is clearly less judgemental than the essentialist one. However, like all historicist narratives, it suffers the persistent hazard of falling into a determinist version of events: whatever happened had to happen. It is useful to be conscious of this and be aware that, within determinate circumstances (this is not a minor proviso), things could have proceeded differently. In particular, it is worth reminding ourselves that while it is true that the socialist movement arises with the inception of industrial society and tracks its development, it is never a necessary component of it. There have been, there are, and in all likelihood there will be, industrial societies without a significant socialist movement. Similarly, there have been societies with a powerful socialist movement where the process of industrialization has barely begun.

The two socialisms

At the beginning of the twentieth century socialists knew that their movement was contingent to capitalist society. It is true that the version of Marx's theory most of them adhered to implied that socialism was a state of affairs that would succeed capitalism, but they had noticed that the fastest growing capitalist society in the world, the USA, did not have a socialist movement. They were also equally aware that the most developed capitalist state in Europe, Great Britain, home of powerful trade unions, had, at most, only an embryonic socialist party. From their point of view, Britain was an advanced capitalist society with a backward socialist movement. Conversely, some of the still mainly agrarian societies of Europe – such as Italy and Finland – had fairly strong and electorally success-ful socialist parties.

In Russia the movement appeared divided – like the whole of the Russian intelligentsia – between westernizing and slavophile tendencies.[1] The westernizers assumed that the duty of socialists was to accelerate the development of capital-ism, because only capitalism could provide the terrain for a further advance towards socialism. The slavophiles surmised that Russia would be able to skip western-style capitalism. Populist anti-capitalists – such as V. Bervi-Flerovski, author of *The Situation of the Working Class in Russia* (1869), a book much praised by Marx – held the view that the *mir*, the Russian peasant commune, provided communal principles which could and should be made universal. Russia could avoid the iniquities of capitalism and offer the rest of the world the example of a superior social system based on nation-wide solidarity and co-operation. This mirage of overtaking and outstripping the West remained a fundamental feature of nearly all revolutionary Russian beliefs. A century later, the abandon-ment of this 'Great Idea' coincided with the collapse of the entire communist system.

The westernizing and slavophile positions converged towards a notable con-sensus: the real problem facing Russian society was one of modernization, which was then regarded as being co-terminous with industrialization. The issue was whether this should be left to the capitalists themselves or should be undertaken directly by socialists. Those who held the second view were inevitably pushed towards the proposition that to achieve socialist-led industrialization it was nec-essary to be in charge of the political apparatus itself, that is, to be in command of the state. It did not follow that the state should necessarily own the means of production. There were various possibilities: the state could substitute itself for a class of capitalists visibly unable to perform its historical task; alternatively the state could encourage the capitalists and help them to industrialize the country; or, again, it could stimulate some entrepreneurs, for instance in agriculture or in new or/and smaller concerns, or it could provide financial incentives to a mana-gerial class operating in a quasi-market even where private property had been abolished. The appropriate mix of state and market was never an issue settled once and for all and it certainly did not follow inevitably from the October Revolution. After all, much of the subsequent history of Russia – from war com-munism, to the New Economic Policy, to Stalin's five-year plans, to the limited and inadequate economic reform of the 1960s and 1970s – can be seen as a dispute over the relationship between markets and politics.

This version of socialism or *developmental socialism* can be described as an ideol-ogy of modernization or development. Though its final goal was a socialist society, its practical tasks consisted in developing an industrial society under conditions where it was felt that if socialists did not do it either no one would (and the country would stagnate) or foreigners would do it (and the country would be like a colony). This kind of socialism – one is tempted to define it as capital-building socialism – coincides, more or less, with communism and its state socialist variants.

The other variety of socialism – the main concern of the rest of this essay – can be conceived as a form of regulation of capitalism.[2] Its task is not to develop an industrial society; the capitalists themselves are busy doing just that. Far from requiring any 'help' from socialists, they can do it better and faster without them – as nineteenth-century Britain and twentieth-century America and Japan amply demonstrate.

This coincides with what came to be known as social democracy. The contrast between developmental or modernizing socialism and socialism as capitalist regulation is, of course, far more profound than this. The former, whether in the USSR or in Cuba or in China and North Korea, exhibited marked authoritarian features and intolerance of dissent and of pluralism which matched and in some cases exceeded those of capitalist authoritarian regimes. The latter brand of socialism co-existed, in all instances, with democracy, pluralism and human rights. Such a comparison is often, quite legitimately, made by social democrats themselves, who point out that developmental socialism (i.e., communism) was never liberal while social democracy was never dictatorial. It is tempting to agree and to follow convention by distinguishing communism from socialism, and to leave it at that.

Unfortunately this would leave a number of problems unsolved. The passage from pre-modern to modern society, at least in its initial phase, has seldom been accompanied by democracy and human rights in their twentieth-century meaning. Even in Britain or the USA, not to speak of Germany and Japan, the pattern was one in which the suffrage was non-existent or severely restricted, freedoms were seriously limited, and trade unions were banned or subjected to harsh control.[3] In some instances the process co-existed with slavery and genocide (the USA), racism, colonialism, rigid authoritarianism (for instance in Japan) and one-party rule (for instance in Taiwan and South Korea until relatively recently). Full democracy and human rights were established later. They were, in other words, the outcome of a *political* struggle, and not an imperative accompaniment of the first phase of the process of modernization. Social democracy, where it existed at all, was in the forefront of the political struggle for democracy and human rights, goading along the liberal parties, then far less democratic, and even the conservative parties, then barely democratic, towards political reforms.

Social democrats, however, when capitalism was not fully developed, were usually in opposition. The modernization of the country, the development of capitalism, its profitability and productivity, were not their concern. They came to power only when the first phase of industrialization was over, unlike the communists who came to power facing the problem of industrializing the country (with a few significant exceptions such as Czechoslovakia and East Germany). It does not follow from this that the degree of authoritarianism exhibited by communist rule was justifiable or inevitable. In principle, other, less harsh and cruel, forms of modernization could have been devised. The point is that the two forms of socialism which have characterized the twentieth century are not comparable. Ideologies are shaped by the kind of societies within which they operate and the relationship they have to political power, that is, to the state. Social democrats ruled only when capitalism was well-established and democracy had become the common property of the main political parties. Communists had to develop an industrial society. Social democrats (or socialists; I shall use the two terms inter-changeably) had to manage it. Communists prevailed in less developed societies, socialists in developed market economies.

Individualism and collectivism

One of the many paradoxes confronting the historian of socialism is that the notion of managing market societies was not part of the ideological armoury of socialists although this is what they all ended up doing. At the turn of the century, socialist ideology distinguished between an end-goal and short- or medium-term demands. The end-goal was a socialist society vaguely defined as the abolition of private property. The short-term demands were varied but, on the whole, they aimed at achieving three aims: the first was the democratiza-tion of capitalist society, the second was the regulation of the labour market (for instance, the eight-hour day), and the third was the socialization of the costs of reproduction of labour: free medicine, pensions, national insurance – in short, costs which would have had to be absorbed by individual workers. This third goal is what we now call the welfare state.

The values which informed this politics were those of equality, social solidarity and the establishment of minimum standards of life. If all citizens were to be of equal worth, they all (including women) had to have the vote, had to be treated equally, and had to have the same rights. Illness, unemployment and old age were to be protected by a common fund, centrally administered and financed. The definition of what would be the minimum standards of civilized life could not be left to the sphere of civil society, that is to the arbitrariness of the market. It had to become a political matter. The state was to be called upon to enforce a system of protection which would not exist or would exist in a rudimentary form if left to market forces. This was the basis for subjecting the conditions of work to state regulation: health and safety procedures were to be strengthened and enforced and a limit placed on the length of the working day. To force the state to operate in this way, it was necessary to democratize it, i.e., to detach it from the exclusive control of the dominant classes.[4]

The extension of democracy that socialists advocated was not based on class principles but on the principle of individual rights. Universal suffrage, after all, assumes that all individuals have exactly the same worth when voting: each, literally, counts as one. The ballot had to be secretly cast by a lone individual making an individual choice. In the domain of politics, socialists, far from being class-conscious, were staunch individualists. It is worth reminding ourselves of such unexceptional views, historically well-documented, at a time when socialists are criticized (and supinely accept to be criticized) for their alleged class collectivist position. Those who, at the turn of the twentieth century, defended a class con-ception of democracy were the liberals and the conservatives not the socialists.

Liberal or conservative parties defended an electoral system which allocated votes in terms of the wealth possessed or earned by each individual. Throughout Europe they also accepted and defended an upper chamber which over-represented or represented only the members of the upper classes. As I write, such an institution still exists, incredibly enough, in Britain, the 'mother of democracy'. Furthermore, liberal and conservative parties were not only guilty of 'class-ism', but also of sexism. Not only did they oppose the enfranchisement of the working class, they also opposed that of women. Their opposition to working-class suffrage may have been based on opportunism: workers, they felt, would have increased the electoral weight of dangerous socialists. Women, on the other hand, were believed to be more likely to vote for conservative and traditional parties, yet these resisted female suffrage – a rare instance of ideology and principle prevailing over self-interest.

Socialists, of course, often did not fight for female suffrage with great vigour, but this had little to do with principle. Some were moved by their commitment to gradualism and moderation (the modern requirement to keep everyone happy, jolly them along, upset no one and remain united). It was thus essential to proceed by stages and to achieve full manhood suffrage before extending it to women. Other socialists were moved, quite simply, by political opportunism: it was clear to them that the enfranchisement of women would give a distinct advantage to religious parties. When it came to principles and values, however, all socialist parties stood firmly on the side of real universal suffrage.

Thus socialists were far more consistent defenders of individual democratic rights than liberals and conservatives. However, in the pursuit of their second aim, the regulation of the working day and, more generally, the regulation of the conditions of work, socialists took a clearly collectivist position. The contractual relation which associated capitalists and workers was one of individual to individual. In exchange for agreed wages, each individual worker undertook to perform a determinate operation, in determinate conditions and for a determinate length of time – a situation Marx and his followers described as 'formal' equality, meaning that such agreement was between juridically equal parties, a contractual relation between equals which disguised a massive inequality in power. Furthermore, capitalists had substantial advantages, especially where there was a considerable surplus of labour – which, in the initial stages of industrialization, was the norm.

The formation of trade unions was a collective means of redressing this inequality of power. Their chances of success depended on a variety of factors, the most important being the absence of legal impediments to their effective functioning. Here, the unions were in favour of retrenching the state and might well have adopted the latter-day slogan of 'getting the state off their backs'. When it came to the political enforcement of minimum standards, however, the unions were in favour of bringing the state back in to create (to use, once again, modern terminology) a level playing field among entrepreneurs, preventing them from competing at the expense of the workers.

The third aim, the creation of what was later called the welfare state, entailed the socialization of some of the costs of reproduction of the working class. The collective tax fund (to which the middle classes were expected to contribute disproportionately) or the forcible extraction of contributions from the capitalists could be used to help finance pensions, national insurance and medical expenses. This would have had obvious beneficial effects for the workers and their families, but it also allowed the entrepreneurs to pay them less. While wages are necessary for the reproduction of the working class, the development of non-wage benefits meant that monetary wages (as opposed to real earnings) could be lower than they would have been if there were no other benefits.

The success obtained in reaching these aims differed from country to country. Much depended on the relative strength of the two contending classes, capitalists and workers, the wealth of the economy, the power and dominance of landed aristocratic interests, the prevailing political ethos, the position of the Church. For instance, at the turn of the century, the USA had the most rapidly developing economy in the world, but wave upon wave of immigrant labour acted as a brake on the formation of powerful politically-inclined trade unions, and the competition among capitalists enabled some to opt for a high wage strategy (Fordism) which helped the formation of a larger market for consumer goods than would have been the case otherwise. While the American political élites were also largely impervious to trade-union pressures, they were less resistant to those stemming from the large class of small farmers. The ensuing polarization more or less isolated the trade-union movement and weakened its political development; hence the development of a peculiar anti-big-business populism.

Britain followed a different path. In the nineteenth century its working class was large and well-organized, and had, by the standards of the time, a long history of struggles and militancy. No established party could ignore the workers. The religious fragmentation of the country and especially of the working class contributed to preventing the formation of a confessional party along the lines of continental Christian democracy. The result was that, in the second half of the nineteenth century, liberals and conservatives competed with each other for the support of the labouring classes and incorporated in their own programmes aspects of a social democratic platform before that could find an outlet in an organized political party. This helped delay the formation and growth of a large British socialist party along the lines of the German SPD. On the continent, a similar process of co-optation was under way: nation-building required the incorporation of demands emerging from the lower classes and took the form of what was called in Germany a form of 'state socialism' – built by Bismarck and supported by the socialist leader Ferdinand Lassalle. Liberal, conservative and nationalist parties were in the forefront of this movement. They were eventually joined by Church-based parties, particularly when the Roman Catholic Church abandoned its intransigent defence of the ancient regime and adopted a new position towards what it called the 'social question' with the publication in 1891 of Pope Leo XIII's encyclical *Rerum novarum*.

Socialists, liberals and the state

By the beginning of the twentieth century the three key aspects of the medium-term programme of social democracy could be found in some form in other parties. It follows that it was no longer possible, if it ever was, to establish a clear and permanent distinction between socialists and non-socialists in terms of practical policies. There were, of course, also massive differences: socialists remained committed to the long-term aim of achieving a post-capitalist society, possessed a set of distinctive symbols, advanced their demands in a more radical way, pursued and explored new forms of struggle, such as the political strike, remained opposed to overt co-operation with other parties, and, with the exception of Britain, expounded anti-clericalism. In other words, socialists tried to distinguish themselves in all possible ways from what they persisted in regarding as a monolithic bourgeois bloc.

The continuous attempt by anti-socialist forces to incorporate socialist demands should be regarded as evidence of the success of socialists and of their ability to shape and influence political developments. But it also makes it impossible to construct a fool-proof definition of socialist policies. The extension of democracy, the institution of the welfare state and the control of the working day were socialist aims and policies, but one can always find, at any moment, similar demands advanced and implemented by non-socialist parties, be they right, centre, conservatives, liberal, Christian or nationalist. From the outset, 'socialism' was not the prerogative of socialists.[5]

It is true that socialists were forced, in their everyday practice, to trim their demands and accept compromises, but so were the conservatives and liberals. The extension of democracy and the advance of mass society meant that no political party could hope to obtain sufficient support either by defending the *status quo in toto* (the essential conservative position) or by proposing to return to the *status quo ante* (the essential reactionary position). Reformism triumphed. It was adopted by the most varied forces: in Germany by Bismarck and the later Wilhelmine nationalists as well as the 'social' Christians of the Zentrum party; in Italy by the majority wing of the Liberal Party (Giovanni Giolitti) and the emerging forces of political Catholicism; in France by the Radicals of the Third Republic; in Britain by both Disraeli's and Salisbury's conservatives as well as Joseph Chamberlain, Gladstone, the New Liberals, Asquith and Lloyd George; in Austria by the anti-semitic Social Christians of Karl Lüger; and in Holland by the new confessional parties in alliance with the more enlightened Liberals.

The impact of this turn to the social was more visible at the local level than at the national. Local authorities were busy devising imaginative schemes to improve the social conditions of urban life through public health programmes, housing developments, slum clearance, poor relief – that is, by developing an important local public sector. This evolving 'municipal socialism' was seldom, if ever, the work of socialists. The success of reformist socialism, like the success of all political ideologies, lay in the fact that it did not have a monopoly of what it stood for. In politics success consists in ensuring that what one thinks of as normal or desirable or possible becomes the shared attitude, the common property of the entire polity. To achieve this, however, it is necessary to formulate demands which are detachable from the ideological package (the symbols and language) which accompanies it. This can only be realized when the connection between ideological values and practical policies is vague and loose, and thus ready to be endlessly re-negotiated. It is precisely because it is perfectly possible to be in favour of adequate pensions without signing up to the end-goal of socialism that adequate pensions can be fought for by liberals and conservatives. Consistency and coherence may enable small political sects to survive indefinitely, but they spell certain ruin for parties and movements with real hegemonic ambitions.

Approaching socialism as a political programme which overlaps with that of other parties helps to highlight the importance of the long-term aims, of the symbols used, of the privileging of a particular class. Socialist parties, like other parties, had to advance contradictory positions. On the one hand they put forward a realistic programme which could appeal to as many people as possible; on the other they stressed what was absolutely distinctive and unique. They knew successful policies were likely to be imitated and popular demands taken over. To counter the probable dispersion of support, socialists presented themselves as the authentic champions of reforms. At the same time, they emphasized that these were not ends in themselves but steps to a situation – socialism – where they would no longer be necessary because the social problems had been eliminated. Thus the insistence on the final end was not only part of a recruitment strategy aimed at intellectuals and others with millennarian aspirations. It was also a convincing way of reinforcing the appeal of what might otherwise appear as limited reforms. Similarly, the insistence on the working class was not just derived from Marxist theory – the non-Marxist British Labour Party was a far more vociferous advocate of a 'proletarian' consciousness than most of its continental counterparts. It was the recognition that that particular social group represented the most likely source of support for social and economic reforms.

The struggle for democracy, for the welfare state, and for the regulation of the working week thus created a wide arena of struggle in which all the main parties participated. It also brought about a fundamental feature of twentieth-century socialism: its étatism. It is only relatively recently that socialists themselves have come to question it. The growth of an exceptionally strong centralized state in the USSR and the development, between the wars, of so-called totalitarian states offered those opposing socialism an ideal platform. Fascism, Nazism and Stalinism may have been extreme forms of state-worship, but did not socialist thought itself come perilously close to it? Had not socialists developed a 'love affair' with centralized control? Was not the welfare state itself – often depicted as the product of a compassionate and socially concerned ideology – but the moderate face of an obsession with controls, bureaucracy, and top-to-bottom direction? Was it not in fact a systematic onslaught against individual freedoms and incentives?[6]

Socialists have now accepted, partly out of political opportunism, partly out of conviction, partly out of that chronic ignorance of their own history that blights modern political movements, that there is an element of truth in such criticisms. In fact étatism was an inseparable and inevitable part of the practice of social- ist (i.e., of reformist) practice, but not of its ideology (i.e., of its revolutionary commitment to a socialist end-goal). Throughout the nineteenth century, when socialists were in opposition and the movement in its infancy, socialism was against the state. The reasons are so obvious and have been investigated so thoroughly that here they can merely be restated: the state was – to Marxists and non-Marxists alike – a bourgeois state which deprived workers of the right to vote and produced legislation which, by and large, favoured the entrepreneurs, the aristocracy and the middle classes far more than the workers. The anti-state position of the socialists had some substance. For similar reasons the European confessional parties, where they existed, and the Roman Catholic Church also regarded the state as an alien force. It was, after all, in the hands of disbelievers and rationalists (as in France and Italy) or 'state-worshippers' (Bismarck and German nationalists). The Church realized perfectly well what liberal propa- ganda has always attempted to disguise, namely that the power of the state was usually the inevitable counterpart of the cult of the individual. In the nineteenth century the state was regarded by liberals as the essential means with which to break down the resistance of traditional privileges or local power and clear the way for the development of national markets and hence for the accumulation of capital. Similarly, conservatives regarded the state as the main instrument to be used to slow down the advance of liberal reforms. The real *étatistes*, in the nineteenth century, were the liberals and the conservatives.

Gradually, at first imperceptibly at the beginning of the twentieth century, more overtly between the wars, and conspicuously after the Second World War, socialists came to recognize that the state was the best political weapon available for the implementation of the three components of the original political pro- gramme – democracy, welfare, and regulation of the labour market.

It is rather surprising that this acceptance of the state – not just the state as a concept, but the state as a machine, as a coercive apparatus – came so late in the development of twentieth-century socialism. There was, in the years before the First World War, an optimistic view of the possibility of forcing the bourgeois state to implement the socialist reform programme. In principle they were not wrong. Without the state there could not have been a socialization of some of the costs of reproduction of the working class (the welfare state) and a regulation of the working day. Powerful trade unions, without a political party, could have struggled alone and negotiated with employers over the length of the working day, the conditions of work, holiday pay, etc. They could have acted as a pres- sure group and wrested concessions from governing political parties. This was, prior to the Second World War, the British experience. Two patterns emerged: on the continent, the length of the working day and similar labour market regulations were obtained from the state; in Britain these were left to the 'class struggle', that is, to the trade unions' confrontation with the employers.[7] The continent followed the principle of universal rights: where the eight-hour day was won, it was won on behalf of all citizens. In Britain any gain would be confined to union members.

The endorsement of the state was thus not part of the ideology of socialists. It was instrumental to the achievement of their medium- or short-term aims. The commitment of socialists to the state grew as these aims became more significant and as the final aim of a post-capitalist state receded ever more into the future. Universal suffrage made the state more receptive to the demands made by the socialists on behalf of all citizens. It also made it more legitimate and hence more powerful. It enabled socialists to achieve political power by 'capturing the state machine'. This facilitated the implementation of the rest of their reform programme – the regulation of the working day and the socialization of some of the costs of production and reproduction. This transformed industrial society.

Socialists and liberals shared equally positive assumptions about industrialism, but had different views on what the relationship between the political system and industry should be. As far as liberal *theory*, as opposed to its practice, was concerned, the purpose of the state was to remove obstacles to the advance of industrial society. Once this was achieved, industry – as part of civil society – should be allowed to develop without interference. It is noteworthy that this was precisely the position reached by some of the early socialists, in particular Saint-Simon.

The socialists were ambivalent about civil society. On the one hand they wanted to be as free as possible to organize and use collective action to achieve their demands, thus joining with the liberals who wanted broad market freedom. On the other hand they viewed civil society as a space where the distribution of power and money was so uneven as to dilute considerably the equality of rights achieved in the political arena.

After the First World War

Socialists thus regarded the state either as an alien force or as a machine which could be used for the redistribution of power. They hoped that they could control capitalism and eventually replace it. What they did not assume is that they could manage capitalism. And here lies the other substantial zone of agreement between socialists and liberals. Before the First World War, no socialists, whether Marxist or non-Marxist, moderate or authoritarian, contemplated a planned economy. How socialism should be organized was an issue on which socialist parties were quite silent, or resorted to vague generalizations of no practical value. The intellectuals were of no help. Marx somehow thought that the socialist economy would run itself: it would be 'the administration of things' whatever that meant. Lenin piously suggested that a cook would be able to run it. Kautsky, like most social democrats of the time, simply believed that the question could be resolved only when capitalism had fully developed and when the working class had acquired a superior culture and intellect. Bernstein, as he declared more than once, was not much interested in a socialist society, preferring to fight for the improvement of the conditions of the working class under capitalism. There were no plans to create a large public sector, or to nationalize the economy.[8]

The war changed matters, and not only for socialists. Politically it broke the isolation of socialists from bourgeois parties in all the contending countries, as socialists in France and Germany put the defence of 'their' state over international solidarity. In economic matters, states were forced to manage the economy, regulating labour markets, production and distribution to an unprecedented extent. The idea of managing the capitalist economy was firmly installed on the agenda of liberals, conservatives and socialists alike.

In Russia the collapse of Tsardom and the ensuing military débâcle created a power vacuum which allowed the Bolshevik seizure of power. Even then the automatic response of the Bolsheviks was not the abolition of private property and the construction of a planned economy. During the civil war the forcible top-to-bottom control of the economy was due to requirements of the military situation, not to ideological preconceptions. The 'step back' towards the adoption of the New Economy Policy was seen as a return to a market economy, not as the harbinger of new forms of economic management. The planning mechanism installed by Stalin in the late 1920s was not the inevitable consequence of the Bolshevik victory (ten years after their seizure of power!) but the outcome of a vigorous political conflict which saw the victory of the planners over their more gradualist opponents. In other words, even in what had become the USSR, socialism had not always been identified with the abolition of market forces or with a state monopoly of the economy.

Elsewhere in Europe, socialists turned out to be reluctant economic interventionists. One of the effects of the Russian revolution was to remove from socialist parties their more radical cadres, who formed communist parties. Nowhere were these able to secure the support of a majority of the socialist electorate, even where, as in France, they were able to rally the majority of party activists. The upshot was that some socialist parties, though radicalized by the war, were freer to pursue more conciliatory policies towards parties of the centre and the centre-left. Before the war all socialist parties, without exception, accepted the political principle that under no circumstances would they co-operate with 'bourgeois' parties. During the war, and even more so afterwards, this principle was abandoned. In the 1920s and 1930s socialists were finally able to achieve political power and to form governments. In all instances they were able to do so only in alliance with other parties: in Sweden, in France, in Germany, in Britain, in Spain.[9]

Some of the ideological barriers which had been erected to distinguish socialists from the rest came tumbling down. As we have seen, in terms of practical politics, these barriers had been flexible all along. After the war and particularly in the 1930s, key aspects of the reform programme of social democracy came to be accepted by other political forces. Radical organizations of the right (fascists and right-wing populists) incorporated some of the social demands of the left, including major features of welfare reform, but rejected the democratic politics which accompanied them. Liberal, Catholic and centrist forces accepted the principle of universal suffrage, though in some cases (France, Belgium and Switzerland) they still excluded the female half of the population. The principle of the regulation of the working day became almost universally accepted.

The incorporation of some aspects of the welfare state while repressing the political forces which most strongly advanced it became the hallmark of the populist authoritarian regimes which prevailed in areas of central, southern and eastern Europe, such as those of fascist Italy and Nazi Germany. In some of the remaining democratic states of Western Europe a period of uneasy compromise between labour and capital characterized the inter-war period.

The existence of a communist movement forced the socialist parties to develop ideological barriers to their left. They did so by stressing the importance of political democracy. This they no longer regarded only as the best political shell for the implementation of their economic and social demands but also as the thing that fundamentally distinguished them from the communists. Socialists, however, were also influenced by key aspects of the new communist ideology, namely the importance of the expansion of state ownership. The regular re-interpretation of the famous Clause Four of the Labour Party is emblematic. Adopted in 1918 almost as an afterthought, it vaguely referred to the 'common ownership' of the means of production, distribution and exchange. How this would work in practice remained unclear. To some, it referred clearly to a socialist future. To others it became part of a gradual process towards a socialist society: capitalism would eventually be abolished as firms and entire industries came to be absorbed into an ever-expanding public sector. To others again, public ownership would compensate for market failures, eliminate inefficient firms, prevent private monopolies.

The process of osmosis between left and right which had started before the First World War continued and was accelerated by the crisis of 1929. Liberals were no longer so certain that the state which interfered the least was the best. The rapidly developing unemployment which had destabilized Germany and threatened France and Britain was seen as evidence that the socialists had been right at least on one point: market forces did not naturally lead to an equilibrium but to chronic instability. In Italy the fascist regime reacted to the crisis by taking over most of the banking system, but limited state intervention became acceptable even in liberal and conservative Britain.

Nevertheless, the old pre-First World War view that capitalism and socialism were rigidly separated – one shared with the communists – remained in place almost everywhere between the two wars. When socialists came to power they refrained from extending the public sector, and did not attempt to direct the economy. Capitalism, they believed, could not be managed except by capitalists – hence the respect for orthodox economics exhibited by socialists in Weimar Germany after 1928, in Britain when Labour was in power in 1929–31, and elsewhere, such as in Belgium and in the Scandinavian countries. The most that could be done was to set up systems of conciliation and negotiation between capitalists and trade unions, one of the many schemes of 'partnership' between the two sides of industry which are still – at the beginning of the twenty-first century – hailed as the *dernier cri* in socialist modernity: from the Stinnes-Legien pact of 1918 which established in Germany the joint labour–management board for economic regulation, to the 'Whitley Councils' in Britain, from the Matignon Accords of 1936 following the victory of the Popular Front in France, to the National Recovery and Wagner Acts of 1933 and 1935 in the USA, from the Saltsjöbaden agreements in Sweden (1938) to the Main Agreement in Norway (1935).

Nevertheless, to most socialists, then as later, practical socialism meant protecting the workers and their families by developing the tried and tested policies of welfarism and regulation of the conditions of work. The victory of the Popular Front government in France was a clear sign that whenever they could socialists should 'occupy power' – and implement needed reforms – even though the time had not come for the 'exercise of power', to use Leon Blum's famous distinction. In opposition some socialists advanced schemes for planning the economy – as in Belgium with Hendrik de Man's *Plan du travail*, or, to use its more appropriate Flemish title, the *Plan van den Arbeid* – and advocated a mixed economic system including, in addition to a private sector, a nationalized sector consisting of credit institutions and former private monopolies.[10] This obviously required a strong and efficient state. Conservatism, right-wing authoritarianism, the technocratic liberalism of Keynes and Lloyd George, and all shades of socialism, converged on this. The only main ideology still defending the minimal state, classical liberalism, was on the run after the collapse of 1929, even in its Anglo-Saxon heartland.

After the Second World War

After the Second World War, European social democrats became leading contenders for power in virtually all the democratic countries of Western Europe. Of their three-pronged platform, the first – universal suffrage – had become the unquestioned basis of all politics with some significant exceptions, which all occurred where socialist parties did not wield any powers: the southern states of the USA, which, until the early 1970s, prevented blacks from exercising their right to vote in most elections; Switzerland where many cantons (in which socialists were weak) restricted suffrage to men until 1971; and South Africa, where – until the collapse of the apartheid regime – a multi-party system excluded blacks from effective political participation. So strongly recognized was the principle of universal suffrage that it was adopted or maintained – albeit in principle only – in most of the newly decolonized countries and in all communist states; dictatorial rule was secured not by disfranchisement but by the elimination of all effective political opposition.

The principles of welfarism and full employment never had such universal legitimacy. They became state policies prevalently in Western Europe and where socialist parties were strong, such as in Australia. As for the public sector, it was expanded throughout Western Europe, but there was little connection between the extension of the public sector and the strength of socialists. Post-war national-

izations occurred under the impetus of conservatives (Gaullism), Christian Democrats in Austria and Italy, and socialists (in the UK). One of the smallest state-
owned sectors in Europe was in the social democratic Nordic countries.

No common foreign affairs principle was adopted in the post-war period.
The pre-World War One rhetorical commitment to pacifism remained, after the
Second World War, a sub-culture within the socialist parties. These were divided
between Atlanticists and neutralists and between those in favour of the political
integration of Europe and those who remained committed to a national conception of socialism. Only in the 1990s did Europeanism become a factor uniting all
socialist parties – unlike Atlanticism which, even after the collapse of the USSR
and the eastward expansion of NATO, was not accepted by major socialist
parties such as those in Sweden, Finland and Austria.

The international organization the socialist parties had formed was never more
than a symbolic forum. Its pronouncements simply reflected in general terms a
vague consensus on matters of principles. In fact each socialist party behaved
strictly as a national organization whose priority was to safeguard its own national
polity and, consequently, the requirements of its own national capitalism.

As we have seen, the connection between modern socialism and its state and
hence with its own capitalism had started to be established towards the end of
the nineteenth century. It is thus hardly surprising that, as socialists proved
successful in reforming their capitalist societies, they were reluctant to let go of
the existing regulatory institutions: a large public sector, a powerful central bank,
a mechanism of exchange control, a complex system of subsidies and regional
policies, and an intricate mechanism for the control of the labour market. This
regulatory aspect became the fundamental relation between socialism and capitalism and further reduced the importance of the older goal of abolishing capitalism. This, in fact, had become largely of symbolic value. It stood to represent
that, however indispensable was a thriving economy for the success of all other
intermediate socialist goals, and however distant were the prospects for a post-
capitalist society, socialists still stood in an antagonistic relationship to capitalism.
However, the popular appeal of this symbolic message had been much reduced.
The prosperity associated with capitalist growth, the establishment of full employment, the protective apparatus of the welfare state, the patent incapacity of
communist states to develop consumer societies comparable to those in the West,
had almost eliminated the deep-seated antagonism towards capitalism which
had existed previously. Other political parties, such as those committed to Christian and conservatives values, who, in the past, had not been major proponents
of capitalism, discovered its virtues. The socialists did the same. Thus, gradually
but constantly, at varying speeds depending on differing political conjunctures
and, above all, on electoral vicissitudes, the parties of the left dropped their
radical anti-capitalist symbols. This process, generally referred to as revisionism,
accelerated in the late 1950s with the German SPD Bad Godesberg Congress. It
continued in all parties, dividing both activists and leaders amidst the indiffer-
ence of the electorate at large whose remarkable electoral stability is one of the
most significant factors of post-war West European history.

The victory of revisionism was almost inevitable. We have just alluded to one of the reasons: the left's electorates were never seriously concerned with the long-term aim of abolishing capitalism. They were far more interested in medium-term demands, and in a generic social justice, particularly in education and health. Consequently the revisionists, even when weak inside their parties, had always a fairly strong following among voters. This could not fail to have an impact on those radical activists who wanted their parties to maximize the chance of winning elections. There were, however, other reasons for the victory of revisionism. In almost all instances, socialists could only hope to achieve power by forming a coalition with parties of the centre. Such accords would have been more difficult if socialists had persisted with their anti-capitalist rhetoric and radical schemes of redistribution (which would require a high level of taxation). There were, of course, instances where socialists could achieve power only by reaching an understanding with parties to their left – for instance in France in the 1970s between socialists and communists. Here the agreed manifesto was radical, but the French socialists were able to use other symbolic events to signal that they would be the dominant partner and that they would be able to keep the communists under control – which is indeed what occurred. More generally, revisionists could always mount a successful challenge because they always enjoyed a vital advantage: their conservative opponents (the parties to the right) and the media and power structures which backed them could always be relied upon to stigmatize the radical left as hopelessly out of touch with modern realities. In other words, revisionism had the advantage that all centrist positions have: they can play a game on two fronts. As part of the left they can denounce capitalist iniquities; as part of the centre they can distance themselves from radicalism.

This underlines the main ideological achievement of modern socialism and also its failure. The achievement lies in the fact that free untrammelled market capitalism has never been able to establish itself as the dominant ideology of European politics. It manifestly failed to do so throughout Catholic Europe (Spain, Portugal, Italy, Austria and southern Germany) where the leading non-socialist ideologies have always taken a traditionalist form (Christian democracy) or a national-popular one (Gaullism) or an authoritarian-populist one (fascism). It also failed to do so in Protestant, Nordic countries where the agrarian parties actively co-operated in the establishment of social-democratic hegemony. Only in Britain – the original home of *laissez-faire* ideology – did free market conservatism gain a position of relative hegemony during the 1980s. Yet even there it did so almost by stealth, thanks to an electoral system which worked to the advantage of the largest party, disarray in the left and centre, and the retreat of traditional 'one-nation' conservatism.

The main ideological failure of social democracy is linked to one of the causes of its original success: having correctly identified the state as the principal regulator of the capitalist economy it sought, successfully, to democratize it and use it. As long as the state held that position, social democratic strategy retained its full coherence. But as various aspects of capitalism (especially its financial organization) developed in a global direction, this state-oriented strategy began to falter. Social democrats and the larger communist parties of the West remained wedded to a nationalist conception of politics and reinforced it constantly, ring-fencing their achievements (welfare, education, civil rights) within the territorial boundaries of the state, while capitalism set out to stride the globe.

Conclusion

To predict whether socialism has a future is a futile exercise which is nevertheless undertaken with astonishing regularity by intelligent and well-informed people. As we have seen, what socialism 'really' is has always been a matter of dispute; as its precise meaning can be endlessly re-defined and re-negotiated, there is no reason why the term could not be used indefinitely – or at least as long as capitalism exists. The only condition for its survival is the existence of significant political forces ready to associate themselves with it. As long as the term 'socialism' is used to denote any form of political regulation of capitalism, socialism will live on, frightening some, comforting others, regularly dying and yet reviving, the endless centre of debates and disputations.

Socialism – as an anti-capitalist force, aimed at overcoming the present economic arrangements of society and establishing an alternative social order where resources are allocated on the basis of need – has been a dead force in Western Europe for decades. The claims of socialism to be a modernizing force (socialism in its communist guise) able to catch up with capitalist industrial societies has been completely routed over the last twenty years. The collapse of the USSR constituted the most conspicuous evidence of this defeat. Developments in China, where a communist party is striving to establish capitalist relations, further confirms the historical collapse of the idea of communism.

At the beginning of the new century, socialism as a distributive force aimed at allocating vital resources, such as health, culture and education, outside of market mechanisms and on the basis of social citizenship, that is, without excluding anyone, is still surviving with no loss of support. Its recent electoral successes may be seen as a conscious or unconscious recognition by a majority of voters of the necessity of some kind of re-negotiation with a new kind of capitalism, more assertive, more confident, more powerful, more global, and a tacit acknowledgement that it may be better to entrust such re-negotiation to political forces that, historically speaking, have always been suspicious if not hostile to the ideology of the untrammelled market.

The difficulty facing those who still call themselves socialist is that, while they need capitalism and the economic growth and prosperity which it can generate, capitalism does not need them. Capitalist societies can be organized in an economically sustainable way by offering only minimal protection to some marginal groups (the USA) or by devolving welfare activities to organizations of civil society such as large firms, families and social groups (Japan). These alternative models, particularly the American one, whose capacity to use each crisis to re-emerge greatly strengthened is striking, have good prospects of a victorious outcome. Such expectations are greatly strengthened by the increasing reluctance of socialist leaders and followers to identify themselves with the term socialism. Such reluctance is a reflection of the uncontrollable multiplicity of meanings the term has been encumbered with, and of the incapacity of socialists to produce their own dominant meaning of the term. It is as if they had accepted that the 'hegemonic' definition of socialism is that which has been given by its enemies, one which disparages socialism for its alleged illiberalism, statism, anti-individualism, and dogmatism; for rewarding inefficiency and mortifying initiative. No ideology can survive for long if its followers are embarrassed to identify themselves with it.

Notes and references

1 The classic text is still Franco Venturi, *Roots of Revolution*, New York, Grosset and Dunlap, 1960.
2 This is the main thesis of my *One Hundred Years of Socialism. The West European Left in the Twentieth Century*, London, Fontana, 1997.
3 On the weak roots of European democracy in the first half of the twentieth century, see Mark Mazower, *Dark Continent*, New York, Knopf, 1999.
4 I take this to be the essential meaning of T.H. Marshall, *Citizenship and Social Class and Other Essays*, Cambridge, Cambridge University Press, 1950.
5 Peter Baldwin, *The Politics of Social Solidarity. Class Bases of the European Welfare State 1875–1975*, Cambridge, Cambridge University Press, 1990.
6 For a classic critique of socialism as a collectivist and anti-libertarian ideology see Ludwig von Mises, *Socialism*, Indianapolis IN, Liberty Fund, 1981.
7 Gary Cross, *A Quest for Time. The Reduction of Work in Britain and France, 1840–1940*, Berkeley CA, University of California Press, 1989.
8 On Kautsky see Dick Geary, *Karl Kautsky*, Manchester, Manchester University Press, 1987. On the wider debate see H. Tudor and J.M. Tudor (eds) *Marxism and Social Democracy. The Revisionist Debate 1896–1898*, Cambridge, Cambridge University Press 1988.
9 On the German Social Democratic Party see Susanne Miller and Heinrich Potthoff, *A History of German Social Democracy. From 1848 to the Present*, Leamington Spa, Berg Publishers, 1986. On Sweden see Steven Koblic (ed.), *Sweden's Development from Poverty to Affluence 1750–1970*, translated by Joanne Johnson, Minneapolis, University of Minnesota Press, 1975. On Britain see Robert Skidelsky, *Politicians and the Slump. The Labour Government of 1929–1931*, London, Macmillan, 1967 and Ben Pimlott, *Labour and the Left in the 1930s*, Cambridge, Cambridge University Press, 1977. On France see Julian Jackson, *The Popular Front in France. Defending Democracy, 1934–38*, Cambridge, Cambridge University Press, 1988.
10 Erik Hansen, 'Hendrik de Man and the theoretical foundations of economic planning: the Belgian experience, 1933–1940', *European Studies Review*, 1978, Vol. 8, No. 2.

5 The doing of conservatism

Robert Eccleshall

Introduction

Does oblivion beckon? This is the kind of question which, though sometimes favoured by authors in search of a snappy headline – 'Is . . . ism dead?', 'Does . . . ism have a future?', and so forth – is probably best avoided, particularly in a chapter which casts a centennial eye on an ideology whose adherents have often been fastidious in their reluctance to predict the future. I raise the question because the argument of much recent writing is that conservatism, particularly in Britain, is in a terminal condition. In doing so my intention is neither to sketch the likely nuances of conservative thinking nor to consider whether this century, like the last, will be a 'conservative' one in which centre-right governments are in power for much of the period. It is the more modest one of suggesting that much recent prognosis of conservatism rests on a shaky analysis of how the ideology operated in the past, and that it perhaps underestimates the capacity of conservatives for self-renewal.

John Gray attributes 'the undoing of conservatism' to the New Right's crusade of bourgeois modernization which swept through much of Western Europe in the final decades of the last century. The consequences of a project of radical individualism have been particularly damaging to British conservatism on this account, because its adherents customarily claimed to be custodians of an *ancien régime*. In relentlessly pursuing a neo-liberal programme of minimal government, Thatcherites cast themselves adrift 'from the larger tradition of European conservative philosophy of which British conservative thought has always been a part',[1] and instead aligned themselves with the American right by embracing an alien form of Enlightenment rationalism. In doing so they 'hollowed out' the culture in which a coherent mode of conservative discourse and political practice had flourished. Traditional institutions were dissolved by market forces, and with them went those attitudes of deference which had sustained the claim of Tory patrician statecraft to govern by evolutionary adaptation rather than by schooling in the techniques of permanent revolution towards a free-market brutopia.

Gray, a lapsed convert from the New Right project, is inclined to make an intellectual splash, and his apocalyptic pronouncements about the obsolescence of conservatism ought to be treated with caution. Yet other commentators, perhaps more prudent in their judgement, concur that conservatism is in crisis because of ideological exhaustion.[2] A common view is that conservatives have cut themselves free from their ideological and cultural moorings in a strained bid to unite certain antinomies which are usually referred to as 'neos' – though there is little agreement about the exact ingredients of this odd ideological mixture. While most commentators, according to Andrew Gamble, portray the New Right as an uneasy interplay between neo-liberal individualism and neo-conservative social authoritarianism,[3] others contend that the strands themselves are self-contradictory. In *The Third Way*, the intellectual flagship of New Labour in Britain, Anthony Giddens claims that 'neo-liberalism is in trouble' because 'its two halves – market fundamentalism and conservatism – are in tension'. In substance, however, Giddens's argument is close to that of Gray, whose influence he acknowledges:

> Conservatism always meant a cautious, pragmatic approach to social and economic change – an attitude adopted by Burke in the face of the messianic claims of the French Revolution. The continuity of tradition is central to the idea of conservatism. Tradition contains the accumulated wisdom of the past and therefore supplies a guide to the future. Free market philosophy takes quite a different attitude, pinning its hopes for the future on unending economic growth produced by the liberation of market forces . . . The dynamism of market societies undermines traditional structures of authority and fractures local communities, neo-liberalism creates new risks and uncertainties which it asks citizens simply to ignore. Moreover, it neglects the social basis of markets themselves, which depend upon the very communal forms that market fundamentalism indifferently casts to the winds.[4]

Commentators are unclear, then, whether the crisis of conservatism is due to an unsatisfactory attempt to fuse a couple of 'neos', the incompatibility of the nostrums of political economy with a traditional scepticism about promises of indefinite social progress, or inherent contradictions within neo-liberalism itself. The problem with this kind of approach is that it characterizes current conservative thinking as primarily a cerebral activity that entails an unsatisfactory struggle, sub-Hegelian manner, to synthesize intellectual strands that are ultimately irreconcilable.

Yet conservatism has always consisted of diverse strands whose consistency, either internally or in relation to one another, does not necessarily match standards of intellectual rigour. Throughout the last century free-market conservatives in Britain were accused, often by opponents within the party, of succumbing to what is now referred to as neo-liberalism. In 1912 Pierse Loftus feared that the party would be deflected from a programme of social amelioration by the presence within it of those who, 'saturated with the *laisser-faire* principles of the Manchester school', used as 'a main argument against improvement of the conditions of the people the old phrase, "The survival of the fittest"'.[5] Yet the Social Darwinists he had in mind were not on the whole classical liberals. Like the New

Right seventy years later they tended to put a conservative gloss on the theme of a self-help society by advocating a disciplinary state to curb individuals who failed to respond to market imperatives. Free-market conservatives have usually been crusaders, dogmatic in their adherence to the laws of political economy and raucous in their demand for radical measures to reverse a drift to collectivism. What was novel about the New Right was neither their convictions nor their zealotry but their electoral opportunity to make 'authoritarian individualism' a sustained political project.

Conservative critics of unfettered capitalism have usually located themselves in that patrician, one-nation tradition which emerged from Benjamin Disraeli's attempt in the 1880s to regroup the party for a democratic age. Some have certainly exhibited those attitudes which Giddens and others consider to be essential features of conservatism: an inclination to improve social conditions by measured statecraft and piecemeal reform rather than by grand design, and preference for orderly procession along some safe route between the rugged terrains of socialism and pure capitalism. Yet on occasion – Joseph Chamberlain's tariff reformers at the beginning of the last century, for example, and Keynesian conservatives in the 1930s – they too have claimed that something more dramatic than the quiet art of cautious statecraft was needed to avert the country from revolutionary socialism or worse. And sometimes their campaigns to capture the party – that of the tariff reformers, for instance – led to the kind of internal divisions and electoral débâcles that are said to be the death-knell of modern conservatism.

The impression given by Gray and others is that conservatives were once unified in articulating certain pristine ideas in a cogent manner, but that the ascendancy of the New Right precipitated a post-lapsarian plunge into intellectual muddle because the doctrine became contaminated by some 'neo' that is certainly alien and may be electorally fatal. This sort of analysis is weak on historical perspective. There is little correlation between intellectual purity and electoral success because conservatism in its various forms has always been something of a patchwork. A more valid approach is to consider what has been distinctive about the doing of conservatism as an ideological rather than an intellectual activity.

Discreet decontestants

Common to the varieties of conservatism has been an affirmation of the need for an orderly, disciplined and unequal society which benefits from appropriate leadership. Differences have tended to focus on how leadership should be exercised. For free-market conservatives a properly constituted society is a hierarchy of talent and achievement in which an entrepreneurial minority reaps the rewards of its endeavours, and in doing so has the incentive to continue creating the prosperity from which the many benefit. Thatcherites were not the first to extol the 'trickle down' effect of wealth creation. Socialism, as a Unionist free-trader put it in 1908, 'would injure instead of benefiting the poor. You will never be able to give every man on a hot day a bigger drink of water if you begin by stopping up the pipe that feeds the cistern.'[6] For patrician conservatives society is more of an ascriptive hierarchy of privileges and obligations that are manifested in legislation to safeguard the majority from the excesses of capitalism. Common to both is an affirmation of the need for a firm framework of law and order to counteract the frailties of human nature which, unless curbed, would tear society apart.

Conservatives have often been robust and unambiguous in vindicating inequality. David Stelling, writing during the Second World War, compared the political order to a military command structure.

> Perhaps one man in every ten will have the capacity for leadership, or the enterprise to back his own ability with his savings. The other nine will be the workers in the hive. Democracy needs its officers and NCOs no less in civil life than in the military field, and as a good Tory Democrat, I set my face firmly against the idea of equality which is sometimes mistaken for sound democratic doctrine.[7]

In 1978 the cerebral Salisbury group, unduly anxious that the market rhetoric of the emerging New Right would deflect attention from the need for measures to preserve a disciplined, organic community, published a collection of essays insisting that conservatism was about attending to ordered hierarchy rather than extending liberty. The only 'sort of freedom' that conservatives 'want', according to one contributor, is the kind that 'will maintain existing inequalities or restore lost ones';[8] whilst another suggested that the 'outstanding minority' found in any society 'should exercise more influence over public affairs than the untalented majority; should form, that is to say, a ruling class'.[9]

Other conservatives have been more reluctant to flaunt what is pivotal to their conception of a sound society. The desirability of inequality is perhaps not the most electorally potent message to convey to a democratic age. Raphael Samuel, in his marvellous essay on Thatcherism, suggests that 'Victorian values' provided an idiom for playing out intra-party differences between market individualists and one-nation Tories in the 1980s. The invocation of Victorian Britain provided each faction with a means of claiming the mantle of authentic conservatism. 'The rhetoric of Victorian Values could be seen as an example of what the post-modernists call "double-coding" . . . i.e., words which say one thing, while meaning another and camouflaging, or concealing, a third.'[10] Besides facilitating internal squabbles, double-coding has enabled conservatives to draw a veil of discretion over the basic message they wish to transmit to a wider audience. Among the euphemisms used to express the need for inequality have been an 'enterprise culture', 'the responsible society', an 'opportunity state', a 'property-owning democracy', and even a 'classless society'.

'Double-coding' is another way of expressing what is characteristic of all ideological activity: the process of decontesting the shared concepts of political discourse by attaching them with ideologically specific meanings. Michael Freeden has illustrated how the meaning of various concepts is fixed by their ideological association with one another. What distinguishes an ideology is its particular configuration of core, adjacent and peripheral concepts.[11] Conservatives, however, do not operate quite like their rivals. Others are prone to parade their core beliefs, even when using secondary values to qualify their significance. Equality is central to the language of socialism, for example, though care is usually taken to demonstrate that its achievement does not require revolutionary upheaval. Conservatives, by contrast, are inclined to use surrounding concepts to conceal their commitment to inequality. If we may borrow Freeden's image of a room in which the significance of each conceptual unit derives from the overall arrangement, conservatives are inclined to shuffle their furniture around to conceal the principal items within it. Rather like those decorous Victorians, who hid some of their basic functions by placing picturesque screens in certain rooms, conservatives are apt to be discreet decontestants.

Their discretion is revealed in a penchant for putting some item other than equality on prominent display, while busily arranging the other conceptual furniture around it to intimate what they have in mind. A favourite concept for exhibition has been that of ordered liberty.

The New Right professed commitment to the kind of liberty which lifts restrictions on competitive individualism while restoring the foundations of an organic community. On their account a free society encourages entrepreneurial ambition while taking firm measures against its unruly members who are disinclined to imbibe bourgeois virtues. Those who persisted in habits of welfare dependency or had been corrupted by permissive values needed to be restrained by a stricter regime of social discipline. As Norman Tebbit, a vociferous exponent of Thatcherite values, proclaimed in 1985:

> The Conservative party shares the British people's attachment for freedom. It is to the free society that we are committed. That is a society in which the unavoidable derogations of individual liberty are minimized and take place only under the rule of law.
>
> Of course, many of our opponents also claim to be friends of freedom, but the freedom they offer is always at best highly qualified. They do not understand or acknowledge that political freedom will not long be maintained if it is divorced from economic liberty . . . And, above all, they refuse to face their supporters with the awkward truth that the moral and material benefits of freedom itself cannot be enjoyed free from the risks and difficulties of freedom and the burdens of personal responsibility . . .
>
> I believe that by the 1990s we shall see the effects of a revulsion against the valueless values of the Permissive Society. The public are demanding stiffer sentences for criminals . . . I know that at the front of that campaign for a return to values of decency and order will be the Conservative Party for we understand as does no other party that the defence of freedom involves a defence of the values which make freedom possible without its degeneration into licence.[12]

Ordered liberty entailed competitive individualism within the framework of a strong state.

There have been other variants on the theme. Bernard Braine, writing in 1948, was critical of socialist egalitarianism. As a one-nation Tory, however, he believed that an unfettered market consigned some individuals to appalling poverty. And so, reflecting the Keynesian mood of the post-war party in Britain, he dwelt not so much on the inevitability of inequality than on the conservative responsibility 'to seek a middle course which brings the claims of order and freedom into proper balance'.[13] Here was an expression of the Whig view of statecraft.

Conservative discretion is also revealed in a tendency to represent the doctrine as a form of naturalism. Free-market conservatives have always contended that society becomes economically and morally stagnant whenever government tampers with a natural economic order. More generally, conservatives have indicated that they are more aware than their opponents of the intricacies of the human condition. F.E. Smith, who before the First World War feared that his party would lose working-class support unless it found some basis other than discredited tariff reform for progressive social legislation, was critical of individualists and socialists alike for constructing their doctrines on false preconceptions about human behaviour. Few people were disposed to engage either in an incessant struggle for self-advancement or in some grand project to eliminate private property. 'On the contrary, most individuals tread in the accustomed paths, and demand of life that it shall give them security and prosperity in the state in which it has pleased God to call them.' The 'essence of Tory Social Reform', of course, was its sensitivity to 'the real aptitudes of the people'.[14]

Conservatives have also claimed a unique grasp of the flow of history. Their gloss on Britain's *ancien régime*, for example, has depicted a small island race of self-reliant and adventurous individuals who, unconquered for a millennium, developed administrative arrangements that were eventually exported to much of the rest of the world. On this account conservatives are the legitimate custodians of the empire state: in touch with the cultural residues of a thousand glorious years because they know, unlike their opponents, that government 'should be designed to allow us to be *ourselves*. And what are we in this country', continued the whiggish Bernard Braine, 'if we are not strangely obstinate, individualistic folk chafing at restrictions and contemptuous of slavery'.[15] Margaret Thatcher, in a speech delivered nearly a decade after she was deposed as leader of the Conservative party, acknowledged the influence on her government's policies of free-market economists, such as Friedrich Hayek and Milton Friedman.

> But the root of the approach we pursued in the 1980s lay deep in human nature, and more specially the nature of the British people. If you really believe, as a matter of passionate conviction, in the talents and character of your nation, of course you want to set it free. And we British have a true vocation for liberty – all our history proves it.[16]

There have been two conservative versions of this heroic tale of the enduring virtues of the people of this land of hope and glory. In the free-market one, scrutiny of a thousand years reveals epic moments – the first Elizabethan age, for example, and the era of 'Victorian values' – of exceptional achievement when governments gave ample scope to the vigorous virtues of an ancestral people by declining to stifle the natural laws of supply and demand. The Whig version is of the incessant adaptability of an unfolding organic community in which institutions and liberties have emerged unplanned from accumulated experience rather than being concocted by political alchemy. Each version has enabled conservatives to profess membership of a 'national' party because of its peculiar capacity to preserve or restore features of this great inheritance. In both, the room of conceptual furniture has been lavishly adorned with murals and tapestries commemorating various events in the triumphal procession of old Britain.

Traditionalism

The discretion of conservatives in attending to their ideological activity helps to explain some of the misconceptions of what they have been about. One mistake is to suppose that the Whig endorsement of cautious statecraft reveals the essence of the doctrine. On this account, conservatism is to be understood as a 'defence of a limited style of politics, based upon the idea of imperfection'.[17] For conservatives the state is not an enterprise for promoting socialist equality, capitalist efficiency, humanity's fundamental rights, or any other utopian project. Sceptical of any scheme for vastly improving the human condition, conservatives are allegedly suspicious of the kind of programmatic politics which claims anchorage in universal guidelines for human conduct. Eschewing the rationalism of the social engineer, they prefer to find their way through the complexities of the practical world by picking up signals from political arrangements that have worked themselves out in the course of history. They realize, unlike their opponents, that the task of the politician is to engage in the art of pursuing what Michael Oakeshott called the 'intimations' of a settled way of life rather than planning for some utopian dawn. 'Politics is not the science of setting up a permanently impregnable society, it is the art of knowing where to go next in the exploration of an already existing traditional kind of society.'[18] In this conception of political activity, society yields no unambiguous rules for amending its practices, there is no single line of direction to be followed, and certainly no ultimate objective to be achieved. Politics instead is about timely accommodation within an organic community whose rulers are attentive to the social dangers of a fallen human nature.

The Whig version of conservatism has a certain resonance in Britain's *ancien régime*. It has also revealed a surprising capacity to travel beyond the confines of a state in which some are inclined to cherish its feudal inheritance. Even in a relatively new country such as the United States, which is supposed to have fallen prey to rationalism by committing itself to a limitless future, commentators have been inclined to suggest that conservatism counsels the art of prudent statecraft. According to Clinton Rossiter, in his classic but inchoate account of American conservatism:

> the genuine Conservative is not a crusader, he goes upon his mission not zealously but dutifully . . . The Conservative is always the prisoner of the social process as it exists in the traditions, institutions, needs, and aspirations of his own country – and thus the prisoner of men who, knowingly or unknowingly, keep that process in motion. They act, he only reacts.[19]

Russell Kirk's *The Conservative Mind*, first published in 1953, is a ringing endorsement of Edmund Burke's politics of prescription, and the impression given by the book is that its author would have relished life among the squirearchy of eighteenth-century England.

The commitment of some conservatives to a politics of imperfection has prompted the claim that conservatism is qualitatively distinct from other ideologies. At its silliest, and usually within a British context, the equation of the doctrine with traditionalism has led to the suggestion that conservatives are not ideologues at all, which at face value implies that they are incapable of coherent thinking about the nature of a sound polity. The message, of course, is that ideologues indulge in an 'alien' form of knowledge because of their conviction that the political order can be analysed, and subsequently transformed, according to the certainties of science.[20] Ideologues seek refuge from the contingencies of a settled way of life in rationalism. Because of their sensitivity to the crooked timber of humanity, however, conservatives are suspicious of promises to steer the ship of state to some island paradise. Their scepticism about utopian projects inclines them to a non-programmatic, un-ideological form of politics which takes its bearings from the peculiarities of a particular culture rather than from some dogma about the universal needs of humanity.

Beyond a British context, scepticism about promises of a new dawn has led to the claim that conservatives, although ideologues, nevertheless operate somewhat differently from their rivals because of their reluctance to provide a blueprint of the ideal society. Conservatism has been characterized as a 'positional' ideology that is articulated only when others beckon with promises of some golden age,[21] a fixed catechism of basic ideas that is recited when anyone produces some fresh formula for eliminating the imperfections of existing arrangements.[22]

The assumption of those who contend that British conservatism is unravelling is that the New Right went astray in capitulating to rationalism. In doing so they abandoned the scepticism of their predecessors in a bid to 'yoke conservatism, perhaps for the first time in its history, to an Enlightenment utopia'.[23] In demanding an 'enterprise revolution', Thatcherites were inclined to depict their project as a crusade to restore the features of a golden moment in the past, that of the Victorian era, when institutional arrangements and native characteristics coincided in a display of national greatness. In doing so they revealed a preference for dogmatic certainties, the nostrums of political economy, which genuine conservatives allegedly detest.

If the New Right were heretical in preferring to be guided by the infallible laws of supply and demand instead of the art of prudent statecraft, they were not the first 'conservatives' to urge dramatic measures for resisting encroachment upon the minimal state. The emergence of the New Right as a serious political project was preceded by the establishment of various organizations and think-tanks dedicated to reversing the tide of collectivism by the propagation of a free-market philosophy. At the beginning of the twentieth century similar organizations were formed with the intention of arresting what was perceived as a drift from individualism.

One of them was the British Constitution Association which, influenced by Herbert Spencer's Social Darwinism, was founded in 1905 with the intention of countering 'political socialism', among the manifestations of which were said to be proposals for a minimum wage, old-age pensions, and free school meals for poor children. One of its committee members contended that such measures derived from a misguided philanthropic desire to improve the condition of the poor. But sound policies emanated from a scientific understanding of human behaviour which demonstrated the general benefits of inequality:

> The inequality of wealth now existing must often cause deep pain to sym-pathetic minds, but if we give way to sentiment we must be aware of the danger of laying up far greater evils for future generations. There is no exception to the rule that where sentiment and emotion come in, science goes out . . .
>
> Liberty and equality are mutually exclusive and cannot live together. The reason is very clear. Mankind are born unequal; unequal in physical strength, in intellectual strength, and in moral strength. If we disregard the facts of human nature, and say 'All men *shall* be equal', we can only attain the end by a profound subversion of the methods of Nature.[24]

Members of the Association were sure that they had to be combative in defend-ing minimal statism. Lord Hugh Cecil's *Conservatism*, published in 1912, is a classic account of the doctrine as a form of scepticism that is wary of Enlighten-ment promises of a bright new tomorrow. As President of the Association, however, he encouraged its members to engage in a mighty endeavour to resist the perils of the age:

> The forces we have to face are considerable, but as we look over the long course of history we know that the principles for which we are contending have been threatened before in one way or another and have survived. We know the principle of liberty has long been the inheritance of the English people, and that it has been defended from some very pressing dangers – successfully defended and handed down to our own time. Now it is menaced by the divine right of the State . . . But we must rely upon the English spirit of the past to prevail now as then.[25]

There have been numerous examples of conservatives in crusading and scientific mood. Between 1880 and 1920 W.H. Mallock sought in a plethora of books to formulate a 'scientific conservatism' which demonstrated the folly of confiscating the wealth of an exceptional minority without whose entrepreneurial activity everyone would be poorer. Ernest Benn became a fervent minimal stater in 1921 after what John Gray would no doubt consider to have been an unfortunate visit to the United States. Some years later he switched allegiance from the Liberal to the Conservative Party, and for a quarter of a century waged a campaign through his publications and organizational activities to retrieve the natural liberty that had flourished in the Victorian golden age of unfettered enterprise. 'The peril which menaces us owing to the growing sense of dependence is enormous, and can never be removed until we have developed in the breast of everyone the old spirit of Individualism and independence.'[26] And this required a crusade to roll back the state in order to release the native characteristics of the British people.

Instead of stigmatizing those who are inclined to scientific certainty and crusading zeal as heretical, we ought to consider the kind of society conservatives have had in mind when calling for ordered liberty or presenting their doctrine as a form of naturalism. Conservatives are no more reluctant than their rivals to provide a social blueprint, though as discreet decontestants of the shared concepts of political discourse they have often misled commentators with regard to what they are about. A preference for evolutionary adaptation is not an essential characteristic of conservatism. The Whiggish art of prudent statecraft has been merely one of the strategies recommended for sustaining the good society, one that is usually favoured when the pillars of ordered hierarchy are judged to be in sound condition. When these pillars are considered to be in danger of erosion conservatives are often as eager as other ideologues to urge dramatic measures for either preserving or restoring their ideal of how society should be organized.

British exceptionalism?

In declining to be guardians of national continuity, according to John Gray, the British New Right abandoned the preference of European conservatives for cautious statecraft by aligning themselves with the American dream of indefinite social progress. Gray is unusual in suggesting that British conservatives in the last century had an affinity with the European right. A more typical assessment, one particularly favoured by Oakeshottians, is that British conservatives have little in common with their counterparts in either Europe or America.

On this account Britain has been exceptional in avoiding rationalism in politics. Its institutions, unlike those of many countries, evolved from historical experience instead of being created by the dogma of some founding document. 'It is no accident', according to the impeccable Whig Bernard Braine, 'that the British constitution is unwritten and that it has survived the test of time while the near-perfect written constitutions of other countries have been short-lived. Our constitution has survived the test of time precisely because it is a natural growth, dependent much *less* upon outward forms than upon the spirit with which it is operated.'[27] Michael Oakeshott made the same point when vindicating the organic community that had unfolded in Britain (or rather England). In the USA and continental Europe political institutions were 'coeval with the blood of rationalistic politics'.[28] But the English, suspicious of the 'foreign clap-trap' that sometimes drifted across the Channel,[29] were on the whole immune to utopian promises. They knew that their arrangements had emerged gradually, even though the English attachment to liberty had been transformed elsewhere into an obsession with humanity's universal requirements. 'What went abroad as the concrete rights of an Englishman have returned home as the abstract Rights of Man.'[30] The Oakeshottian academic industry has produced absurd claims about the specificity of the English preference for timely accommodation. Gordon Graham, for example, contends that a sceptical disregard for utopian projects 'is a decidedly English doctrine with little appeal and no following in other countries' because only 'British institutions have been decent enough to allow a decent man to be conservative'.[31]

There is some validity in the claim that English scepticism does not travel well. Rebellious American colonists in the eighteenth century were influenced by ideas that had taken shape in the English commonwealth period and were subsequently refined by John Locke, and the Declaration of Independence ensured their entry into the ideological mainstream. But in England commonwealth ideas remained marginal because their prospect of a democratic republic frightened even most Whigs. Hence the tendency of Americans to seek the ideological origin of their country's separatist nationalism in some region of the British Isles other than England; and to find it in late seventeenth-century Ireland where ideas emanating from a clash with the Westminster government are said to have forged an 'essential link' in 'the development of a radical chain of thought' which eventually prompted Americans to secede from the imperial monarchy.[32]

But is the ideological gap between American foundationalism and English reverence of an *ancien régime* as wide as Gray suggests? Gray, like other commentators, argues that the ideals of the Declaration of Independence shackle all Americans to a project of classical liberal rationalism. Yet the foundation of the American Republic has always been contested ideological territory, and conservatives have been careful to put their own gloss upon it. In one version it constituted a condition of pre-lapsarian purity – rather like the Victorian age celebrated by the British New Right – a godly commonwealth that decent citizens must campaign to restore.

> The only option the traditionalist and the conservative have, then, is never to cease struggling – until we have re-created a government and an America that conforms, as close as possible, to our image of the Good Society, if you will, a Godly country.[33]

In another version it embodied the ideas not so much of the English commonwealth as of ancient republics in which care was taken by prudent statecraft to attend to the frailties of human nature. The founding fathers, like ancient republicans, knew that societies are inclined to degenerate unless effort is made to cultivate a virtuous citizenry. 'Virtue was defined according to stern Roman values, with something of the sober English ones thrown in.'[34] In both versions the message is that the American nation will become corrupt unless measures are taken to instil thrift, self-discipline and patriotism in its people. Is the message being transmitted so different from that of British conservatives who in their various ways have called for ordered liberty?

Conclusion

Finally, what should we make of the claim that British conservatism is a spent force? The contention is that the New Right project of bourgeois modernization demolished the intricacies of class, respect for tradition and other features of an *ancien régime* in which the Whig conception of statecraft had resonance. Conservatives, as we indicated, have certainly been inclined to depict themselves as the custodians of national continuity in a land of hope and glory. There is also a tendency among commentators of the left to suggest that Britain's long past has been the ideological preserve of conservatives: that the residues of an 'empire state' have lent themselves to the articulation of a culture of subjecthood in which the mass of people are invited to defer to wise leadership.

Yet Britain's long history has provided enormous ideological resources for parties across the political spectrum. Labour politicians, including Tony Blair, have been no less disposed than conservatives to invoke a thousand glorious years, promising to preserve or restore the nation as a global leader by harnessing the enduring qualities of its people to some fresh challenge. Their promise, like that of the New Right, has been to use British grit to reinvigorate an old country.[35] Even if the Thatcherite project did destroy Britain's lingering feudal roots, which is debatable, there is no reason to suppose that conservatives have been deprived of a context for constructing plausible narratives of the sound polity. In this century, as in the last, they will probably continue to call for the kind of ordered liberty which rewards risk-taking while curtailing social indiscipline, and to represent their doctrine as a form of naturalism which flows from the native characteristic of robust individuality.

Notes and references

1 John Gray, *End Games: Questions in Late Modern Political Thought*, Cambridge, Polity Press, 1997, p. 6. See also 'The undoing of conservatism', in John Gray, *Enlightenment's Wake: Politics and Culture at the Close of the Modern Age*, London, Routledge, 1995, pp. 87–119.
2 Andrew Gamble, 'The crisis of conservatism', *New Left Review*, 1995, No. 214, p. 24.
3 Andrew Gamble, 'Legacies and meanings of the New Right', *ECPR News: The News Circular of the European Consortium for Political Research*, 1999, Vol. 10, No. 2, pp. 9–10.
4 Anthony Giddens, *The Third Way: The Renewal of Social Democracy*, Cambridge, Polity Press, 1998, p. 15.
5 Pierse Loftus, *The Conservative Party and the Future: A Programme for Tory Democracy*, London, Stephen Swift, 1912, p. 110.

6 J. St Loe Strachey, *Problems and Perils of Socialism: Letters to a Working Man*, London, Macmillan, 1908, p. 20.

7 David Stelling, *Why I am a Conservative*, London, Conservative Headquarters, 1943, p. 8.

8 Maurice Cowling, 'The present position', in M. Cowling (ed.), *Conservative Essays*, London, Cassell, 1978, p. 9.

9 Peregrine Worsthorne, 'Too much freedom', in ibid., p. 141.

10 Raphael Samuel, 'Mrs Thatcher and Victorian values', in Alison Light, Sally Alexander and Gareth Stedman Jones (eds), *Theatres of Memory*, Vol. II, *Island Stories: Unravelling Britain*, London, Verso, 1998, p. 342.

11 Michael Freeden, *Ideologies and Political Theory: A Conceptual Approach*, Oxford, Clarendon Press, 1996.

12 Norman Tebbit, *Britain's Future: A Conservative Vision*, London, Conservative Political Centre, 1985, cited in R. Eccleshall, *English Conservatism Since the Restoration*, London, Unwin Hyman, 1990, pp. 246–8.

13 Bernard Braine, *Tory Democracy*, London, Falcon Press, 1948, p. 84.

14 F.E. Smith, *Unionist Policy and Other Essays*, London, Williams and Norgate, 1913, p. 44.

15 Braine, *Tory Democracy*, p. 84.

16 Margaret Thatcher, Speech at the International Free Enterprise Dinner on 20 April 1999.

17 Noel O'Sullivan, *Conservatism*, London, J.M. Dent, 1976, p. 13.

18 Michael Oakeshott, *Rationalism in Politics, and other Essays*, London, Methuen, 1962, p. 58.

19 Clinton Rossiter, *Conservatism in America: The Thankless Persuasion*, second edition, New York, Alfred Knopf, 1966, pp. 53–4.

20 Kenneth Minogue, *Alien Powers: The Pure Theory of Ideology*, London, Weidenfeld and Nicolson, 1985.

21 S.P. Huntington, 'Conservatism as an ideology', *American Political Science Review*, 1957, Vol. 51, pp. 454–73.

22 Albert O. Hirschman, *The Rhetoric of Reaction: Perversity, Futility, Jeopardy*, Cambridge MA, Harvard University Press, 1991.

23 Gray, 'The undoing of conservatism', p. 100.

24 Hugh Eliott, 'Man versus the state', in Mark E. Judge (ed.), *Political Socialism: A Remonstrance*, London, P.S. King, 1908, pp. 166–7.

25 Ibid., p. 49.

26 Ernest J.P. Benn, *The Return to Laisser Faire: The Case for Individualism*, London, Ernest Benn, 1928, p. 20.

27 Braine, *Tory Democracy*, p. 74.

28 Michael Oakeshott, 'Scientific politics', *Cambridge Journal*, 1947/48, Vol. 1, p. 352.

29 Oakeshott, *Rationalism in Politics*, p. 50.

30 Michael Oakeshott, 'Contemporary British politics', *Cambridge Journal*, 1947/48, Vol. 1, p. 490.

31 Gordon Graham, *Politics in its Place: A Study of Six Ideologies*, Oxford, Clarendon Press, 1986, p. 188.

32 Nicholas Canny, *Kingdom and Colony: Ireland in the Atlantic World, 1560–1800*, Baltimore MD and London, Johns Hopkins University Press, 1988, p. 22.

33 Patrick J. Buchanan, *Right from the Beginning*, Washington DC, Regnery Gateway, 1990, p. 342.

34 Clyde N. Wilson, 'Citizens or subjects?', in Robert W. Whitaker (ed.), *The New Right Papers*, New York, St Martin's Press, 1982, p. 108.

35 See R. Eccleshall, 'Party ideology and national decline', in Richard English and Michael Kenny (eds), *Rethinking British Decline*, London, Macmillan, 2000, pp. 155–83.

6 The ideology of Christian democracy[1]

Paolo Pombeni

During a lecture broadcast by the BBC in November 1945, the historian A.J.P. Taylor offered an interesting, and at the time entirely original, analysis of the ideological panorama of post-war Europe (in which, incidentally, he did not include Great Britain).[2] But the most novel feature was not Taylor's description of the change then taking place in political parties of Marxist, socialist or communist inspiration, which he viewed as offering a broad range of catch-all ideological proposals:

> They want a strong government which will run economic life; but they want also to be able to grumble against it. They want the state to do things for the good of individual human beings; they do not want individuals to have to do things for the good of the State. In other words, they want socialism, but they also want the Rights of Man.

Perception of this transformation was already quite widespread, and it rested, as Taylor himself pointed out, on the contribution made by these parties to the struggle against fascism. Rather, the novelty of Taylor's analysis lay in its understanding of the importance assumed by the Christian democracy parties in a context where, he believed, the ideology of capitalism had now been marginalized, reduced to nothing more than a hangover from the war: 'Nobody in Europe believes in the American way of life – that is, in private enterprise; or rather, those who believe in it are a defeated party and a party which seems to have no more future than the Jacobites in England after 1688'.

For Taylor, the novelty was Christian democracy, although he placed it in the category of the 'conservative' and 'peasant' parties (a judgement which, as we shall see, cannot be historically justified). Although the Catholic parties had garnered votes from the old right, Taylor regarded them as anti-capitalist and not opposed to nationalization. They comprised a section of the popular classes marked out by a boundary that was 'not social, but religious'. It was this feature that most forcefully struck Taylor, who rightly pointed out that the Roman Church had taken the side of the fascist dictators.

> Now, for almost the first time in modern history, it seems to be taking a democratic, indeed revolutionary line. Instead of demanding a privileged position for itself, the Roman Church is beginning to defend toleration

for everybody; it is trying to make its peace with what has hitherto been regarded over the Continent as an anticlerical, atheistic doctrine – the principle of liberty and the Rights of Man.

When viewed with the hindsight of today, Taylor displayed considerable acumen, at least in the light of subsequent events in large areas of Europe and Latin America. Although in his concluding remarks he made no further mention of Christian democracy, the problem he evoked also comprised the role fulfilled by that ideology in many of the countries tied to the culture of the 'Western' world.

> That is the point to which I am brought back in considering both the communists and the political Catholics. Both start from totalitarian doctrines, both claim exclusive inspiration, but when they seek mass support, they have to recognise that most Europeans want individual liberty, not freedom alone, but freedom as well as socialism. Can you have freedom without capitalism? Can you reconcile economic collectivism and intellectual individualism? That is the question underlying the European revolution. For my part, if I have confidence in anything, I would have confidence in this: the continent which was the birthplace of both Rousseau and Marx, which produced both the Declaration of the Rights of Man and the Communist Manifesto, will produce an answer to the problem of our time.

Europe was therefore the continent that was to blend liberalism and socialism. But why did Taylor include the ideology of the Catholic parties which now wrapped themselves in the banner of Christian democracy – a label once in odour of heresy? To an orthodox British intellectual (from the point of view of his academic background) like Taylor, the Roman Church appeared 'totalitarian' in its ideology, and the feature that he deemed most positive of the Catholics' political presence was their inclination towards nationalization and anti-capitalism: a factor which would have given impetus to the general movement towards socialism.

Those who consider the two Christian democracy parties that remained longest in power after 1945 – those of Germany and Italy – may have doubts as to the accuracy of Taylor's analysis, given that both the Christliche Demokratische Union/Christliche Soziale Union and the Democrazia Cristiana have been depicted by historical research as the protagonists of the reconstruction of Western capitalism in their respective countries. And yet Taylor's thesis comprises more than one important point.

In order to analyse this ideological perspective thoroughly, we must first impose some sort of order on the confused panorama of religiously-based political ideologies. Secularization and the general anti-religious prejudice displayed by a substantial part of academic research often make it impossible to grasp the diverse layers of the phenomenon. Christian democracy, in fact, was the final outcome of a process that was by no means linear; and it was moreover a typical 'ideology of transition'. Its goal was not so much to fashion a new explanation (and perhaps a new organization) of public space as to move a cultural community (in this case a religious community) towards a new organization of public space hostile to it; and to do so in such a way that this community not only found protection for its identity on this new terrain but could also act with its heritage recognized and thus potentially assume leadership. If one does not take account of this context, it is difficult to understand either the exact position of the ideology in the overall panorama or the historical process of its growth and current decline (irreversible, in my view).

It is first necessary to examine the relationship between the denomination Christian democracy – which may theoretically refer to Christianity in its entirety – and the specific position occupied within it by Catholicism. This is an important point because in the post-war period an 'interconfessional' form of Christian democracy arose in Germany which appealed to the Catholic world and the reformed churches alike. As we shall see, this development was exceptional, and in a strict sense the phenomenon of 'Christian Democrat' ideology has been closely bound up with Catholicism.

At the origin of the problem, obviously, lies the Roman Church's traumatic relationship with the modern political organization. When writing about *Azione Cattolica*, Antonio Gramsci noted that it bore a resemblance to 'monarchical legitimism': only when the monarchical ideal ceased to be a peaceably shared political form did it become necessary to have a 'monarchical party' that defended it.[3] This explanation, propounded in various forms, has long been used by a large part of modern culture to account for the phenomenon of the Catholic parties: they were, it is contended, formed to defend the social space of the Roman Church and to enable it to regain the influence that it had lost over society. Of course, there is a great deal of truth to this explanation, but it does not comprise the whole truth. Today, it seems even more difficult than in the past to discard it, because the present-day attitude of all the Christian Churches – and no longer only that of the Catholic Church – largely inclines towards their transformation into a sort of organization of 'lobbies' to promote their political presence. Moreover, mainly in Europe but elsewhere as well, the experience of the great dictatorships between the two wars, combined with the definitive secularization of the public sphere, almost entirely destroyed the illusion that the non-Catholic Christian Churches could have a 'natural' relationship with the state – whether it was based on their nature as national public services (state churches like the Anglican Church or the reformed German one prior to 1945) or on their participation in the liberal sphere of free individual choice (the various forms of non-conformity).[4]

However, this was not the original context. The great liberal constitutional revolution substantially destroyed the 'communitarian' fabric on which European politics were based. The medieval idea of the political sphere as *communitas communitatum* gave way to the celebrated definition of the Le Chapélier law which abolished every form of corporation (June 1791): 'now there is nothing but particular interest and general interest . . . Between the state and the citizen there is nothing.'[5] It should be borne in mind that the communitarian fabric that had been lost was not the one that usually goes by that name today: in fact there was no problem regarding the existence in lawful form of any association of individuals (as envisaged and indeed protected by all the liberal constitutions). The community called into question by the new constitutional order was a legal entity able to dictate its own rules and to demand compliance with them regardless of the will of its members, who no longer exerted control over the existence of the 'corpus' to which they belonged. Liberal constitutionalism in its original form found this a concept difficult if not impossible to handle: consider its aversion both to political parties in their 'modern' form (as something more than and different from generic ideal movements with which individuals could identify or otherwise as they wished) and to trade unions as the general representation of workers' interests.

Operating in the world that arose from the liberal revolution was much more difficult for the Catholic Church than it was for the reformed Christian ones: in fact, the Roman Church claimed to be, in the language of its jurists, a *societas perfecta*, an original legal entity which stood on an equal footing with the other original legal entities (by now reduced to states alone).[6] The pope was just as much a 'sovereign' as the others (for which reason he had never accepted the loss of his right to 'territory' as the essential prerequisite for sovereignty); and he stood at the apex of a system of diplomatic and judicial government no different from that of any other state. Of course, the presence of this sovereignty in parallel with state systems which also demanded the exclusive loyalty of their members created almost insoluble problems.

It was this model that underpinned the Catholics' public political presence, and its eventual overturning worked to the advantage of both churches and states – this being the beneficial and ideologically valuable contribution of Christian democracy. The process, however, was a long and tortuous one. After an initial phase in which the papacy directed its energies towards a simple restoration of the system of relationships between state and Church assumed to exist before the French Revolution (recognition by states of the ecclesiastical structure as an autonomous legal entity and as an equal partner in the management of public space), it concentrated on defending the sovereignty of the pontiff, in the aftermath of the events in Italy that had led to the demise of the ancient papal state. This development, together with the doctrine of papal infallibility propounded at the same time (1870) by the First Vatican Council, radically reduced the impact of the organized political forces which asserted the social presence of the Catholics. The only two notable exceptions, in Belgium and in the new German Empire, can be explained by local peculiarities. In Belgium, the Catholic movement had formed a *de facto* alliance with the liberals during the revolution of 1830 in order to sever the union with Holland, which had a Protestant monarchy. In Germany, as a result of national unification, the Catholicism which had previously enjoyed privileged status in many of the federated states was now a minority under the sway of a Protestant dynasty with its own state church (in the previous German Confederation the presence of the Catholic Habsburg monarchy meant that the Church's circumstances had been very different). Consequently, in those two countries the presence of a Catholic party as an instrument of defence against Protestant dominance assumed an exceptional significance.

In other countries the apparent objective was not to found a Catholic party to participate in the constitutional system but to create a Catholic social force which would support and legitimize the Pope's position. Since the Church had somehow to explain to the faithful how the present situation had come about, it chose to employ the traditional apocalyptic message of the 'disorder of the times'. The 'modern state', constitutionalism and liberalism were nothing but visible manifestations of the collapse of the principles that underpinned co-existence and they were bound to perish in the final tragedy that would inevitably ensue from this cancellation of the ordering principles of social life. The maximum expression of this 'social disorder' had been the exclusion of religion, together with its institutional structure which regulated human society.

On this basis the Catholic Church developed a social doctrine of its own which in certain respects was radically critical of liberal society. Since the ultimate purpose was to marshal all available evidence of the 'disorder' and 'dissolution' which weakened the constitutionalism that had severed its ties with the Church, the latter set about denouncing the shortcomings of the system in terms that often seemed closely akin to those of the socialist ideologies.[7] It is this that accounts for the anti-capitalist strictures that often attracted the sympathy of socialist and radical thinkers, and also for the distrust in the values of the liberal system and its constitutionalism that induced the Catholic Church to see little wrong with the fascist revolutions.

Against this background, however, historical developments profoundly altered the ideological world just described. First, political events in Belgium and Germany proved particularly beneficial for the Catholics. Especially in Germany, liberal parliamentarianism enabled one of its constituent parts, the Zentrum party, to win its battle even though the entire might of the Prussian bureaucratic state was ranged against it. Not only did Bismarck lose the *Kulturkampf* (which, incidentally, the liberal left had initially supported) but the Zentrum constantly increased its political weight. In a system where, like it or not, laws had to be approved by parliament before they came into force, and where the government, despite all rhetoric to the contrary, could not function without a majority,[8] a parliamentary party with a hundred-odd deputies exerted considerable influence. On the other hand, the experience of social movements in opposition – cases in point being France and Italy – had shown that the liberal constitutional system offered ample room for manoeuvre and substantial opportunities for action to organized movements which operated on the terrain of political agitation.

A split thus opened up between the doctrinal orientation of the Roman Church and the ideology deployed by the Catholic political movements. For a long period, the Church continued to reject the liberal political system, although it moderated its views on the constitutional legal system while instead accentuating its antipathy to capitalism, which it regarded as that system's economic form of organization. As regards the former point, the 'rule of law' proved favourable to the Church as well, when it was in the minority or marginalized. In order to deal with the problem raised by previous condemnations, after the events surrounding the celebrated case of Catholic *ralliement* in France, the Church in the person of Leo XIII announced that it was neutral with regard to political regimes, and that it would judge them only in the light of their ability to work for the common good. On the latter point, matters were more complicated. The so-called 'social question' – the imbalance that had arisen in European societies between participation in the production process and entitlement to an income that ensured an acceptable standard of living – was a problem that was universally apparent. Today, one may dispute that the situation was due to liberal principles,[9] but the 'social doctrine of the Church' as set out in the encyclical *Rerum novarum* of 1891 nevertheless started from that assumption.

The anti-capitalist critique of the pontiffs differed from those from the socialist camp because the social reference model was not the mythical community of equals that existed in the primordial stage of humanity – and which was now to be re-established on technological bases – but the equally mythical community of orders and social corporations that had allegedly existed in the Christian Middle Ages. In this case, too, the myth was then widely manipulated (and effectively minimized) in the light of more realistic notions of social evolution. Nevertheless, it remained in the background as the basis of a view of the social order founded on an ethic much more communitarian than individualistic.

There are two different ways to treat these ideological developments: they can be regarded as resulting from the backwardness of Catholic religious culture, or they can be viewed as intuitions of a crisis then traversing European society (suffice it to consider the Tönnies of *Gemeinschaft und Gesellschaft* or the Maitland of the 'body politic'). Even those who maintain that both components were contained in this ideological context must acknowledge that these contaminations fostered dialogue with other cultures of the time: nostalgia for a principle able to restore a unitary texture to the political-social fabric was very strong.

In this period, however, the Roman pontificate kept itself very distant from the concept of democracy. The notion had begun to circulate among various Catholic intellectual groups (mainly those more directly engaged in politics) at the turn of the century, especially in France and Italy. For these groups the concept of democracy – to which official liberalism was hostile – brought a number of advantages: not only did it relate more incisively to the concept of the 'people' as the totality of political subjects (and in which the Catholic component was therefore numerically much larger), but by protecting social articulations alternative to the state to which it gave full citizenship rights, it opened up a significant space for the Catholic forces to assert themselves (not coincidentally, these groups became substantially close to certain aspects of socialist theory). The Church, however, firmly rejected such an interpretation and censured Christian democracy on numerous occasions, the most important being when, in terms of general doctrine, the ideology of Christian democracy was included in the condemnation of modernism pronounced by the encyclical *Pascendi* (1907), and politically when, in 1910, the Sillon (furrow) movement in France was accused of evading 'the laws of the doctrinal and directive power of the ecclesiastical authority by moving to the political plane' so that 'it wrought confusion between evangelization and the promotion of democracy'.[10]

This accusation has its own peculiar story within the general history of the relationship between Roman orthodoxy and Catholic movements (it has most recently been levelled by John Paul II against the 'theology of liberation' in Latin America), but it is not of present interest. Here I shall instead seek to explain why this condemnation reached the point that the theory of Christian democracy became the fulcrum for the revival in the fortunes of political Catholicism.

To understand the phenomenon from an ideological point of view, one must examine not so much the histories of Catholic movements as that of the papacy and its relationship with the policies of the modern states.[11] Advancing secularization and the growth of liberal hegemony (of which, from a certain point of view, socialist ideology was a radical variant) long hampered the papacy's ability to intervene in the political sphere. However, once the anti-modernist obsession of Pope Pius X had been superseded, and the watershed of the First World War had passed, the new Pope (Pius XI, 1922–39) realized that the cultural scene had changed: there was growing uncertainty as to the value of progress, the rationality of the political order was doubted, salvational doctrines were once again demanded. From his first encyclical (*Ubi arcano*, 1922) onwards, Pius launched the thesis of civil society's return to 'the kingdom of Christ', which was manifest 'in civil society when it recognizes and reveres the supreme and universal sovereignty of God' and when 'the Church of Jesus Christ is accorded the place in human society to which He himself assigned it'. This centrality of the power of the Church not only as the repository of Christ's message but also as a practical means to achieve salvation, amid the crisis of society and politics, initially prompted the Vatican to compromise itself with authoritarian or dictatorial regimes willing to pay a certain (and usually purely formal) tribute to this position. Relationships were tense (consider the encyclicals against fascist statism, *Non abbiamo bisogno* of 1931, and *Mit Brenneder Sorge* of 1937 against pagan conceptions of the state, and therefore against Nazism), but the Church's attitude towards the Spanish Second Republic and the official position pronounced, again in 1937, against atheistic communism and against the ecclesiastical policy of the Mexican government redressed the balance.

However, the essential text for our present purposes was the encyclical *Quadragesimo anno* published in 1931 to mark the fortieth anniversary of *Rerum novarum*. In this encyclical the pontiff once again raised the problem of the best social order, which he envisaged as based 'on the precepts of correct reason, to wit, Christian social philosophy' and governed by a quest for the 'common good'. Promulgated together with this general principle was the one that later came to be known as 'subsidiarity': 'It is not rightful to remove from individuals what they are able to achieve with their endeavour and industry in order to give it to the community, it is unjust to assign to a larger and higher society what can be done by smaller and lower communities.'[12] This stance rested on two key principles: (i) the equivalence between natural rationality and the social doctrine of Catholic *magisterium* (which derived from the theology of Aquinas); (ii) the defence, in opposition to the statism of the time, of civil society's capacity for self-organization, which was to be supported by the state, not abolished by the latter in order that it might take its place.

These directives were flanked by developments in Catholic thought during the inter-war years, especially in France through the works of Jacques Maritain and Emmanuel Mounier, both of whom (albeit from different points of view) put forward a positive vision of the contemporary political crisis. The latter was not to be interpreted as the poisoned fruit of abandonment of the *ancien régime*'s 'correct reason' which united religion and politics; rather, it was to be viewed as the positive offspring of an age seeking to leave the 'disorder' of liberal capitalism behind and which – perhaps even by going to the extreme of embracing entirely erroneous ideologies like communism – testified to mankind's yearning for a return to the happy equilibrium of a society founded on the common good rather than on reciprocal exploitation.

The new version of Christian democracy that predominated during the post-war years in many European countries, and then spread to several Latin American ones, was rooted in this passage from a negative to a positive consideration of the crisis of modern man. Now, in fact, a number of important novelties became apparent. The connection between 'natural' political philosophy founded on reason ('good' reason, of course) and the Church's political theory enabled Catholics to take part in the general process of the development of political society, without immediately having to claim 'confessional' positions, in that every political order and system correctly understood according to reason was also a contribution to the construction of God's kingdom. Moreover, Catholics believed that they had found a new compass with which to locate their bearings in the crisis of modernity: the idea of the 'person'. Few concepts have been as controversial as this one, but in broad outline it can be defined as follows: the modern philosophical revolution since Descartes, and then liberal ideology, had shifted attention to the central importance of the individual, but they had also highlighted his/her fragility. This was due to the loss of centrality of that complexity of the individual which derived from the interaction between the social roots of individuals and their higher need to be led beyond the material sphere. Consequently, one had no longer to talk of the 'individual' – a non-existent monad (a criticism of liberalism) – but of the 'person'. This was the single subject considered not in his/her individuality, in the separateness of his/her existence as a monad, but in terms of the subject's relationship with society, understood both as the relationship with the formative roots of subjects and as the projection of their rights to develop in a manner which fulfilled their potential and was beneficial to the social context to which they belonged.

By means of this formulation a number of difficult tasks were accomplished: humanism was re-launched in sharp contrast to totalitarianism; a defence was provided for the ability of elementary social and generally non-state organisms (like the Church) to provide the environment necessary for the human person to develop; a critique was waged against the growing weight and importance of state apparatuses, and against the loss of control over economic development that had become evident in recent decades (thus linking up both with socialist thought and with recent economic analysis).

This ideology, which had drawn strength from the pontificate of Pius XI, but cannot be entirely identified with it, received a certain amount of support from the new Pope, Pius XII (1939–58). Pope Pacelli was a diplomat by training who had done work of crucial importance in Germany during the Weimar crisis and the advent of Nazism, and then in the Vatican as chief policy-maker on the eve of the Second World War. In the process he had changed his attitude: he no longer shared Pius XI's illusion that the Church could dispense with the Catholic political movements and deal at first hand with states; he now believed that in a political structure dominated by mass organization, the only actors that mattered were those able to mobilize mass political parties and ideologies which exerted a forceful grip on the public.

In order to undertake this new mission, however, the Church had to devise a language able to penetrate a society in crisis but still poisoned by anti-ecclesiastical prejudice. It is not surprising to find these elements of judgement in the early stages of a papacy that culminated in a curious mixture of hardening theocratic positions and the re-launching of the Catholics' view of themselves as surviving warriors beleaguered in their fortress. In the years between 1943 and 1947, Pacelli sought to impose the leadership of the Catholic Church as the precondition for restoration of a generic 'Christian civilization' increasingly identified with an ideal vision of the restoration of the 'Western' world (in which he even included the USA). That world was dominated by shared values in which post-war reconstruction signalled a return to the 'natural order' that a liberalism – still regarded with substantial hostility – had sought in vain to gainsay.

On this basis Pius XII legitimated democracy (officially in a radio address broadcast at Christmas 1944) as the natural political form which came closest to the Church's thinking: on the one hand because it was an alternative to communism in that it guaranteed the freedom of social bodies (and consequently *imprimis* that of the Church); on the other because it was simultaneously governed by the principle of the imposed will of the majority and the protection of minorities, and thereby favoured Catholicism in whichever of the two positions it might occupy. This evolution enabled the Catholic political movements reborn in the post-war years to enter the political scene with a substantially increased capacity to wield influence. In some countries – France, Italy and Germany for instance – they were the protagonists of the first attempts to re-think the liberal constitution; in others – like Belgium and Holland – they nevertheless made a significant contribution to post-war reconstruction.

At the constitutional level, Christian democracy was able to introduce into various constitutions – that of France in 1946–7, Italy's of 1948, Germany's of 1949 – the principles just outlined: the centrality of the 'person' with its new and momentous meaning as a judicial subject, conceived of as a social entity possessing concrete attributes and rights that could be enjoyed as part of the process of social and cultural evolution;[13] a predominantly 'social' view of the economy with a moderate amount of control over the capitalist system; the defence of non-state social entities, from the family to churches; and the consequent valorization of forms of organization, both political (parties) and corporative (trade unions).

This ideology was often presented as a break with the previous liberal system. This was a curious cultural phenomenon, given not only that liberal groups, in Britain for example, had devised quite similar proposals,[14] which were entirely ignored, but also that these theoreticians adopted at the level of constitutional legal theory the tenets of mature liberalism embraced by European political thought in its entirety (separation of powers, rule of law, parliamentarianism and jurisdictional controls, and so on). However, it was precisely this myth of a purported break with the past that enabled the Catholic world quite rapidly to absorb the features of the modern liberal state in its final stage of evolution, and of which most Catholic politicians then became the most convinced proponents. On the contrary, the anti-liberal ideology still alive in Catholic social doctrine enabled Catholic movements to accept the planned economic system which in all countries arose from their wartime experiences. A certain amount of centralized economic regulation seemingly fostered that pre-eminence of the 'common good' over individual acquisitive appetites preached, as we have seen, by the Vatican.

Finally, the ecclesial basis of these ideologies favoured the 'neo-communitarian' ideas so earnestly desired by many Europeans in the period following 1945. By appealing in the first instance to the ecclesial community as their reservoir of consensus, the Christian democracy parties based themselves on an idea of the people as underpinning the political community. In keeping with the Marxisant language of the time, they deployed the term 'inter-class party' to emphasize that they drew on a pool of consensus comprising diverse social strata. Once again, the ideology of the 'common good' and a reference to co-living in the same cultural container (Catholicism) enabled them to rationalize this notion, elevating it to a model of modern politics whose purpose was to merge the classes into a single cultural and social entity. By so doing, the Church and the Catholic movements reduced ecclesial membership to a pure form of endorsement of average cultural values shared by society as a whole; a sort of secularized and minimal Christianity readily accepted by the masses for traditional reasons, but also entirely devoid of the militancy that had initially galvanized Christian democracy. This levelling process greatly enhanced the social leverage of the Catholic parties in countries where they had a well-established tradition; but it also transformed them into lay groupings, separating them from their grounding in authentically religious movements.

It is evident even from this brief outline that the ideology of Christian democracy helped to integrate a large proportion of the European population into the political system created after the war. I do not believe it necessary to dwell on how this process was thereafter secularized by the gradual removal of its religious affiliations, so that in the end it merged with the mainstream of what we may call 'European social democracy'. However, I believe it would be an error to underestimate the historical value of this ideology in ensuring the success of the European liberal constitutionalism that, alternatively, it may have been intended to defeat. Initially, the Catholic Church was still one of the leading forces of social acculturation in continental Europe, and the state (and I dare say civil society in general) did not have those instruments of mass socialization that have only become completely available to it in recent decades (mass compulsory education, standardized consumption, television). As it pursued this tortuous course, not only did the Catholic Church, through its associated political movements, foster the definitive and uncontested installation of liberal democracy (or, if one prefers, post-liberal democracy) as the only legitimate political system because it was founded on the protection of 'social man', but Catholic intellectuals contributed importantly to building the consensus for the 'new democracy' which political theory, perhaps unconsciously, still uses today as a standard of reference.

However, with this process Christian democracy dissolved as an ideology typical of the contemporary system. It had to a certain extent accomplished its task of conveying a substantial proportion of the European population into the new political arrangement that arose from the dissolution of the *ancien régime*. The question of the political order was settled once and for all (at least in those particular historical circumstances) with the form typically assumed by Western democracy in the 1950s and 1960s: a mixture of social democracy based on a certain degree of equal access to the consumer goods made available by the affluent society, and on the individual and social rights produced by the astonishing growth of the regulatory powers wielded by the state in the relational and moral sphere. There was no room in this context for the re-shaping of the system by forces that distanced themselves from some of its founding values. The only alternatives were either to become part of the establishment or to return to the purely religious problem of finding 'consolation' for the 'evil' inherent in history.

Notes and references

1   The author is grateful to Adrian Belton, who translated this article from the Italian.
2   The text of the broadcast was subsequently published: A.J.P. Taylor, 'The European revolution', *The Listener*, 22 November 1945, Vol. 34, pp. 575–6.
3   See A. Gramsci, *Quaderni dal Carcere*, edited by V. Gerratana, Vol. III, Turin, Einaudi, 1975, pp. 2081–6.
4   In this essay I shall not consider the Orthodox Church. As a student of Western political systems, my work concerns what can be called 'liberal constitutionalism', as a cultural system profoundly endorsed by Western political cultures (even in the extreme reaction to it that takes the form of tyranny). The areas in which the Orthodox Church mainly operates (the Russian–Slav part of the world) lie, I believe, outside this context.
5   The problem, of course, is highly complex and can only be outlined here. For more detailed treatment, see my *Partiti e sistemi politici nella storia contemporanea*, Bologna, Il Mulino, 1994. Cf. the French translation of a previous edition, *Introduction à l'histoire des partis politiques*, Paris, PUF, 1992.
6   On this evolution see P. Prodi, *Il sovrano pontifice*, Bologna, Il Mulino, 1982; English translation, P. Prodi, *The Papal Prince*, Cambridge, Cambridge University Press, 1987.
7   Although there was little affinity. Essentially, the socialists believed that the evils of industrial society could be remedied by 'radicalizing' development and its dynamics. By contrast, Catholic social thought long believed that these evils could be remedied by restoring political life to the archetypal relations distinctive of a rural society (and in many respects inscribed in the culture of the Holy Scriptures).

8 To meet the objections always raised when I argue this thesis, I would point out that the fact that the German Chancellor did not need 'parliamentary confidence' did not mean that he could work without a parliamentary majority. Defeat on a bill did not force the government to resign, but this did not allow for the bill to be passed and converted into law.

9 Not only does Britain, from the radicals to Gladstone, demonstrate that re-equilibrating intervention by the public powers (at least by fiscal means) was considered necessary, but also it has been shown that one of the foremost proponents of political liberalism, Alexis de Tocqueville, embraced an economic doctrine highly critical of the free market and preoccupied with establishing equilibrium among the social classes: Eric Keslassy, *Le Libéralisme de Tocqueville à l'épreuve du pauperisme*, Paris, L'Harmattan, 2000.

10 See E. Poulat, *Intégrisme et catholicisme intégrale*, Tournai, Casterman, 1969; J. Caron, *Le Sillon et la démocratie chrétienne*, Paris, Plon, 1967.

11 For new light on, and an acute interpretation of, this secular evolution, see the recent book by Paolo Prodi, *Una storia della giustizia: dal pluralismo dei fori al moderno dualismo tra coscienza e diritto*, Bologna, Il Mulino, 2000.

12 For a treatment of subsidiarity from a standpoint closely akin to the traditional doctrine of the Church, see G. Morra, *Teologia politica e Religione civile*, Bologna, Barghigiani, 2000, pp. 119–43.

13 On this, see P. Pombeni, 'Individuo/persona nella costituzione italiana: il contributo del dossettismo', *Parole Chiave*, 1996, Vol. 10, No. 1, pp. 197–218.

14 Though the Christian democracy groups were unaware of them. This curious phenomenon is illustrated by the behaviour of the Italian Catholic left led between 1945 and 1951 by Giuseppe Dossetti: although a fervent supporter of Keynes's theories, it was entirely unaware of his convinced endorsement of liberalism, believing him instead to be some sort of non-Marxist socialist.

7 Fascism

Reflections on the fate of ideas in twentieth-century history

Zeev Sternhell

A reflection on the extreme right is not only a reflection on the twentieth-century European catastrophe but on the culture of our time.[1] But despite the fact that the Great War is more and more commonly seen as the end of the nineteenth century, the twentieth century I am referring to is not the so-called 'short' twentieth century which began with the Great War, the fall of the multinational empires and the Russian Revolution but the twentieth century which came into being with the intellectual, scientific and technological revolution of the 1880s and 1890s.[2] The idea that the First World War was the beginning of the twentieth century has, perhaps, a certain logic – although to a very limited degree – in connection with Russia or Austria-Hungary, but it is not really applicable to Western Europe. The nineteenth century did not end on the day that Lenin got off the train at the Finland Station but with the construction of the first electrical power plant, with the invention of the automobile, the telephone, the wireless telegraph, the cinema, and the X-ray, and with the opening of the Paris Métro. It ended when the first motor-driven bus went forth into the streets of London, and with the discovery of the tuberculosis bacillus and the vaccines against diphtheria and typhus. The nineteenth century died when the European worker, that beast of burden who lived in conditions often worse than those of the slaves in the American South, became a citizen enjoying universal suffrage and who was able to read and write, and whose children, instead of going down into the mines at the age of eight, went to school where, as in France, there was free and compulsory education.

The century of *The Phenomenology of Spirit*, of *Capital* and of *Democracy in America* came to an end when, right in the midst of a period of unprecedented scientific and technological progress, the rejection of the heritage of the Enlightenment, of rationalism, universalism and the idea of progress – in other words, the rejection of ideological modernity – reached a point of culmination and, becoming a mass phenomenon, acquired its disruptive force. Our century began when Nietzsche and Bergson, Le Bon and Freud, Pareto, Mosca, Durkheim and Dilthey created a new conception of morals, man and society, when the impressionists, followed by the cubists and futurists, created a new aesthetics, and when Max Planck and Albert Einstein propounded a different vision of the universe.

Thus, in the last years of the nineteenth century, most of the systems of thought and most of the political and social forces which make up our contemporary world were already in existence. The ideologies which, a quarter of a century later, were to contribute so mightily to changing the face of the world, were then reaching maturity. Because it was a period of incubation and because, in the sphere of intellectual evolution, it had all the characteristics of a revolutionary epoch, the last quarter of the nineteenth century was a time of exceptional richness and intensity. The years between the deaths of Darwin and Marx and the outbreak of the Great War were among the most fruitful in the intellectual history of Europe. This rare flowering not only reflected the quality of the scientific, literary and artistic production of that period but also its variety, contrasts and contradictions.

The more clear-sighted and sensitive figures of that time were conscious of living in an extraordinary period, and each in his own way expressed this sense of novelty and upheaval. 'The birth of new gods has always marked the beginning of a new civilization, and their disappearance has always marked its decline. We are in one of those periods of history when, for a moment, the skies are empty. Owing to this very fact, the world must change', wrote Gustave Le Bon in 1894.[3] Thirty years later, glancing backwards at the very first years of the century, Virginia Woolf would say:

> On or about December 1910 human character changed. I am not saying that one went out, as one might into a garden, and there saw that a rose has flowered, or that a hen has laid an egg. The change was not sudden and definite like that. But a change there was, nevertheless; and since one must be arbitrary, let us date it about the year 1910.[4]

Indeed, the world was changing as it had never done before. The technological revolution, while transforming the face of the continent, greatly changed the nature of existence. There was a hitherto unprecedented rhythm of life, the product of out-and-out urbanization. The scientific revolution overturned the view men had of themselves and of the universe they inhabited. A real intellectual revolution prepared the convulsions which were soon to produce the European disaster of the first half of the twentieth century.

That is how the fascist impregnation is to be explained: the extreme right, the pre-fascist and already fully fascist right were the direct product of this crisis of civilization on an unprecedented scale. This is the explanation of the attraction of the different varieties of fascism for both uneducated strata of the population and for some of the greatest figures in the intellectual life of the twentieth century. This is the reason why fascism could be a mass movement and simultaneously an élitist intellectual phenomenon capable of attracting some of the most advanced elements of the avant-garde of the time.

Here certain basic questions must be asked: has this fascination of fascism something to teach us about our civilization, or can one say, on the contrary, that fascism was no more than a simple parenthesis in the history of our time, as Benedetto Croce asserted?[5] Is it reasonable to suggest, as many people still do, that fascism was just an unfortunate accident which happened after the First World War, a phenomenon strictly limited to the interwar period, linked to economic catastrophe, unemployment and depression, born in 1918 and dead in 1945? Was it simply a shadow cast by Marxism, a defensive reaction to communism, a vague imitation of Stalinism?[6]

Such an explanation is an easy one, probably too easy. Fascism appealed to people's imaginations because it was concerned with a real problem: the nature of social relationships. Fascism provided attractive answers to some of the questions which preoccupied people in the last two centuries: first of all, what makes a group of humans into a society? What is the nature of the relationship between the individual and the collectivity, and thus, what is the basis of political legitimacy? What constitutes a nation? Is it a freely-expressed option of individuals with equal rights, as the French Revolution in its first years maintained, or history, culture, religion, the ethnic group? What is the real basis of collective existence? What, precisely, is the nature of the common factor which enables men to develop the minimum of solidarity which makes a life together possible? What gives life in society a meaning? To these questions, there are many answers, but, when they are reduced to their essence, these answers belong to two basic categories. There is the answer deriving from the tradition of the Enlightenment and there is the historicist answer.

The attractiveness of the solutions offered by the radical right was all the greater because the fascist ideology was simply the hard core and the most radical variety of a far more widespread, far older phenomenon: a comprehensive revision of the essential values of the humanistic, rationalistic and optimistic heritage of the Enlightenment. At the end of the nineteenth century, the rejection of the Enlightenment assumed truly catastrophic proportions and swept away a large part of cultured Europe. It was this rejection of the Enlightenment adapted to the conditions of the mass society of the turn of the nineteenth century which produced the fascist ideology. Thus, before it became a political force, fascism was a cultural phenomenon. Everywhere in Europe, the cultural rebellion preceded the political and was the essential precondition of the political rebellion. Fascism was not only a cultural phenomenon, but it was primarily a cultural phenomenon.[7]

I wish to insist on this: fascist ideology developed long before the First World War.[8] The war enabled the cultural revolt to be translated into political terms, but it did not create fascism as such. The war produced favourable conditions: it provided the intellectual revolt, after half a century of incubation, with the opportunity and means to become a political force, but the basis for the rise of fascism is not to be found in the post-war crises but in the struggle against ideological modernity, which means, against the French and Kantian tradition of the Enlightenment. Essentially, fascism's roots lay in the reaction against the principles expounded by Kant in his justly famous reply to the question, 'What is Enlightenment?' (*Was ist Aufklärung?*) in December 1784: 'Enlightenment is man's emergence from his self-incurred immaturity. Immaturity is the inability to use one's understanding without the guidance of another . . . The motto of Enlightenment is therefore, "*Sapere aude!*". Have the courage to use your own understanding'.[9]

The reaction against the Enlightenment began at the time of the Enlightenment itself. Just as the Enlightenment was a political movement, so the movement against the Enlightenment was a political movement as well. As was well known since Herder and Burke, the most potent threat to the *Aufklärung* came from the rise of historicism and Johann Gottfried Herder was the intellectual father of historicism, and consequently of nationalism. His philosophy of history, his defence of the past cultures, his historical relativism also introduced by him to other fields of activity like aesthetics, were first and foremost intended as a virulent attack on modern civilization. As such, his work refutes any rationalist interpretation of social development. His essential purpose was to reconstruct the values of a culture, the spirit of a nation and its character, the instincts and the feelings which hold a people together, which are the spiritual substance of laws and manners, and which make up the 'happiness of a people'.[10]

All the basic theses of historicism can be seen as a consequence of applying an organic metaphor to society: society being considered as a living organism. Hence, historicism is frequently and properly associated with organicism, the notion that society can be explained by laws applicable to living creatures. Obviously, fascism cannot be understood without historicism: I am not claiming that there was a direct relationship of cause and effect between historicism and fascism, but the formation of the fascist ideological corpus is incomprehensible without taking into account the enormous influence and the extraordinary attraction of historicism.

I am using the term 'historicism' in its literal sense, as defined by Friedrich Meinecke in 1932, in his famous *Die Entstehung des Historismus*: 'The essence of historicism is the substitution of the process of *individualizing* observation for a *generalizing* view of forces in history'.[11] As in the case of all broad concepts, there were various types of historicism, which were either of a national kind or were differences of degree. All these varieties of historicism, however, had a common basis. Over and beyond the positive value given to history viewed as human progress in its immanent reality, over and beyond the rehabilitation of history there was a basic hostility to natural law, to intellectualism and to rationalism. The result was that historicism demolished the idea of a common human nature, of a universal reason which gives rise to a universal Natural Law, regarding this way of thinking as empty, abstract, and, above all, hypocritical. From Herder to Ranke to Meinecke, historicism, in Meinecke's own words, was thus a revolt against the idea that man

> had remained basically the same in all periods of which we have any knowledge . . . in particular, it was the prevailing concept of Natural Law, handed down from antiquity, which confirmed this belief in the stability of human nature and above all of human reason. Accordingly, it was held that

the pronouncements of reason . . . did speak with the same voice and utter the same timeless and absolutely valid truths, which were in harmony with those prevailing in the universe as a whole.[12]

Historicism, therefore, was a global attack on the rationalism, universalism and the idea of progress of the French Enlightenment. In Meinecke's view this was the specificity of German culture, its most important contribution to Western culture and the basis of the great difference between the intellectual and political development of Germany and France since the French Revolution. Meinecke had no doubt that German historicism constituted 'the highest stage so far reached in the understanding of human affairs'.[13]

Here a question arises which Meinecke did not answer after the Second World War, when he considered the 'German catastrophe' in a book which bore this title.[14] The question is: is not this *Sonderweg*, this 'special road' taken by German history, the chief reason for the failure of German liberalism from the beginning of the nineteenth century onwards? Does not Germany's long imperviousness to universal values, to the idea of natural law have something to do with the fact that Germany never had a liberal revolution, and that until the second half of the twentieth century democracy was regarded by its élites as a foreign concept? Was it not, after all, this cult of the particular as opposed to the universal, this view of the nation as an ethnic and racial entity, which contributed to making Germany, precisely, the instrument *par excellence* of the war against the Enlightenment?

Historicism is thus not only an innocent appreciation of the value and legitimacy of variety and multiplicity; it not only strongly developed the idea – the famous idea we owe to Vico – that the human spirit does not know any reality except for history, since it created it, but it also produced certain principles whose influence on our century has been crucial and generally disastrous. The violence, the scale and the depth of the reaction were commensurate with the greatness of the phenomenon against which it was reacting: the man of the Enlightenment wanted no less than to recreate the myth of Prometheus. His immediate enemies replied by appealing to Providence, to destiny, to history and to the profound roots of the collective subconscious.

Germany was undoubtedly the place where historicism gained an overridingly dominant position, where it reached its full development and from where it radiated outwards. But if historicism was the dominant current in German thought, if it was the German ideology *par excellence*, historicism was by no means confined to Germany. It was a European phenomenon that also took root in France and Italy, and it has had enormous influence, in the two centuries from the French Revolution to the present.

Herder gave Europe the idea of the unalterable individuality of the nation, which found its norms of life within itself, transcending universal laws. He taught that the nation was a living organism, not a collection of individuals; he believed it had a soul, and this soul was both a natural phenomenon and entirely individual. All cultures were organic and unique totalities, with unique and inimitable languages, values, traditions, institutions, customs. All values, therefore, were individual and historical: as such they were relative values. The Herderian idea that there is a national 'essence' whose purity has to be protected and whose special character has to be promoted was fundamental to the whole of the revolutionary right in the first half of the present century. This concept fused with an idea developed even more enthusiastically by Justus Möser: that of the ancient, barbarous and pure nation.[15] Throughout the nineteenth century, the cult of the national past involved the rehabilitation of the Middle Ages: the national rebirth required the medieval heritage to be substituted for the classical heritage.[16]

The conclusion the first wave of Romanticism and, later, the generations of 1890 and 1930 drew from the Herderian conception of history and culture, is that one cannot enter a family in the way in which one buys a share on the stock exchange. The cult of the national genius, the organic conception of the nation, the view of the nation as the source of all truth meant, first, that membership of this body could not be a matter of choice and second, that talking about universal values was pure nonsense. All men may be brothers, but those who speak the same language, pray in the same church and whose ancestors are buried in the same cemetery share values which are special to themselves, and they are consequently infinitely closer to each other than they are to anyone else. The individual, seen in this way, is the product of a unique environment, different from any other. It follows that people who are the product of the same geographical environment, the same climate, and who heard the same tales and legends at their mother's knee possess a mentality which is unique of its kind. Thus, there are natural collectivities on the one hand, and artificial ones on the other. A community of citizens, a society based on the social contract or simply on some utilitarian principles, must necessarily be artificial and is consequently inferior. In reality, the idea of a citizen could be useful in providing people with more liberty, but it is no more than a legal fiction.

Herder saw each nation as the manifestation of a collective spirit which spends itself in expressing itself; this collective spirit grows old, but nevertheless remains the same. It is precisely because it is incapable of renewing itself that it ages. The genius of a people, precisely because it is unalterable, can neither change nor regain its youth, but only fulfil and exhaust itself. In this context, Herder used an image that was to become classic: that of a plant which springs up, flowers and withers.[17] A century and a half before Oswald Spengler, and more than a century before the reflections of Hippolyte Taine and Ernest Renan and of the generation of the 1890s, Herder's writings on decadence gave form to a certain kind of cultural pessimism, a certain vision of history whose impact would only be felt at the turn of the nineteenth and twentieth centuries and which finally contributed to the creation of a new hierarchy of values.

In addition, this notion of a variety of national characters inevitably destroyed the idea of a universal human nature based on reason. History, it was said, is not the domain of reason, as reason is incapable of understanding life. That is why irrationalism was already basic to the thinking of this school. 'Does not reason, used carelessly and unnecessarily, weaken – has it not already weakened? – inclination, instinct, activity?'[18] Here, Herder was the great prophet of vitalism: reason, he argued, weakens the instincts. The Herderian aesthetic presupposes the superiority of creative vitality over reflectiveness, of spontaneity over study. The eighteenth century, Herder thought, was characterized by a fatal predominance of intelligence over vitality. His great argument against 'the spirit of Modern Philosophy' was that ideas engender ideas rather than life.[19]

This was Herder's contribution to the *Sturm und Drang* movement, to German and French romanticism and to the philosophy of history of some of the major figures of the nineteenth century. 'Germany owes to him more than to any one man between Luther and Bismarck' wrote one of his best biographers in the English-speaking world many years ago.[20] It should be emphasized here that while it was dominant in Germany, the influence of Herder was enormous in France as well. Ernest Renan called Herder '*le penseur-roi*'. He considered Herder, who had been translated into French by Edgar Quinet and was very much admired by Quinet's friend, Jules Michelet, to be 'one of the finest geniuses of modern times': greater than Kant, Hegel or Fichte.[21] Certainly, Renan had no need of Herder in order to condemn 'the idea of the equality of human individuals and the equality of races,' as he did in 1871.[22] But it was undoubtedly from Herder that, without speaking of *Volk*, he took his organic vision of culture and society.

However, as long as the attack on the Enlightenment had not descended from the cultural heights into the public arena, the political significance of this phenomenon in France was limited. This, on the other hand, was clearly not the case in Germany. It was the wars of liberation against Napoleon, waged not only against the French armies but also against the French Enlightenment, that, for the first time, enabled the intellectual corpus associated with the essential principles of historicism to become a political force.

France was affected politically only much later, in the context of industrialization and the rapid democratization of European society. The Dreyfus Affair was the first act of a drama continued and ended forty years later, with the Vichy racial laws. It was at the turn of the nineteenth century that we see the dividing-line between an aristocratic, conservative rejection of the Enlightenment and the translation of these attitudes into the truly popular, revolutionary terms of the nationalism of *la Terre et les Morts*, the French equivalent of *Blut und Boden*. The conception of society as a body, the idea of the nation as a living organism, a great family governed by a new morality, led to a closed, ethnic and racial conception of nationalism.[23]

It was the anti-Dreyfusard intellectuals who turned the cultural rebellion into a mass product. When the rejection of universal values and natural rights, the Herderian critique of modernity, the philosophy of history expressed in Hippolyte Taine's *Histoire de la littérature anglaise* and *Les Origines de la France contemporaine* or Ernest Renan's *L'Avenir de la science* came down onto street-level, the reflections on egalitarian decadence, the explanation of history first in cultural and then in racial terms became a war-machine of unexpected effectiveness. It was undoubtedly the anti-Dreyfusard intellectuals who did the work of vulgarization and popularization, but in the cases of both Renan and Taine this vulgarization communicated at least certain aspects of the essential teachings of these two giants who dominated the second half of the French nineteenth century, for Taine was a convinced social Darwinist and Renan had a definite anti-semitic side.

In the last thirty years of the nineteenth century, the rejection of the Enlightenment and the French Revolution exploded in the context of out-and-out industrialization and the rapid democratization of European society. It was then that one had the new wave of rejection of the 'modern values' which Nietzsche, the greatest of anti-Enlightenment figures of his time, defined so clearly: universalism, humanism, progress, utilitarianism, egalitarianism.[24] 'In all essential points,' wrote Nietzsche referring to *Beyond Good and Evil*, 'this book is a criticism of *modernity*, including modern science, modern art, even modern politics'.[25] It was then that Renan and Taine, whom Nietzsche considered 'the foremost living historian',[26] described the French Revolution as a real cultural disaster and saw the intellectual corpus which had made it possible as the origin of modern decadence in general and of that of their country in particular. The code-word most often used to describe this absolute evil was 'materialism': which meant utilitarianism, egalitarianism, the rights of man. Translated into political terms, materialism meant democracy, liberalism and socialism. 'Materialism' was the term most often used until the end of the Second World War to describe the sickness that was eating away at Europe. It was truly a general European phenomenon and not a specific reaction to any particular event, however important.

But let there be no doubt about it: the rise of fascism was only possible because the liberal bourgeoisie did not succeed in creating a new spiritual base and fully satisfying people's emotional and intellectual requirements. An emotional void, an intellectual malaise at the supremacy of reason and science were already discernible in the heart of the eighteenth century: Herder and his friend and teacher Hamann, and Burke, Maistre and the German romantics were the most famous representatives of this new trend. This sense of inadequacy deepened as the industrialization of the European continent increased, together with its well-known social ills. Democracy itself came to be regarded as an evil: it was accused of conceiving society as only an aggregate of individuals, without any common beliefs, without any emotional solidarity. It was accused of fostering alienation. It was this void which at the turn of the nineteenth century, contributed to the birth of fascism.

At the cusp of the century, in a world transformed by the technological and scientific revolution of the thirty or forty years preceding the First World War, by compulsory primary education, by the dissemination of knowledge and by a widespread participation in political life, the shift took place from philosophical reflection to ideology. It is in this context that one may perhaps see most clearly all that differentiates the work of some of the greatest figures of the century from its application in politics, and at the same time all that links philosophical reflection to politics. When the revolt against the heritage of the Enlightenment descended into the street, it became, in the hands of Sorel, Le Bon, Barrès, Drumont and Maurras, or of Langbehn and Lagarde, and later Spengler, Moeller van den Bruck or again, Marinetti, Corradini, d'Annunzio or Hulme, and so many others, an extraordinarily effective weapon of war. We should not forget that at the turn of the century, Langbehn's *Rembrandt als Erzieher* and Drumont's *La France Juive* were among the greatest best-sellers of their time, and that Gustave Le Bon was translated into sixteen languages. Drumont's and Langbehn's success was later equalled only by that of Spengler.[27]

One must insist on this point: on the one hand, the onslaught on modernity of Nietzsche, Renan or Taine already included a merciless condemnation of democracy – or, in other words, equality – and a preference for hierarchy. But, on the other hand, it is clear that an aristocratic, highly individualistic and often conservative rejection of the Enlightenment was profoundly different from the translation of these ideas into truly revolutionary terms by the generation of 1890. It is clear that when Nietzsche's philosophy, Renan's, Taine's or even Gobineau's philosophy of history came down into the street, when the reflections on slave-morality, the Christian and egalitarian decadence are translated in terms that fit the needs of readers of popular literature and daily newspapers, these observations take on a new dimension and a quite different significance. At the twilight of the nineteenth century these reflections on the fate of civilization were fused with racial nationalism, authoritarianism, the cult of the state and the leader, and the new art of politics: the manipulation of people in a context of political democracy. It is cultural rebellion which gives political rebellion its conceptual depth, and it leads to political rebellion as soon as circumstances allow.

The generation of 1890, however, only took from Nietzsche the elements it wanted and needed. 'All this modernity is what I am fighting against, modernity as defined by Nietzsche', said Maurice Barrès, the chief intellectual leader of French nationalism, the father of the French political novel, and one of the most intelligent founders of the fascist synthesis.[28] His entire opus is devoted to the struggle against the 'rationalist idea', which he considered 'antagonistic to life and its spontaneous forms', and he berated Rousseau for sterilizing life by attempting to rationalize it. For a quarter of a century, Barrès waged a Nietzschean struggle against the French Enlightenment, Cartesian rationalism, the Kantian categorical imperative, the rights of man, humanism, liberal democracy, the idea of progress and democratic education. But where Nietzsche favoured an extreme individualism, Barrès advocated the complete subordination of the individual to the community; where Nietzsche declared his horror of the masses and extolled an aristocracy of thought and will, the primacy of culture, intellectual independence and nonconformism, Barrès took the side of the multitude, the sole depository of great collective values. Nothing could be more foreign to Nietzsche than the historical, cultural and racial determinism of Barrès, his tribal nationalism, his cult of a strong state. Nothing was more agreeable to the nationalists of the generation of 1890, than a national, Catholic, Proudhonian, xenophobic, authoritarian and often anti-semitic state.

The centrality of anti-semitism resided in its role in the struggle against the Enlightenment: anti-semitism was an integral part of the intellectual revolution of the turn of the previous century. It was not, as such, a necessary precondition for the growth of fascism. It was almost unknown in Italy at the time, in Spain or in Portugal, but it played a role of prime importance in Germany, France, and the Austro-Hungarian Empire. Throughout the nineteenth century, the emancipation of the Jews was in France and Germany the very symbol of the Enlightenment. There was consequently no better way of signifying the death of the values of the Enlightenment than by casting the Jews, whose very capacity to survive in Europe depended on the fate of liberalism, out of the national community.

It is interesting to note the political function or the similarity of the role played by anti-semitism in Germany and in France, the nation-state *par excellence*. In Germany, the nation preceded the state: the cultural identity preceded the political identity. In France, the nation was forged by the legal and administrative structures created by a powerful monarchy. There it was the state which made the nation, and the political identity preceded the cultural identity.

Despite this essential difference, at the end of the nineteenth century both countries had an identity problem. The German nationalists felt that national unity still had to be achieved, while the French ones thought it had to be regained. In France, one of only three countries in the world to have had a liberal revolution, the nationalists saw with desperation how the unity built up for 700 years had been shattered by the Enlightenment and the Revolution. In order to regain that lost unity, in order to bridge the gulf between the old France and post-revolutionary France, between the France of the regicides and that of the Restoration, between Catholic France and lay France, the nation had to be purged of all causes of dissension: universalism, the categorical imperative, the rights of man, the supremacy of reason. From the nationalist viewpoint, truth and justice had no existence in themselves. Justice only existed among the same species. For the theoreticians, journalists and ringleaders of nationalism on either side of the Rhine, only people of the same blood, sharing the same long history, could participate in the same cultural heritage. The nation, they believed, was not a collection of citizens but a *volk*, a body, a family, a product of a specific landscape. Herder, and after him Renan, were now being translated into the language of politics, a highly sophisticated philosophy of history was being vulgarized, and the conclusion was that nothing could bring it to pass that the heart, mind and spirit of a Jew could become the heart, mind and spirit of a Frenchman or a German. Anyone can acquire a French or German passport, but not anyone is a Frenchman or a German. Anti-semitism, as Charles Maurras pointed out, was a methodological necessity. Thus, despite dissimilar histories, the two nationalisms, at the turn of the century, found themselves at the same point.

Around 1910, the same became true for Italian nationalists, revolutionary syndicalists, futurists: for them too, very often as a result of French and German influence, the nation was an enduring historic, physical, and moral reality. For Mussolini in 1915, the nation, united in culture and tradition, enjoyed the prerequisites of long-term viability. It was the 'great product of history',[29] and the war had revealed it to be a primary object of loyalty for the vast majority of the national proletariat.

Here we must introduce very briefly another element of the revolt against the heritage of the Enlightenment, the Sorelian revolutionary revisionism. As T.E. Hulme, the true ideologist of vorticism, the translator in English of Bergson and Sorel, and an admirer of Maurras, the theoretician behind T.S. Eliot, Ezra Pound and Wyndham Lewis, has put it, Sorel, the anti-Enlightenment revolutionary, the anti-rationalist classicist, was a key figure of European intellectual life of the beginning of the century.[30] Following Sorel, at the end of the first decade of the twentieth century, the French and Italian revolutionary syndicalists reached the conclusion that the working class of the great industrial centres of Western Europe corresponded to the portrait Le Bon had painted of it: it was only a crowd and a crowd is conservative. The proletariat of universal suffrage, of the eight-hour working day, of compulsory education, and of compulsory military service was no longer, and would never be, an agent of the anti-bourgeois revolution. All those socialists who wanted to destroy the humanist, rationalist bourgeois civilization could not follow the proletariat into social democracy: all those who remained revolutionaries but had lost their faith in the logic of Marxist economics had to find an alternate revolutionary force capable of saving the world from decadence.

The Sorelians needed the proletariat only as long as they believed it capable of fulfilling its role as the agent of revolution. Listen to Lagardelle, the editor of the review *Le Mouvement socialiste*, who thirty years later was to become Pétain's minister of labour, writing in the summer of 1912: 'The labour movement interests us only to the degree that it is the bearer of a new culture. If the proletariat trails along in demagogy or egoism, it no longer has any attraction for those who seek the means by which the world is transformed.'[31] Having to choose between the proletariat and the revolution, they chose the revolution: they opted for the non-proletarian revolution, the national revolution.

Thus it was quite natural that a synthesis would arise between the revolutionaries who discovered the nation as a revolutionary agent and the nationalist movement which also rebelled against the old world of the bourgeois and which believed that the nation would never be complete until it had integrated the proletariat. A socialism for the nation as a whole, a revolution for the nation as a whole, a nationalism that despised the bourgeois world, that believed in a civilization of monks and soldiers, came together to form an attractive, powerful and successful ideological synthesis.

To this combination Marinetti, with the publication of the *Futurist Manifesto*, brought the enthusiastic support of cultural avant-gardism. One can hardly exaggerate the significance of the avant-gardist element in original fascism, the importance of the revolutionary aesthetic it contained. Futurism was, at this period, the first intellectual current to give a political formulation to an aesthetic conception.[32] One can explain the attractiveness of fascism for large segments of European intelligentsia when one understands that they found in it an expression of their own nonconformism, and that in addition to proposing a conception of the relationships between the individual and society, fascism represented a new ideal of the beautiful and the admirable. This is the answer to the question why, everywhere in Europe, from the London of Ezra Pound, Wyndham Lewis, and T.S. Eliot, to the Bucharest of Mircea Eliade and Emile Cioran, and from the Lisbon of Fernando Pessoa to the Brussels of Hendrik de Man, and of course in Germany, Italy and France, did fascism have such a strong hold on men of stature? Why did it exercise such a profound fascination on so many highly cultivated people?

Thus, the thirty years preceding the First World War constituted the laboratory of fascist thought. The intellectual crisis of the end of the nineteenth century was expressed in concrete terms by the crisis of liberal democracy. Naturally enough, this crisis first struck the most advanced liberal society of the continent, the one where the regime proudly claimed kinship with the Enlightenment and the French Revolution. It was precisely in a society in which liberal democracy, because it was a tangible reality, had already had time to give rise to much disappointment and animosity, that the cultural rebellion became a mass ideology and began to take the form of a political revolt. This was the real historical significance of the Dreyfus Affair. Following on the heels of the prologue of Boulangism in the 1880s, the Dreyfus Affair was an extraordinary attempt to undermine the intellectual basis of the regime and its legitimacy. This was the first time that the attack upon liberal democracy had been made in the name of the people. The Boulangists and the anti-Dreyfusards advocated the destruction of democracy in the name of the masses. They all condemned both liberalism which, in their opinion, set one individual against the other, regarding them as simple merchandise in the labour market, and Marxism, which broke the natural solidarity of the nation in the name of class struggle.

Marxism and liberalism were forms of materialism, and fascism was anti-materialism in its clearest form: it was a rejection of the rationalist content of liberalism and Marxism, those two heirs of the eighteenth century. But, fascism cannot only be defined in negative terms: it was a third revolutionary option between liberalism and Marxism. Although an ideal prototype of a disruptive ideology, fascism offered its own vision of the world and created a new political culture. Fascism was an original, nonconformist answer to the question of how to overcome certain seemingly insurmountable social conflicts.

Liberal democracy never claimed to provide a global, clear-cut answer to these questions. It could only propose very partial and limited solutions, and it was concerned with the results of social phenomena rather than with their causes. Liberal democracy never aimed at eliminating the conflicts that tore society apart – economic, social, ideological – it merely attempted to control them.

From the seventeenth century onwards, conflict had been regarded as integral to the very essence of human society. The whole of liberal thought was based on the acceptance of conflict as a permanent phenomenon. On this, liberalism and its heirs, democracy and democratic socialism, were in agreement: they only differed on the question of how conflict should be regulated. Up to this very day, the whole question of state intervention in the economy and in society comes down in reality to the problem of regulating conflict. Fascism, on the other hand, wished specifically to eliminate the conflict as such. It was here that its great originality and its specific character resided, and, of course, its final disastrous consequences.

In this respect, its founders believed fascism to be an invention of genius. Whereas communism, destroying social structures, a way of life and age-old practices, launched out on a gigantic adventure, fascism claimed it could confer a comparable harmony on the social fabric without touching in any way the social and economic reality. In order to bring this about, it was sufficient to regard society not as an aggregate of individuals or a juxtaposition of antagonistic groups, but as a single entity whose organic, biological and cultural unity, destroyed by modernization or at least strongly endangered by it, could and should be restored. Fascism could come into being when the idea began to be entertained that man, in the final analysis, was not the *homo economicus* of liberalism and Marxism. A fascist view of the world took hold once the conclusion was reached that men's lives could be transformed without touching social and economic structures. This was an idea that the revolutionaries of the eighteenth and nineteenth centuries had never thought of. It was based on the assumption, as Hendrik de Man put it, that 'the concept of exploitation is ethical and not economic'.[33]

Once one accepts the idea that social and economic problems are psychological phenomena, one can change the relationships between people, one can transform life without touching the social and economic system. If exploitation is a psychological and not an economic phenomenon, it is sufficient, in order to end it, to give everyone the feeling of working for the good of the country, of being in the service of some higher cause rather than their personal interests. As if by a miracle, exploitation and alienation disappear. One has only to add fascist camaraderie, uniforms and grand parades to give a sense of belongingness and equality. One can destroy the moral and intellectual content of liberalism while preserving the capitalist economy and its social structures together with all the benefits of modernization and technology. Fascism showed that the world could be changed by the force of will, that a moral and political revolution, a revolution involving the nation as a whole, was sufficient to give a whole generation the feeling of entering into a new era. It was sufficient to regard the leader as a new Christ and to commune in him, and the nation would be restored to its natural unity. This was an essential aspect of the novelty of fascism and of its attraction.

In the period between the two world wars, the rebellion against the basic values of the eighteenth century changed very little since the years before the First World War. When Mussolini attempted to define fascism in 1932, he described it as a revolt against 'the materialistic positivism of the nineteenth century'.[34] A year later, when the fascist movement was founded in Spain, its leader, José Antonio Primo de Rivera, began his opening speech by launching an attack on Rousseau.[35] In 1940, Drieu La Rochelle declared that 'France had been destroyed by rationalism'.[36]

The fascist revolt of the feelings and instincts, of energy, of the will, and of primal forces, this search for new values that could ensure the integrity of the community, this rejection of materialism, excited, impressed, and influenced a great many Europeans. For many Europeans to serve society while being at one with it, to identify one's interests with that of the nation, to share in a cult of heroic values, was a far more satisfying way of participating in the life of the community than slipping a voting paper into a ballot box. For all of that generation, the spread of fascism throughout Europe was proof that a culture could exist based not on privileges of birth or wealth but on the spirit of the group. The war waged against the 'bourgeois spirit', as opposed to the spirit of the community, was a fundamental aspect of the fascist temptation.

The anti-Enlightenment culture made the élites more vulnerable than ordinary people: the collapse of liberalism and democracy in Europe was first and foremost the collapse of the élites. Spengler and Jünger, for example, were contemptuous of the Austrian corporal who took over their country, but they and their friends from the 'revolutionary conservative' school of thought gave Nazism the legitimacy it needed in the eyes of the upper middle classes.[37] Alfred von Martin wrote: 'Spengler is capable of something Nietzsche was not yet able to achieve: to opt for barbarism without seeing it as a fountain of youth'.[38] Carl Schmitt served the regime faithfully and Heidegger spoke of the 'great inner truth of Nazism'. In this connection, Jürgen Habermas was correct in saying that if a Nazi intelligentsia as such never came into being, it was for one reason only, namely, that the Nazi leadership was incapable of appreciating the intellectuals and thus unable to exploit their readiness to serve the regime.[39]

The same was true in Italy and France. In Italy it was the liberal establishment led by the former prime ministers Giolitti and Salandra, and backed by major intellectuals like Croce, Marinetti, D'Annunzio, Pirandello, Michels and Mosca that handed over the country to Mussolini. If he had not died in 1923, Pareto, whose whole oeuvre expressed a profound contempt for democracy, would have been in the front rank of the fascists. If one wishes to understand the reasons for the ascendancy of fascism in Italy, one must turn to the man who is rightly regarded as the most important Italian intellectual since Vico. Croce is a representative figure, for in his time he was the living symbol of all the ambiguities of fascism.

After having contributed, together with many other leading figures of Italian liberalism, to the rise of fascism, Senator Croce did not hesitate in 1924, after the assassination of the socialist deputy Giacomo Matteotti, when there was an opportunity of overthrowing Mussolini and the King might have shown himself favourable, to raise his hand in support of the government. After experiencing fascism in power, Senator Croce nevertheless gave a vote of confidence in its leader. Despite the fact that Mussolini publicly accepted responsibility for the crime, the greatest living Italian still felt that fascism, in saving Italy from democracy and socialism, still had an important role to play. Just before the King invited Mussolini to form the new government, Croce did not hesitate to assert that, all things considered, fascism was compatible with liberalism.[40] It was only later that Croce entered into opposition and from the 1930s onwards began to see history as the history of liberty.

But, before reaching the point where he decided that there was no longer any room for fascism in his system of thought, Croce, from the turn of the twentieth century, long persisted in opposition to democracy. His conduct was not the result of opportunism any more than his attitude was due to an incorrect understanding of fascism. On the contrary, no one understood fascism better than Croce; no one had a more exact idea of its intellectual content and political purpose. In May 1924, Croce wrote an article in connection with the assassination of Matteotti, that heroic figure of the anti-fascist opposition. Published in the review *La Critica* and much reproduced in the Turin daily *La Stampa*, it says more about the reasons for the ascendancy of fascism than the long and tortuous explanations given in the years following the fall of Mussolini:

> My rejections, like those of any reasonable man, are always *secundum quid*, and do not rule out the possibility that things that are reprehensible in some respects may be admirable in others, and that things that are not valid with regard to some of their effects may be valid in other ways. I have denied that futurism, a voluntaristic, vociferous and vulgar movement, can give rise to poetry, which comes into being among certain solitary and contemplative spirits in shadows and in silence, but I have not denied and I have even recognized the practical advantage of the futurist movement. To make poetry is one thing; to use one's fists, it seems, is another, and there is no reason to assume that someone who does not succeed in the first activity will not succeed in the second, nor that an avalanche of blows of the fist cannot in certain cases be usefully and suitably delivered.[41]

These reflections are a remarkable example of the way in which a philosophy of history can be translated into terms accessible to the reader of a daily newspaper, or the way in which historical relativism can be applied to ordinary politics. Croce, who is often regarded as an Italian Meinecke, had the same historicist vision as the German historian: Croce's motto, 'Against the Eighteenth Century,' exactly describes the aims of his intellectual criticism. His historical vision was based on the idea that humanitarian 'preconceptions' were the main obstacles to the power of the state and the protection of the country, and hence to historical progress.[42] Like Mussolini and his syndicalist colleagues, he drew a classical conclusion from the Great War: 'The makers of world history are peoples and states, not classes'.[43] Croce was close to the German school of historians both in his sense of individuality and in his anti-positivism. From the last decade of the nineteenth century he insisted in a similar way to the Germans on the inalienable individuality of historical facts. There is no doubt that at that time German historical relativism had great influence on Croce's thought. At the same time, he was interested in Marx, but, like Sorel, what he took from Marx was above all his opposition to bourgeois democracy and the concept of natural rights. What Croce found significant in Marx was, to use Sorel's admirable view, the 'sociology of violence'. In 1917, Croce, who had broken away from Marxism long before, expressed his gratitude to Marx for having helped to 'make him insensible to Justice and Humanity'.[44]

True to this principle, in the twenty years preceding the rise of fascism, Croce waged a daily polemic against democracy, the philosophy of the Enlightenment, natural law and the humanist ideologies. 'Definitely, democracy is mere nothingness! It is the flock leading the shepherd, it is the world upside-down, it is disorder, inanity and organized stupidity!'[45] This was a quotation from the *Mercure de France* of September 1915. Croce liked it so much that he reproduced it as it was, in French, in an article of his own written in October. It was typical of Croce's thought, and he considered it so worthy of quotation that he republished it verbatim in *Pagine sulla guerra* in 1928, in the midst of the period of the 'fascization' of the Italian state. Moreover, in the early years of the century, the author of *Historical Materialism* was a convinced social Darwinist.[46] It took the experience of all those long years of dictatorship to convince Croce that one could not with impunity wage war against intellectualism, abstract and general principles, historical materialism and the heritage of the French Revolution. Croce finally understood that war on democracy had a price and actual consequences. That is why his vote of confidence was so symbolic: nothing can more clearly illustrate the ambiguity of the positions taken up throughout the interwar period by so many European intellectuals in the face of fascism. And not only can nothing better illustrate their behaviour in times of crisis, but nothing can better account for their *a posteriori* explanations.

Things were just the same in France. The origin of this state of affairs, as Pier Giorgio Zunino so well demonstrated in the case of Italy,[47] was the distinction which the intellectuals of the interwar generation made between moral consciousness and historical understanding. The attraction of fascism existed precisely because of the possibility of distinguishing between a fascism which was negative from the moral point of view and a fascism which was positive from the historical point of view. Meinecke could be horrified by Nazism as a system of inhuman oppression while being filled with pride at the victories of the German armies. From the annexation of Austria to the fall of Berlin, his loyalty to Germany and the government which defended its interests – expansion, war against communism – was never in question.[48] That the greatness of the nation had to come at the price of the Nazi barbarism was unfortunate, but was that not precisely what was meant by the 'cunning of history'? Likewise Spengler, one of the finest representatives of the historical relativism of the previous century, did more than anyone else to make possible the rise of Nazism. It is in this perspective that one has to see the French dissidents of the 1930s, for if historicism was an invention Europe owed to Herder, if it owed its immediate application to politics first of all to German romanticism, in the period between the Napoleonic wars and the Second World War the philosophy of history of the Lutheran pastor and his successors spread like wildfire through the European continent.

Certainly, France, in these years between the two world wars – which are put in the shade by the years before 1914 – did not have a Troeltsch or a Meinecke able to formulate the principles of historical relativism in modern terms suitable to the period. It did not have a Max Weber, who was also very ambiguous in his attitude to Western democracy, but the enemies of the Enlightenment, who continually undermined the foundations of French democracy, from the nationalist circles and a large number of Catholics, including those who in the 1930s opposed the Action française, to the most extreme elements of the revolutionary right, professed a moral relativism which was not always totally different from the one in Germany. It was this relativism that played such a dominant role in the 'German catastrophe', in fascism's rise to power in Italy and in the acceptance of the Vichy regime in France.

This moral relativism, coupled with the irrationalism promoted by the theoreticians of anti-Dreyfusism in the 1880s, had gained a wide measure of acceptance in France. The war against liberal democracy was a war against French rationalism and English utilitarianism. The rejection of the Republic was inspired by the concept of the nation as a self-sufficient individual entity with a special spirit of its own, by a denial of natural law, considered an abstract ideology. The long road towards Vichy, the destruction of liberty, dictatorship, the local concentration camps and the racial laws began with the moral relativism of the theory of the Land and the Dead, the war against the Jacobin conception of the nation and the rejection of universal norms, Justice and Truth, always contemptuously spelt with capital letters.[49]

Continuity, however, does not necessarily mean determinism. The rise of fascism or Nazism or the French National Revolution of 1940 was not an inescapable destiny, but neither were they merely the product of circumstances. Continuity is a dynamic process in which there is an acceleration in times of crisis. There is no continuity without change, but the ideology of the revolutionary right at the turn of the century was more than simply a background to the Vichy regime. This ideology was the very essence of the National Revolution. An acceleration took place after the First World War, and there was another after the defeat of 1940. In France as in Italy, the revolt against the Enlightenment, or, in concrete political terms, against liberalism, democracy and socialism, was the common denominator of all the dissidents drawn into the National Revolution, from the extreme fascists who thought the new regime too moderate to those who disliked the totalitarian character of Pétainism while being unable to resist the attraction of the spiritualistic and idealistic aspects of this long-awaited revolution.

Thus, the Vichy regime was no less fascist than Mussolini's Italy, and was in many ways more brutal, with racial legislation harsher than the Nuremberg Laws, applied infinitely more stringently than in Italy. This regime enjoyed the support of the élites and was generally accepted by the mass of the population. The great majority of the intellectuals and the influential sectors of society – the administration, the legal profession, the teachers, the academics, from the provincial universities to the Collège de France, the writers and artists, the business and industrial sectors – enthusiastically placed themselves at the service of a regime and an ideology which not only set about destroying all the institutions of democracy but was determined to kill its spirit.

The case of France is very significant, and also, especially today when the European extreme right not only displays vitality but demonstrates that it is not a simple reaction to communism, contains a lesson which ought to be heeded.

It is especially important to recall these characteristics of the fascist revolution, its origins and above all the reasons for its rise to power, now that a new wave of anti-communism, encouraged by the fall of the Soviet Union, is distorting our sense of historical perspective. The theory that fascism and communism are twins, accomplices and enemies at the same time, and that Nazism was an imitation of Stalinism, an understandable and even natural response to the Bolshevik danger and a simple product of the First World War, is not only a banalization of fascism and Nazism but above all a distortion of the true nature of the European disaster of the twentieth century. This idea, put forward by Ernst Nolte in the 1960s, has had an unusual fate. Though scholars regard it as outmoded, like the 'fascism-as-a-parenthesis' theory, in the sphere of intellectual polemics it is accepted today by a large part of the conservative right in Europe.[50] Just as in the 1940s anti-communism and the Cold War were the gateway through which collaborators and fascists could return to the political and cultural fold, so in the 1990s the factor which has permitted this German apologetic thesis to be revived has been the new wave of anti-communism which followed the fall of the Soviet Union.

This view of fascism has strongly resurfaced recently because it was taken up by François Furet. *The Passing of an Illusion* is a brilliant essay, but not even the talent of this major historian, an expert on the French Revolution, whose recent death has left a great hiatus, can give weight to a theory which not only has worn badly but has generally been considered, everywhere except in German con-servative circles, to be one more attempt to take Nazism out of German history. It is not true that fascism 'came into being as a reaction to communism', and it is difficult, for more than one reason, to imagine that there could have been a complicity between fascism and communism.[51] Fascism and communism un-doubtedly had a common enemy – democracy – and the Great War provided the psychological conditions which permitted them to rise to power, but the two movements were engaged in a fight-to-the-finish, for they possessed a totally different conception of man and society. Together with nationalism, the other main element of fascism was the anti-rationalist revision of Marxism and not the Leninist version of post-Marxism.[52]

The great difference between the two ideologies was in their objectives. Fas-cism belonged to the historicist tradition and was the most dramatic and extreme example of the application of particularistic principles – nationalism, historicism – as well as the most extreme form of rejection of universal and abstract princi-ples: the rights of man, the unity of the human race and class struggle. Applied communism and fascism had in common voluntarism and faith in the power of mobilizing myths and in men's capacity to change the world in which they lived, but the changes they envisaged were completely different. Communism (and in this and this only was it true to its Marxist origins), sought to change society by altering its economic structure. In order to do this, in order to change a form of existence which seemed to be part of the natural order of things, it embarked on a Herculean adventure which necessarily involved a barbaric repression. The communist revolution was the kind of revolution imagined by the nineteenth century: an economic and social revolution. The fascist revolution, however, was quite different: a real twentieth-century revolution, it was a cultural, moral, psychological and political revolution, but one which never touched capitalism, the basis of the existing economic order. This revolution was not carried out on behalf of a social class which spoke for the whole of suffering humanity, but on behalf of the nation and nothing else. Thus, a new human order was created, but social and economic injustices and inequalities were not eliminated. This acceptance of capitalism as the natural foundation of society was a basic characteristic of fascism, for capitalism comes to terms with the worst of tyrannies no less easily than with democracy.

Pure fascists undoubtedly detested the bourgeois order, but they felt they could control the bourgeoisie and harness it in the service of the nation. They thought they could make it work for the benefit of the country. The Sorelian syndicalists and their immediate followers, including Mussolini and the hard core of the founders of the Italian fascist movement, the nationalists and the futurists, could offer no alternative to capitalism. It was a matter of ideology: unlike the Bolsheviks, they did not believe capitalism was the cause of the evil of the bourgeois phenomenon. This explains why Mussolini was not a disciple of Lenin, and, contrary to François Furet's assertion,[53] he broke away from Marxism from 1912 onwards. Lenin came from a small group of Russian and Polish revolutionaries, many of whom, like Rosa Luxemburg, Trotsky and Parvus (pseudonym of Alexander Israel Helphand, inventor of the theory of permanent revolution), were Jewish, which means in most cases anti-nationalists, and who from 1900 to 1914 remained true to the idea of a proletarian revolution.

On the other hand, in Western Europe this type of revolutionary had disappeared long before, and the only remaining violent enemies of the established order were the Sorelians. Thus, in the years before the war, Mussolini began to turn towards this faction: these revisionists who loathed Marxist 'materialism' and rationalism, and the Marxist concept of a revolution which would be the culmination of a long and, generally speaking, mysterious process. This development took place without any connection to the explosion of 1914. Mussolini drew near in these years to the syndicalist revolutionary left, whose relationship with the proletariat was not an essential one, and which only had use for the proletariat if the worker agreed to sacrifice his class interests in order to become the instrument of a great moral revolution. Around 1910, these dissidents of French and Italian socialism had already formed the nationalist-socialist front from which fascism would emerge. Launching out against the Enlightenment, rationalism and utilitarianism, or, in other words, against liberal and Marxist 'materialism', against the universal values of both liberalism and democratic socialism, the Sorelian left wished to save civilization by impregnating society with heroic values. Thus, a civilization of monks and warriors would arise, they hoped, on the ruins of the modernity of the Enlightenment. In order that this should happen, there was no need, they believed, to touch the foundations of capitalism: the evil was not in capitalism but in liberal and Marxist individualism, in the rationalist, hedonist and utilitarian decadence common to liberalism and

Marxism, and in the liberal and Marxist conception of the individual as the ultimate value and the ultimate object of all political and social action.

Thus, if a disdain for an aristocracy of birth or money was common to both fascism and communism, if fascists and communists could be equally scornful of parliamentary democracy, its rules and institutions, there was a world of difference not only between the two ideologies but between the two regimes, for while fascism could inspire fear and contempt in liberals and conservatives, it did not threaten capitalism. Precisely because it did not have the aim of uprooting the existing economic and social system, Italian fascism was a regime which could never be compared to the Stalinist terror. In order to attain the objectives he had set himself, Mussolini and his supporters had no need to resort to excessive brutality.[54] In November 1926, with the abolition of all civil liberties and guarantees of the rights of man, Italy became a police state, but the dictatorship of a monolithic party never came into being there.[55]

It is worth remembering these essential facts, especially when one is speaking of totalitarianism. More than any other concept, totalitarianism is defined by its actions. Fascism, Nazism and Stalinism were all single-party regimes, but they were very different dictatorial systems, and worlds apart in the objectives they set themselves. Here we will do well to go back a little more than forty years and look at an admirable passage from Raymond Aron's *Démocratie et totalitarisme* in which the author put his finger on the essential point: 'In order to assess the relative degree of similarity or opposition, one cannot be content with comparative, sociological analysis. One must be aware of two other means of comprehension: history and ideology.' He added: 'That is why, passing from history to ideology, I would maintain that there is an essential difference between the two [communism and Nazism] because of the difference in the ideas behind them. In one case, the outcome is the labour-camp, and in the other, the gas-chamber.'[56]

In fact, it is historically absurd and morally unjust to make Stalinism responsible for the Nazi horrors. Not only was Nazism not a simple reaction to communism (though the theme of the communist danger did play an important role in the rise of Hitler), but, if the Nazi system fell into barbarism, it was not because it was a reflection of Stalinism, but because it was the most thoroughgoing attack on Western civilization ever conceived. Communism assailed capitalism and its political expression, liberalism; fascism attacked the Enlightenment. Only Nazism attacked the conception of the human being as it has come down to us from Jewish and Greek antiquity, and as conceived by early Christianity. Only Nazism attacked the human race itself. Communism attempted to uproot capitalism and take a staggering leap forward by completely transforming social and economical relations. The human disaster which resulted was commensurate with the greatness of the enterprise.

If, in order to defeat Nazism, one had to go all the way to Hitler's bunker, it was first of all because the Nazi regime was a precise implementation of its ideology. On the other hand, if the fall of communism was the result of a process in which the regime, after the death of the dictator, was profoundly transformed, it was also because the gap between ideology and practice had become intolerable.

Should one conclude from the fate of the communist adventure that any questioning of the social order based on private property and the profit motive must always necessarily produce results of this kind? There is no methodological reason to assume this, just as there is no methodological reason to say that the extreme, fascist or fascistically-inclined right was buried once and for all in 1945. That right, whether of the Pétainist, Mussolinean or Hitlerian variety, that right which included the greatest intellectuals of the day and simple folk from the great European cities, was not born in the trenches of the First World War and did not die in the ruins of Berlin. Whatever we imagine its future to be, that right is still part of our world.

Notes and references

1 This chapter is part of a larger project supported by the Israel Academy of Sciences and Humanities. I am grateful to the Academy for making my research possible. The original article on which this chapter is based was written during the month of September 1999 which I was privileged to spend as a fellow at the Bellagio Study and Conference Centre. I wish to thank the Rockefeller Foundation for the opportunity to work in the ideal conditions provided by the wonderful staff of Villa Serbelloni.
2 This is not intended as a global criticism of Eric Hobsbawm's *Age of Extremes: The Short Twentieth Century, 1914–1989*, London, Michael Joseph, 1994, which I consider to be an important work.
3 G. Le Bon, *Les Lois psychologiques de l'évolution des peuples*, Paris, Alcan, 1894, p. 170.
4 V. Woolf, 'Character in fiction', in *The Essays of Virginia Woolf*, edited by Andrew McNeille, Vol. III, *1919–1924*, London, The Hogarth Press, 1988, pp. 421–2.
5 On Croce and fascism, see D. Mack Smith, 'Benedetto Croce: history and politics', *Journal of Contemporary History*, 1973, Vol. 1, pp. 41–61; G. Stasso, *Per invigilare me stesso: i tacuini di lavoro di Benedetto Croce*, Bologna, Il Mulino, 1989; S. Zeppi, *Il pensiero politico dell'idealismo italiano e il nazionalfascismo*, Florence, La Nuova Italia, 1973; M. Abbate, *La filosofia di Benedetto Croce e la crisi della societá italiana*, Turin, Einaudi, 1955.
6 This is one of the most problematic aspects of Ernst Nolte's 'phenomenological approach' to fascism. See his *Three Faces of Fascism: Action Française, Italian Fascism, National Socialism*, New York, Holt, Rheinhart & Winston, 1965.
7 Z. Sternhell, M. Sznajder and M. Asheri, *The Birth of Fascist Ideology: From Cultural Rebellion to Political Revolution*, Princeton NJ, Princeton University Press, 1995.
8 For the most recent histories and state-of-the-art definitions of fascism, see S.G. Payne, *A History of Fascism, 1914–1945*, Madison WI, The University of Wisconsin Press, 1995; R. Griffin, *The Nature of Fascism*, London, Pinter Publishers, 1991; R. Eatwell, *Fascism: a History*, London, Vintage, 1996. Griffin has also edited an important reader, *Fascism*, Oxford, Oxford University Press, 1995. On fascism as an ideology, see R. Eatwell's highly stimulating article: 'On defining the "fascist minimum": the centrality of ideology', *Journal of Political Ideologies*, 1996, Vol. 1, pp. 303–19. See also A.J. Gregor, *The Ideology of Fascism*, New York, Free Press, 1969, and G.L. Mosse, *The Fascist Revolution: Toward a General Theory of Fascism*, New York, Howard Fertig, 1999. On issues related to the concept of ideology, cf. M. Freeden, 'Political concepts and ideological morphology', *Journal of Political Philosophy*, 1994, Vol. 2, pp. 140–64.
9 I. Kant, 'An answer to the question: "What is Enlightenment?"', in *Kant's Political Writings*, edited with an introduction and notes by H. Reiss, Cambridge, Cambridge University Press, 1970, p. 54.
10 R. Pascal, *The German Sturm und Drang*, Manchester, Manchester University Press, 1953, p. 222.

11 Friedrich Meinecke, *Historicism: The Rise of a New Historical Outlook*, translated from the German by J.E. Anderson, with a foreword by Sir Isaiah Berlin, London, Routledge and Kegan Paul, 1972, p. lv. See the original text: F. Meinecke, *Die Entstehung des Historismus*, Munich, R. Oldenbourg Verlag, 1959, p. 2: 'Der Kern des Historismus besteht in der Ersetzung einer generalisierenden Betrachtung geschichtlich-menschlicher Kräfte durch eine individualisierende Betrachtung'.

12 Meinecke, ibid., pp. lv–lvi (pp. 2–4 of the German text). On historicism and its context, see F.C. Beiser's excellent *Enlightenment, Revolution and Romanticism: The Genesis of Modern German Political Thought, 1790–1800*, Cambridge MA, Harvard University Press, 1992, pp. 30–3 and 37, and G.G. Iggers, *The German Conception of History: The National Tradition of Historical Thought from Herder to the Present*, Middletown CT, Wesleyan University Press, 1983, pp. 124–228.

13 Ibid., p. lvii.

14 F. Meinecke, *The German Catastrophe: Reflections and Recollections*, translated by S. Bradshaw, Boston MA, Beacon Press, 1963.

15 Carlo Antoni, *L'Historisme*, traduit de l'italien par Alain Dufour, Geneva, Librairie Droz, 1963, pp. 54–5. See also C. Antoni, *From History to Sociology: The Transition in German Historical Thinking*, translated from the Italian by H.V. White, Westport CT, Greenwood Press, 1976.

16 Max Rouché, 'Introduction' to a bilingual critical edition of J.G. Herder, *Auch Eine Philosophie der Geschichte zur Bildung der Menschheit, Beytrag zu vielen Beyträgen des Jahrhunderts / Une Autre philosophie de l'histoire. Pour contribuer à l'éducation de l'humanité. Contribution à beaucoup de contributions du siècle*, Paris, Aubier, 1964, pp. 19–23. The French text is translated from the German and presented by Max Rouché.

17 Rouché, 'Introduction', p. 60.

18 Herder, *Auch Eine Philosophie der Geschichte / Une Autre philosophie de l'histoire*, p. 249.

19 Ibid., pp. 242–5. For a probably more accessible German edition, see Johann Gottfried Herder, *Werke*, Vol. I: *Herder Und Der Sturm und Drang, 1764–1774*, Munich, Carl Hanser Verlag, 1984, pp. 639–41.

20 A. Gillies, *Herder*, Oxford, Blackwell, 1945, p. 133. Gillies emphasizes Herder's contribution to the *Sturm und Drang* movement, while R.T. Clark on the contrary considers Herder much more as an *Aufklärer* of the right kind: *Herder: His Life and Thought*, Berkeley CA, University of California Press, 1955. This line was followed by Isaiah Berlin's friendly, if not selective, reading of Herder. See *Vico and Herder: Two Studies in the History of Ideas*, London, The Hogarth Press, 1976, and more recently, 'Alleged relativism in eighteenth-century European thought', in *The Crooked Timber of Humanity: Chapters in the History of Ideas*, London, John Murray, 1990, pp. 70–90. See also F.M. Barnard, *Herder's Social and Political Thought: From Enlightenment to Nationalism*, Oxford, Oxford University Press, 1965. On Berlin as a prominent representative of counter-Enlightenment liberalism, see G. Garrard's brilliant 'The counter-Enlightenment liberalism of Isaiah Berlin', *Journal of Political Ideologies*, 1997, Vol. 2, pp. 281–96.

21 E. Renan, 'Lettre à M. Strauss', in *Œuvres complètes de Ernest Renan*, édition définitive établie par Henriette Psichari, Paris, Calmann-Lévy, 1947, Vol. I, pp. 437–8; E. Richard, *Ernest Renan, penseur traditionaliste*, Aix-en-Provence, Presses Universitaires d'Aix-Marseille, 1996, p. 57. Cf. also H. Tronchon, *Ernest Renan et l'Etranger*, Paris, Les Belles Lettres, 1928, pp. 205 and 217. Another work of interest by Tronchon is his *La Fortune intellectuelle de Herder en France*, Paris, F. Rieder, 1920.

22 Renan, 'Nouvelle lettre à M. Strauss,' in *Œuvres complètes de Ernest Renan*, p. 454.

23 Cf. Z. Sternhell, *Maurice Barrès et le nationalisme français*, new expanded edition, Paris, Fayard, 2000.

24 F. Nietzsche, *Beyond Good and Evil: Prelude to a Philosophy of the Future*, translated by W. Kaufmann, New York, Vintage Books, 1966, pp. 153 and 206. Cf. also pp. 13, 49 and 61.

25 F. Nietzsche, *Ecce Homo*, in *The Philosophy of Nietzsche*, New York, Modern Library, n.d., p. 114.
26 Nietzsche, *Beyond Good and Evil*, p. 193.
27 On the German and French schools of 'conservative revolution' or pre-fascism, see F. Stern's classic *The Politics of Cultural Despair: A Study in the Rise of Germanic Ideology*, Berkeley CA, University of California Press, 1963; L. Dupeux (ed.), *La 'Révolution conservatrice' dans l'Allemagne de Weimar*, Paris, Kimé, 1992; and Z. Sternhell, *Neither Right nor Left: Fascist Ideology in France*, Princeton NJ, Princeton University Press, 1996. On Spengler, see G. Merlio's major work, *Oswald Spengler, témoin de son temps*, Stuttgart, Heinz, 1982.
28 M. Barrès, *Mes Cahiers*, Paris, Plon, 1931, p. 139.
29 Gregor, *The Ideology of Fascism*, p. 144.
30 T.E. Hulme, *Speculations: Essays on Humanism and the Philosophy of Art*, London, Routledge and Kegan Paul, 1954, pp. 250, 254–60. On Hulme's anti-rationalist and anti-humanistic revolutionary conservatism, see pp. 47, 55–8, 60–2 and 68–71. On Sorel as 'the key to all contemporary political thought', see W. Lewis, *The Art of Being Ruled*, London, Chatto and Windus, 1926, p. 128. Cf. also pp. 407–9.
31 H. Lagardelle, 'Les revues', *Le Mouvement socialiste*, July–August 1912, No. 243, p. 153.
32 See F.T. Marinetti, *Enquête internationale sur le vers libre et Manifeste du Futurisme*, Milan, Edizioni del 'Poesia', 1909; F.T. Marinetti, 'Manifesto del partito politico futurista', in M.D. Gambillo and T. Fiori (eds), *Archivi del Futurismo*, Rome, De Luca, 1958, pp. 34–7; G. Lista (ed.), *Marinetti et le futurisme*, Lausanne, L'Âge d'homme, 1977; E. Gentile, 'Il Futurismo e la politica: dal nazionalismo modernista al fascismo (1919–1920)', in R. de Felice (ed.), *Futurismo, cultura e politica*, Turin, Fondazione G. Agnelli, 1988; W.L. Adamson, *Avant-garde Florence: From Modernism to Fascism*, Cambridge MA, Harvard University Press, 1993; M. Affron and M. Antliff (eds), *Fascist Visions: Art and Ideology in France and Italy*, Princeton NJ, Princeton University Press, 1997.
33 H. de Man, *Au-delà du Marxisme*, Paris, Seuil, 1974, p. 329. The original German edition, *Zur Psychologie des Sozialismus*, was published in 1927, and the English translation was published in 1928 under the title *The Psychology of Socialism*, London, G. Allen and Unwin. Ten more translations followed.
34 B. Mussolini, 'La dottrina del fascismo', *Opera Omnia* edited by E. and D. Susmel, Florence, La Fenice, 1961, Vol. 34, p. 118.
35 J.A. Primo de Rivera, *Selected Writings*, edited and introduced by H. Thomas, London, Jonathan Cape, 1972, p. 49.
36 P. Drieu La Rochelle, *Notes pour comprendre le siècle*, Paris, Gallimard, 1941, p. 171.
37 Cf. F. Stern, *Dreams and Delusions*, New York, A. Knopf, 1987, pp. 156–7 and 164–5.
38 G. Merlio, 'The critique of liberal democracy in the works of Oswald Spengler', in Z. Sternhell (ed.), *The Intellectual Revolt Against Liberal Democracy*, Jerusalem, The Israel Academy of Sciences and Humanities, 1996, p. 188.
39 J. Habermas, *Profils philosophiques et politiques*, Paris, Gallimard, 1974, pp. 90–1. On Carl Schmitt and in general on the anti-liberal tradition, see Stephen Holmes's brilliant *The Anatomy of Antiliberalism*, Cambridge MA, Harvard University Press, 1996.
40 Payne, *A History of Fascism*, p. 107.
41 Quoted in Pier Giorgio Zunino, 'The weakness of the democratic tradition in Europe: the case of Italy (1920–1940)', in Z. Sternhell (ed.), *L'Éternel retour: Contre la démocratie, l'idéologie de la décadence*, Paris, Presses de la Fondation nationale des sciences politiques, 1994, p. 238.
42 B. Croce, *Pagine sulla guerra*, second edition, Bari, Laterza, 1928, pp. 105–7; *Materialismo storico ed economia marxista*, preface of 1912, Bari, Laterza, 1968, p. xiv.
43 Croce, *Pagine sulla guerra*, p. 109.
44 Quoted by Antoni in *L'Historisme*, p. 120.
45 Croce, *Pagine sulla guerra*, p. 66. Cf. also Zunino, 'The weakness of the democratic tradition,' in Sternhell, *Intellectual Revolt*, p. 239.

46 D. Gasman, *Haeckel's Monism and the Birth of Fascist Ideology*, New York, Peter Lang, 1998, p. 48.

47 Zunino, 'The weakness of the democratic tradition', in Sternhell, *Intellectual Revolt*, p. 244.

48 With regard to this, cf. Iggers, *The German Conception of History*, pp. 222ff.

49 For a detailed demonstration of this, see the new editions of my *Maurice Barrès et le nationalisme français*, and *La Droite révolutionnaire: les origines françaises du fascisme*, Paris, Fayard, 2000.

50 My criticism of Nolte's thesis is now a quarter of a century old: Z. Sternhell, 'Fascist ideology', in W. Laqueur (ed.), *Fascism: A Reader's Guide. Analyses, Interpretations, Bibliography*, Berkeley CA, University of California Press, 1976, pp. 368–71.

51 Cf. F. Furet, *Le passé d'une illusion. Essai sur l'idée communiste au XXe siècle*, Paris, Robert Laffont/Calmann-Lévy, 1995, pp. 39, 195–9, 213, and the whole of Chapter 6. In English: *The Passing of an Illusion: The Idea of Communism in the Twentieth Century*, Chicago, University of Chicago Press, 1999.

52 See Sternhell, Sznajder and Asheri, *The Birth of Fascist Ideology*, pp. 12–25 and Chapter 1.

53 Furet, *Le passé d'une illusion*, pp. 197–213.

54 Payne, *A History of Fascism*, pp. 112–17.

55 A. Lyttleton, *The Seizure of Power: Fascism in Italy, 1919–1929*, second edition, London, Weidenfeld and Nicolson, 1987, p. 297.

56 R. Aron, *Démocratie et totalitarisme*, Paris, Gallimard, 1965, pp. 294 and 302; pp. 198 and 203–4 of the English translation, *Democracy and Totalitarianism*, London, Weidenfeld and Nicolson, 1968.

8 Interregnum or endgame?

The radical right in the
'post-fascist' era

Roger Griffin

A charred corpse lying unrecognizable in an underground bunker in Berlin, a body hanging all too recognizably upside down from the gantry of a petrol station in Milan: if single images can be worth pages of historical analysis then the fates of Hitler and Mussolini in April 1945 certainly point to a dramatic watershed in the history of the radical right. The Duce's prophecies that his regime inaugurated a 'century of the Right, a Fascist century', and the Führer's claims to have founded a thousand-year Reich had proved catastrophic misreadings of unfolding political realities. The increasingly geriatric personal dictatorships of Franco and Salazar soon seemed grotesque anachronisms. In 1994 the oldest and most successful neo-fascist movement, the Movimento Sociale Italiano, became a 'right-wing party', declaring at its first congress held in Fiuggi that the collapse of actually existing socialism five years earlier had meant the end of an era characterized by the struggle between anti-fascism and fascism, and that parliamentary democracy now remained 'the only solution without negative side effects to the problem of competition between political forces for the conquest of consensus'.[1] In the run up to the congress in December 1993 the MSI's leader, Gianfranco Fini, had asserted that 'Fascism was now irreversibly consigned to history and its judgement . . . Like all Italians we are not neo-Fascists, but post-Fascists'.[2] Symbolically at least, Fiuggi was the Bad Godesberg of the European radical right. Liberal democracy had triumphed.

With its Faustian urge to probe beneath the surface of human phenomena to find 'what holds together the world at its inmost level',[3] political science clearly cannot be content with such punchy story-lines and cinematographic *dénouements*. However, once it is asked to recount how things 'actually have been' for the radical right since 1945 a number of factors come into play which make it hazardous to offer any sort of script at all, even if only in the form of a rough treatment. For one thing, even if the scope of the question is restricted to Europe, the failure of the radical right to achieve hegemony has a different story in every country.[4] Moreover, the conceptual problems involved compound those raised by the sheer quantity of empirical material. Apart from the increasingly contested nature of the fundamental term 'the right',[5] the concept 'radical right' can be defined and delimited in several conflicting ways,[6] and in each case subsumes a number of distinct forms of organization and ideological rationale. Moreover, the specific connotations of the term in different languages (when it is possible to translate it literally) and its significance, both historical and contemporary, vary significantly from country to country and from one part of the world to another (e.g., in German 'radical right' is regarded as still within the bounds of legitimate political debate, while 'extreme right' is not). In some Anglo-Saxon usages it embraces thousands of individual groups, movements, and parties the world over, ranging from the vast and well-established to the ephemeral and minute.[7] In addition, the subliminal political values, not to mention the historical assumptions and shadowy teleological imaginings, of the social scientist who attempts to sketch the 'big picture' cannot fail to influence the way it is composed, which empirical features are highlighted, and what inferences for the future are drawn from it.

Fortunately, three factors operate to bring the remit of this chapter just within the bounds of the manageable. First, it is written as one of a series of essays primarily concerned with general patterns of development discernible over the twentieth century within some of the major modern political ideologies, rather than with specific political formations and the events they helped shape. Secondly, the right–left dichotomy is a product of the French Revolution, and the term 'radical right' acquires its most precise connotations in the context of ideologically elaborated rejections of parliamentary liberalism of the type which first arose in early nineteenth-century Europe. Considerations of traditionalist forces operating outside Europeanized societies in a non-parliamentary context, such as Islamic fundamentalism, or of ideologically vacuous dictatorships, whether military or personal, thus need not detain us. Thirdly, one of the most significant events in the recent history of the radical right arguably concerns not the object of research but the lens through which it is seen. After several decades in which even the most rudimentary agreement over the definition of fascism was lacking, a significant pocket of consensus has emerged about its basic definitional contours. This conjuncture of factors enables an area of empirical data which poses irreducible definitional and taxonomic problems to be cut down to size. For heuristic purposes I propose to consider within the relatively uncontentious conceptual framework of the 'new consensus' those aspects of the post-war radical right which can be seen as outlets or conduits for the same ideological energies which fed interwar fascism. Having cleared some of the terrain it will then be possible to suggest in a more speculative spirit that the most significant development that has taken place since the war in the radical right has occurred outside the parameters of fascism: the spread of 'ethnocratic liberalism'. The anti-liberal currents of ideology it feeds may prove even more insidious than modernized forms of the interwar fascist right in their liberticide effects because they are so easily absorbed into the bloodstream of liberalism itself.

There is now a growing consensus that fascism is best seen as a revolutionary form of populist nationalism which emerged in the interwar period at a time when a systemic crisis seemed to many within the Europeanized world to be affecting not only national life, but civilization as a whole.[8] A necessary precondition for the rise of fascism was a cultural climate saturated with apocalyptic forebodings and hopes for imminent or eventual renewal captured in such works as Spengler's *Decline of the West* and H.G. Wells's *The Shape of Things to Come*. It articulated, fomented, and channelled inchoate but extraordinarily widespread longings for a new type of political system, a new élite, a new type of human being, a new relationship between the individual and society, for a more planned economy, for a revolutionary change in the values of modern life, for a new experience of time itself.[9] The mobilizing myth which can be treated ideal-typically as the definitional core of fascism (the 'fascist minimum') is that through the intervention of a heroic élite the whole national community is capable of resurrecting itself phoenix-like from the ashes of the decadent old order ('palingenetic ultra-nationalism'). It is this myth which informs the obsessive preoccupation with national/ethnic decadence and regeneration in a post-liberal new order which is now widely acknowledged to be the hallmark of all fascism.[10]

After 1945 not only was ultra-nationalism widely identified with war, destruction, genocide, and calculated inhumanity on a horrendous scale, but liberal democracy underwent no serious systemic crises, and was if anything strengthened and legitimated for the bulk of its citizens (in the myth of the 'Free World') by the emergence of the Soviet Empire, which also had the effect of comprehensively denying political space to liberal and right-wing agitation on its own territory. Within a few years of the Axis defeat it had become clear to all of fascism's more astute activists that the age of mass armed parties led by charismatic leaders was dead, and that in order to survive at all as an ideology in the absence of a pervasive palingenetic climate it had to be extensively overhauled. The basic problem was to adapt a revolutionary form of populist nationalism posited on the imminent collapse of Western liberalism and the palpable risk of a communist takeover, to a Western world now divided between a dynamically expanding capitalist and an apparently impregnable communist state system, neither of whose populations were susceptible to mass mobilization by the rhetoric of extreme nationalism, racism and war.

It would be misleading to suggest that all fascists recognized the extent to which their vision had been discredited by events, and have accepted the need for drastic change in their ideology and tactics in the light of the new international situation. The psychotropic power of palingenetic myth to transform despair into hope encouraged many who had believed in a fascist cause at the height of the war to enter a sustained state of denial. For decades pockets of purely nostalgic and mimetic fascism could be found in Europe, like muddy puddles in the bed of a dried-up lake. But the dramatic loss of the historical climate which produced fascism forced its more flexible activists, decimated by events and acutely marginalized within their political cultures,[11] to develop two basic strategies for keeping the dream of national rebirth alive, even if in a state of hibernation, in the bleak winter of liberal and (until 1989) communist hegemony in Europe. They can be summarized ideal-typically as 'internationalization' and 'metapoliticization'.

The internationalization of fascism

Even before the end of the Second World War some Nazis were making plans for the core values of the Third Reich to be perpetuated after its increasingly inexorable defeat. One of the more bizarre schemes may well have involved the setting up of a secret international order through the agency of the Sicherheitsdienst des Reichsführers-SS.[12] Though this particular project came to naught, it was an early symptom of the Europeanization of fascism which has become such a striking feature of the post-1945 fascist radical right. There had been several fascist schemes for a federal Europe before the war,[13] especially emanating from Italy,[14] and the realities of a Nazi conquest made the 'New European Order' a subject of considerable speculation and forward planning in some ministries of the Third Reich when victory seemed a foregone conclusion[15] – one Nazi initiative, Young Europe, was revived after the war as Jeune Europe. Nazi fellow travellers, such as Drieu la Rochelle in France and Szálasi, leader of the Hungarian Arrow Cross, also promoted visions of a Nazi dominated pan-fascist Europe. Once Germany had lost the war, a tempting explanation for the defeat without abandoning fascist principles was to accuse Mussolini and Hitler of being too narrowly nationalistic to realize the true historical purpose of fascism, namely to save European civilization as a whole from destruction at the hands of Bolshevism and Americanization.

Symptoms of the Eurofascism which emerged in the aftermath of 1945 were the launching of periodicals dedicated to the cause such as *The European*, *Europa Nazione*, and *Nation Europa*, the publication of major texts by Oswald Mosley,[16] Julius Evola,[17] Maurice Bardèche,[18] and Francis Yockey[19] calling for a European Federation or Empire of fascist nations, and the creation of pan-European fascist organizations such as The Nouvel Ordre Européen, The European Social Movement, and Faisceaux Nationaux et Européens.[20] However, any notion that the radical right had found in Eurofascism an effective strategy for a co-ordinated assault on the citadels of power is instantly dispelled when it is realized how many incompatible schemes emerged from it: pagan and Catholic, Nietzschean and occultist, pro-Nazi (and anti-semitic), pro-fascist, pro-British, pro-French, and pro-Hungarian. Some saw the new Europe as equally threatened by Russia and America, and hence saw Africa as a colonial hinterland supplying an autarkic Europe with raw materials (the idea of 'Eurafrica' was first formulated in the Salò Republic in the last years of the war). Others linked its destiny with the USA as part of an anti-communist alliance, or with Russia to form a continental bloc against decadent materialism and individualism ('national Bolshevism').

The acute taxonomic difficulties posed by the post-war fascist radical right are brought out clearly when we consider that the Nazi variant of Eurofascism is simultaneously an example of another form that its internationalization has taken. Once stripped of its specifically German connotations of a Third Reich, Nazism became the ideology of the white supremacist struggle to save civilization from its alleged enemies (Jews, communists, the racially inferior, liberals, etc.), whether on a strictly European (Nouvel Ordre Européen, Circulo Español de Amigos de

Europa) or a planetary (World Union of National Socialists, League for Pan-Nordic Friendship) scale.[21] In both cases, as with Eurofascism in general, the national or ethnic dimension of the struggle for regeneration was not abandoned, but subsumed within a wider context, so that Swedish or American Nazis can feel that the struggle for the rebirth of their nation or homeland is but one theatre in an international race war. By the 1970s a new generation of Universal Nazis was thinking globally and acting locally, made up principally of marginalized 'working-class' white racists targeted through propaganda directed at the educationally challenged, a racist variety of heavy metal punk rock and ballads, and, in Europe at least, through networks of organized football hooliganism with a racist agenda. Extensive international links exist between them, not only in the form of ritual congresses (e.g., the annual jamboree in the Belgian town of Dijksmuide, the Hitler or Hess birthday celebrations), but especially at the level of the distribution of propaganda, literature, and merchandizing. The White Noise CD business is a multinational industry in itself whose profits are channelled into financing political activities.[22]

Universal Nazism has retained the original's fanatical belief in the genius of Adolf Hitler and in the innate right of Aryan peoples to take any measures necessary to protect and strengthen the national community, which in practice means fighting the threat posed by Jews, communists, Blacks, and other alleged enemies of racial health, but the showdown between cultural health and degeneracy has generated new variants of Nazism as it adapts to its new habitat. Thus US Nazis present the federal state as ZOG (Zionist Occupation Government), and the United Nations as an agency of enforced racial mixing in a culturally homogenized, genocidal New World Order. Specific groups blend elements taken from the Ku Klux Klan, heterodox Christianity,[23] or Nordic mythology[24] in a spirit reminiscent of the German Faith Movement which appeared under Hitler, though the fusion of radical politics with 'new religions' has its roots deep in the charter myths which inform the national identity of traditionally minded white Americans.

An even more original form of international fascism ideologically is Third Positionism, which, influenced by some currents of Italian neo-fascism, seeks a third way between capitalism and communism, and associates itself with third-world struggles against the global market and a USA–Israel dominated 'international community' (notably Gaddafi's Libya, the PLO, and Hussein's Iraq), 'Zionist' capitalism, and the cultural hegemony of the USA. The English Third Positionist group, the National Revolutionary Faction, for example, promotes its own alternative economics ('distributionism'), and calls for the component parts of Britain (including Cornwall and the Isle of Man) to achieve semi-autonomy within a united (but decidedly not in the EU sense of united) Europe. This combination of regionalist separatism (ethno-pluralism) with supranational federalism reflects a marked tendency in some areas of the modern European radical right to abandon the nation-state as the basic unit of homogeneous cultural energy and promote the idea of discrete ethnic groups or *ethnies* (a principle already familiar from the Nazi equation of nation with *Volk*). This produces the concept of the 'Europe of a hundred flags' to which the NRF subscribes.

Though it presents itself as a vanguard movement of 'political soldiers', the NRF is typical of Third Positionism for the considerable energy it expends on refining its ideological alternative to classic fascism and encouraging a healthy diet of reading among its followers. The books on sale via its magazine *The English Alternative* (formerly *The Crusader*) range in subject matter from Nazism, especially its anti-Semitism and racial politics, the Iron Guard and the Falange, to ecology and the ideas of English visionaries such as Hilaire Belloc and William Morris. Especially significant is its promotion of the socialistic, pro-Russian, and Europeanist brand of fascism evolved by Otto Strasser and (in attenuated form) by his brother Gregor before he became a Nazi leader. Indeed, Third Positionism is sometimes called Strasserism to distinguish it from neo-Nazism, which it rejects as excessively compromised by capitalism, demagogy, and narrow chauvinism. The NRF is informally linked to Third Positionist groups all over the world, all with their own unique syntheses of ideas.[25]

The metapoliticization of fascism

An even more important ideological development within the fascist radical right than its rejection of the nation as the sole or principal focus for revolutionary energies also results from the defeat of the Axis powers in 1945. An outstanding feature of fascism and Nazism which fascist organizers elsewhere attempted to emulate was that they were able to take over the state as a new type of force in modern politics which combined four components: an electoral party, a paramilitary army, a mass social movement, and a prolific artistic and intellectual subculture. The ideological discourse, which under the two regimes became the orthodoxy and hence the basis for the social re-engineering of values and behaviour, was provided by a profusion of texts by intellectuals, artists, and articulate activists (notably the leaders themselves) who felt an elective affinity with a movement which promised to put an end to the decadence in national life and inaugurate a process of renewal. Far from being fully cohesive bodies of doctrine, the ideologies of both movements were alliances (in the fascist case a very loose one) of heterogeneous political, intellectual and cultural currents and ideas which converged on the image of the reborn nation.

A post-war political climate inclement towards all 'extremisms' precluded fascism from attracting anywhere in the world a mass following of sufficient size, momentum, and gravitational pull to bind these four components together under a charismatic leader in a way which had been only possible in the exceptional circumstances of the 1920s and 1930s. As a result overtly anti-systemic cadre movements of revolutionary paramilitaries and radical ideologues split off from ostensibly democratic political parties pursuing a fascist agenda, and it became possible for the ideological production of fascist discourse to operate relatively autonomously without any formal links with organized politics. The situation which emerged was reminiscent of the French or German radical right in the pre-1914 period where party politics, popular passions, extra-parliamentary activism, and ideological agitation were still not co-ordinated into cohesive unified populist movements. As a result of the fragmentation the modern fascist right in Europe presents the spectacle of a small number of political parties with fascist associations existing alongside a much larger number of organizations made up of militant activists dedicated solely to ideas, some of them with minute memberships (the 'groupuscular right').[26] The radical right planets of Europe's interwar political system have broken up into countless asteroids.

The combination of this situation with the universalization of Nazism is that a whole new sector of international cultural production has grown up since the war dedicated to keeping alive Nazism as an ideology, either through books glorifying the Nazi period (memoirs, biographies), or, more subtly, through academic journals, monographs, conference papers and 'scientific' reports which are 'revisionist' in that they offer historical accounts of Nazism denying, relativizing or minimizing the atrocities and human catastrophes which directly resulted from its attempt to create a racial empire in the heart of Europe. The most notorious product of revisionism is 'holocaust denial', which exists in various degrees of pornographic crudity and specious sophistication in its manipulation of historical realities.[27] Its success in re-editing history and making the facts about the Nazis' racial state at least contestable in the minds of post-war generations is crucial to a long-term strategy of elements within the international radical right for normalizing and rehabilitating Nazism to a point where its ideas no longer create repulsion among the general public, and where some anti-Nazi energy is actually deflected towards Jews themselves (who are accused by some vulgar revisionists of 'inventing the lie' of the Holocaust in order to be given a homeland at the expense of the Palestinians).

Some of the more sophisticated examples of revisionism[28] provide fascinating and disturbing case studies in the persuasive psychological power which form can exercise over content. By deliberately emulating a discourse and format of academic production (conferences and public lectures, journal articles and books incorporating footnotes, a strictly analytical linguistic register, the appeal to documentary evidence, the invocation of academic qualifications, etc.) which originally evolved as part of a liberal humanistic quest for truth, revisionists set out simultaneously to pervert the historical record and overcome psychological barriers which any humanist should have towards fascism. Revisionist and holocaust-denial literature is demonstrably part of the staple diet of 'Nazi-oid' fascists the world over and its most prolific producers nearly always have links to known Nazi activists. However, much of its insidious power derives from the fact that it exists as a free-floating discourse in its own right, and is not part of the ideological stance of any particular movement, party, or 'school' of fascism. In this sense revisionism is 'metapolitical'.

The pro-Nazi subtext of revisionism is at least apparent. By far the most sophisticated disguise assumed by the fascist radical right since the war is the (European) New Right. First elaborated as a response to calls for a more 'modern' fascist discourse which became increasingly frequent within the French radical right in the 1960s,[29] the Nouvelle Droite has been responsible for an extraordinary output of high quality ideological material associated with the 'think-tank' GRECE and the periodicals *Nouvelle École* and *Éléments*, most of which only the trained eye (peering through the lens of the 'new consensus') can detect as bearing the traces of a fascist legacy. The New Right's 'metapolitical' critique of liberal democracy has been taken up in several other countries, notably Italy (where it has been fused with a fascination with fantasy literature, especially Tolkien, and with esoteric elements derived from the total alternative 'Traditionalist' philosophy of history bequeathed by Julius Evola), Germany (where the influence of the Conservative Revolution is particularly strong), and Russia (where it has given rise to a new version of Eurasianism). There is even an English branch of the New Right which adds some Celtic and Anglo-Saxon perspectives to a view of the modern world as indebted to Evola as it is to GRECE.[30] The European New Right embraces a large number of academics and freelance autodidacts, journalists, writers, and intellectuals, some of whom are associated with particular magazines, study groups, or parties, while others are essentially loners. Some are overtly fascist, as when one of their number calls for a regenerating explosion of mythic energy of the sort precipitated by Hitler,[31] while others have evolved in such idiosyncratic directions away from any discernible revolutionary position that their fascist expectations of rebirth seem to have melted into a diffuse cultural pessimism about the present world order.[32]

While it is impossible to generalize about its precise ideological contents, the recurrent features of New Right thought are: a 'right-wing Gramscianism' which recognizes that cultural hegemony must precede political hegemony; the extensive use of intellectuals associated with the 'Conservative Revolution', notably Nietzsche, Ernst Jünger, Martin Heidegger and Carl Schmitt, as articulators of principles central to non-Nazi variants of German fascism which emerged under Weimar; the idea of Europe as a unique cultural homeland which can still be revitalized by renewing contact with its pre-Christian mythic roots; an extreme eclecticism stemming from the belief that the dichotomy of left and right can be transcended in a new alliance of intellectual energies opposed to the dominant system of liberal egalitarianism, capitalist materialism, and American consumerist individualism (summed up in the concept of a creeping 'McDonaldization' of the world, which also links in with an idiosyncratic concern with ecology); and the celebration of ethnic diversity and difference ('differentialism') to be defended against cultural imperialism and 'totalitarian' one-worldism ('mondialisme'), mass migration, and the liberal endorsement of a multi-racial society (presented as 'genocidal').

The hallmark of the New Right is its belief that the present world system is not only decadent, but that it will eventually give way to a new type of civilization based on healthy mythic forces (though the new millennium nowadays often seems indefinitely postponed). Contemporary history is thus an 'interregnum' for the spiritually awakened (a concept derived from the Conservative Revolution). New Rightists of an Evolian bent use the alternative image of the 'Kali Yuga' or Black Age which in the Hindu cyclic philosophy of history precedes the opening of a new golden age. Since the Axis powers did not take advantage of the unique opportunity offered by the interwar crisis to install a European empire based on traditional values, those with an intuitive sense for these values have no option but to withdraw into 'apoliteia' (which does not preclude political activism and even terrorism) until the modern world finally collapses.

It is in the copious publications of Europe's metapolitical New Right that the remarkable vitality and originality of the contemporary fascist radical right as an ideological phenomenon is to be found, as well as the most sophisticated expression of its Europeanization.[33] Perhaps the ultimate form taken by fascism's metapoliticization, however, is the extensive use it is now making of the Web. Thanks to the Internet, schemes for the salvation of nations, ethnic groups, Europe, the West, or the White race from their present decadence cease to be located in a movement, party, ideologue, or visionary leader, or even in a particular country or ethnic community: the secular Jeremiads and Evangelia are everywhere and nowhere simultaneously in a suprahistorical electronic reality which has the most tenuous link with the material world. In 'cyberfascism', the zenith of metapoliticization coincides with the ultimate degree of internationalization. To follow up the links to kindred organizations provided on each radical right web-page will take the avid researcher on a virtual journey through literally thousands of sites located throughout the Europeanized world, all presenting different permutations of palingenetic ultra-nationalism. What results is the paradox that as fascism diversifies into an ever greater plethora of factions and sects, it is simultaneously undergoing an ever more intense process of ecumenicalization.[34]

Democratic fascism, ethnocratic liberalism, and the prospects of the radical right

The sheer quantity of *groupuscules*, organizations, and publications which point to the tenacity of fascism in its various modulations might lead the unwary to assume that fascism is growing in strength and still poses a challenge to democracy. Fortunately in the present case, where variants of major ideologies are concerned there is often weakness in sheer numbers, since they point to an absent centre, the lack of dynamic movement which would turn them into mutually intelligible dialects of the same *lingua franca*. Fascist ecumenicalism does not run deep, and papers over radical differences in ideology which would nip in the bud any sort of fascist international (as they did when attempts to 'universalize' fascism formally were made in the much more propitious 1930s). Similarly, its metapolitics mask the fundamental impotence of visions which survive solely because their essential utopianism is never exposed by the acid test of attempted implementation. Creating a European Empire on differentialist lines, for example – leaving aside the preposterously surreal conditions required before such a fantasy could be enacted – would involve a process of enforced resettlement and ethnic cleansing which would soon leave the 'hundred flags' of the new Europe drenched in blood.

The most telling indicator of the structural impotence of the revolutionary radical right today is perhaps the emergence of electoral parties, which, despite euphemizing their fascist agenda for public consumption, have remained firmly marginalized everywhere in the world since 1945. The Nationalsozialistische Deutsche Arbeiterpartei or the Partito Nazionale Fascista used paramilitary force to back up electoral campaigns and negotiations with the state, and made no secret of their contempt for liberalism. The modern parliamentary fascist party (e.g., the British National Party, the Nationaldemokratische Partei Deutschlands) is more like a toothless, emaciated, old nag than a powerful Trojan horse capable of carrying revolutionaries into the citadel of power. The extent to which 'real fascism' is a dead letter is exemplified by the consequence of Fini's decision to move the MSI towards the centre from the right to take advantage of the Italian state crisis of the early 1990s. The price for becoming a legitimate player in the political game was to renounce the official commitment to a post-liberal new order, which meant taking Genesis out of the Bible just as much as it did for the hard left in Britain when Clause 4 was removed from the Labour Party Constitution. In both cases a small rump of intransigents were left (Scargill's Real Labour Party and Rauti's MSI Fiamma Tricolore) to keep the flame of ideological purity burning as a practically invisible point of light in the political spectrum. Despite occasional bouts of media panic about the possibility of massive swings to the right triggered by neo-Nazi violence against asylum seekers or the BNP's winning of a seat in a local election, the structural conditions are simply lacking for any fascist party to 'take off' as a mass force in national politics anywhere in the world as long as the globalization of capitalism continues apace.

Fascists cannot afford to concede this without ceasing to be fascists. Just as communists when confronted by the appearance of fascism in the 1920s had to classify it as another counter-revolutionary form of capitalism in order to 'save' their teleology, so fascists have to believe they are living on the threshold of a new age or in a protracted interregnum (or the 'Kali Yuga'), in order to retain their commitment to the cause intact. They are temperamentally incapable of coming to terms with one of the most psychologically disturbing cosmological implications of liberal modernity: the idea of history as an intrinsically meaningless, neutral medium in which – at least as long as our species survives – an infinite chain of events will continually unfold generated by the largely random interaction of the lives of billions of human beings, events which disclose patterns and trends but no intrinsic purpose or continuous story. In that sense the withering away of fascism in the West marks the victory, not of the 'Open' over the 'Closed Society', but of open-ended, amorphous, plotless time over aesthetic shapes and mythic dramas projected onto events as a palliative to the 'Terror of History' – a term coined by Mircea Eliade, who before becoming a world expert on palingenetic cosmologies, himself succumbed to the need to believe in the myth of politico-cultural rebirth from decadence.[35]

It would be academically irresponsible, however, to give this brief account what is, in a liberal perspective, a happy ending. As many reading this will have been already waiting impatiently for me to point out, another type of radical right has crept up on European society, one which is potentially of considerable virulence, not in its ability to destroy liberalism from without, but to contaminate it from within. Sometimes called 'radical right populism', or simply 'the radical right',[36] its paradoxical qualities perhaps emerge more clearly in the term 'ethnocratic liberalism'.[37] It is a type of party politics which is not technically a form of fascism, even a disguised form of it, for it lacks the core palingenetic vision of a 'new order' totally replacing the liberal system. Rather it enthusiastically embraces the liberal system, but considers only one ethnic group full members of civil society. As the case of apartheid South Africa illustrates only too clearly, a state based on ethnocratic liberalism is forced by its own logic to create institutions, including a terror apparatus, to impose a deeply illiberal regime on all those who do not qualify on racial grounds for being treated as human beings. This contaminated, restrictive form of liberalism poses considerable taxonomic problems because, while it aims to retain liberal institutions and procedures and remain economically and diplomatically part of the international liberal democratic community, its axiomatic denial of the universality of human rights predisposes it to behave against ethnic outgroups as violently as a fascist regime.

The fact that ethnocratic liberalism is a hybrid of ideological extremism and democratic constitutionalism, of radical right and centre (making the term 'radical right populism' misleading), and is a paradox rather than an oxymoron, also makes it more dangerous. It is perfectly attuned to a post-war world hostile to unadulterated fascism, one where the clerks[38] now enthusiastically help man the ideological Maginot Line which has been constructed to stop an openly revolutionary brand of illiberalism ever again achieving credibility. It speaks a language of 'rights' – rights of ethnic peoples, rights to a culture – which addresses deep-seated and understandable fears about the erosion of identity and tradition by the globalizing (but only partially homogenizing) forces of high modernity. It is a discourse which has grown in sophistication thanks to the theorists of communitarianism,[39] ethnopluralism, and differentialism, and in legitimacy in the context of justified concerns over cultural globalization. The ground for its widespread acceptance as a familiar and genuine (if unwelcome) member of the liberal ideological family rather than the offspring of a highly fecund anti-liberal cuckoo, has been well prepared by liberalism's long history of contamination by prejudices which have denied entire groups access to the rights it upholds as 'sacred': women, the poor, children, the handicapped, the nomad, the allophone, the aboriginal, the 'primitive'. If the battle cry of liberalism in theory is Rousseau's 'All [human beings] are born equal and everywhere they live in chains' then its slogan in practice has been Orwell's 'All men are equal but some are more equal than others' (a phrase which is often conveniently identified with the authoritarian 'other' rather than 'our' own brand of totalitarianism).

The Front National, the FPÖ, the Lega Nord, the Vlaamsblok, the Republikaner, the Centrumpartei, the Scandinavian Progress parties, and scores of openly xenophobic parties which have emerged in the countries of the former Soviet Empire[40] vary considerably in their programmes and aspirations, and most can sincerely claim to have nothing to do with historic fascism in the conventional sense of the word. Yet in a world inoculated against openly revolutionary varieties of palingenetic ultranationalism, their axiomatic rejection of multi-culturalism, their longing for 'purity', their nostalgia for a mythical world of racial homogeneity and clearly demarcated boundaries of cultural differentiation, their celebration of the ties of blood and history over reason and a common humanity, their rejection of *ius soli* for *ius sanguinis*, their solvent-like abuse of history represent a reformist version of the same basic myth. It is one which poses a more serious threat to liberal democracy than fascism because it is able to disguise itself, rather like a stick insect posing as a twig to catch its prey. It was arguably because Zhirinovsky's Liberal Democratic Party blended fascism with ethnocratic liberalism that he made such an impact on Russian politics in 1993, even if events since have shown that it is the militarist/imperialist perversion of liberalism familiar from nineteenth-century Europe which still retains hegemony. It was his exploitation of ethnocratic liberalism, not fascism, which enabled Milosovic to carry out ethnic cleansing for years under the gaze of an international community mesmerized by the (procedurally speaking) democratic consensus on which he based his actions. The total number of victims of the calculated atrocities against non-Serbs which resulted far outweighs that of all the outrages committed by post-war fascists put together, suggesting that ethnocratic liberalism has replaced fascism as the form of radical right best adapted to the realities of the modern world.

The Third Reich's citizenship laws distinguished between Germans and non-Germans, but at least the Nazis had never made a secret of their contempt for what one of their number dismissed in 1925 as 'the Jewish-liberal-democratic-Marxist-humanitarian mentality'. He went on: 'as long as there is even a single minute tendril which connects our programme with this root then it is doomed to be poisoned and hence to wither away to a miserable death'.[41] Ethnocratic liberals have genetically modified the radical right so that it thrives in the very soil which once would have been poisonous to it. What are their long-term prospects for success, in the face of the 'ecological' purists within liberalism constantly seeking to cleanse it of toxic additives? Take the way Tudjman's ethnocratic liberal party was eventually ousted by centre-left forces in Croatia.[42] Fukuyamians might read this as a sign that history is still on course for achieving the undisputed hegemony of liberal capitalism which will give birth to the bottomless *ennui* of the 'last man'. A host of less sanguine social scientists such as Anthony Giddens and Zygmunt Bauman would suggest instead a Manichean view which sees contemporary history as a permanent battleground between forces tending to realize liberalism's project of a global humanity and those seeking to thwart and corrupt it. We will continue to live in interesting times.

I must side with the Manicheans. The modern world is not an interregnum, but it is an endgame, one being continually played out, like the eternal recurrence of world snooker competitions and European cup football on British TV, super-imposing a cyclic pattern on rectilinear history. 'It is only our concept of time which causes us to use the phrase The Last Judgment: actually it is a court in permanent session.'[43] Now that millennium hysteria has died down, it might become easier to see that the last act being constantly performed in our age has nothing to do with a particular date or a technological glitch, or even a final reckoning between liberalism and the conveniently alien ideological 'other' provided by fascism, communism, or fundamentalism. Instead it is between genuinely liberal versions of democracy open to global humanitarian and eco-logical perspectives on the one hand, and radical right versions on the other which exploit the profound ambiguity of the concept 'demos'. Nor is it necessary for openly radical right political formations such as the National Front or the Liberal Democratic Party of Russia to triumph for liberalism to be corroded by the ethnocentrism which they represent. Given the evidence of contemporary Europe's continuing implication in forces which, according to some reliable humanitarian monitoring agencies, are generating mounting structural poverty and ecological depredation in the 'South', it is possible to see 'actually existing' liberal Europe not just as a socio-economic fortress, but as an ethno-cultural one as well, protected by ramparts being continually reinforced. It is a concentration of ethnocentric power which, though liberal in its domestic politics, continues to operate prevalently as a radical right-wing force in terms of its total impact on the global community.

The effect of propaganda put out by ethnocratic ideologues and parties can only reinforce this tendency, no matter how marginalized they are from actual government, making it even more impossible for politicians to present populations with policies which would involve a substantial transfer of wealth and resources (back) from the North to the South or address the structural reasons for mount-ing immigratory pressures, for fear of the mass dissent it would arouse. The next few decades should decide whether a healthy liberalism can prevail or whether, in the midst of a deteriorating environment and escalating demographic explo-sion which the new millennium inherits from the old, its contamination takes a permanent hold. Meanwhile, one of the messages transmitted by the protesters against the World Trade Organization in Seattle in the autumn of 1999 for those who habitually treat the radical-right as 'out there' is that it might also be already in our midst. If the radical right is based on a malfunction of human empathy, on an affective aridity, then it might be legitimate to appropriate lines written in a very different context by T.S. Eliot, someone who managed to make the transition from fellow traveller of radical-right cosmologies to a pundit of 'high' liberal humanist culture:

> The desert is not only round the corner.
> The desert is squeezed into the tube-train next to you,
> The desert is in the heart of your brother.[44]

Notes and references

1 *Pensiamo l'Italia: il domani c'è già. Valori, idee e progetti per l'Alleanza Nazionale. Tesi Politiche approvate dal congresso di Fiuggi*, Rome, On Line System, 1995, p. 11. For more on the AN's ambiguous embrace of democracy, see R. Griffin, 'The post-fascism of the Alleanza Nazionale: a case-study in ideological morphology', *Journal of Political Ideologies*, 1996, Vol. 1, pp. 107–46.

2 Quoted in C. De Cesare, *Il Fascista del Duemila*, Milan, Kaos Edizioni, 1995, p. 106. For a more sceptical view of the sincerity of the MSI conversion to democracy, see Piero Ignazi, *Postfascisti?*, Bologna, Il Mulino, 1994.

3 A phrase from Faust's monologue in the first scene of Goethe's *Urfaust*.

4 See especially the impressive country-by-country survey in S.U. Larsen and B. Hagtvet (eds), *Modern Europe after Fascism*, New York, Columbia University Press, 1998.

5 One of the best surveys of the conceptual complexities posed by the term 'right' is still R. Eatwell (ed.), *The Nature of the Right*, London, Pinter, 1989.

6 See, for example, the debate over the comparative value of the terms 'fascism' and 'radical right', in D. Prowe, ' "Classic" fascism and the new radical right in Western Europe: comparisons and contrasts', *Contemporary European History*, November 1994, Vol. 3, pp. 289–313. For another perspective on the word-field associated with the radical right, see Herbert Kitschelt, *The Radical Right in Western Europe: A Comparative Analysis*, Ann Arbor MI, University of Michigan Press, 1995, Chapter 1.

7 C. O'Maoláin, *The Radical Right: A World Directory*, London, Longman, 1987.

8 For a fuller account, see the 'General introduction' to R. Griffin, *International Fascism: Theories, Causes and the New Consensus*, London, Arnold, 1998. The latest (unwitting) convert to the consensus is A.J. Gregor, as shown in his latest book on generic fascism, *Phoenix*, New Brunswick, Transaction Publishers, 1999, in which he refers to it as a 'tortured, enraged, and passionate demand for national renewal' (p. 162). For independent corroboration of the existence of this necessarily partial and contested consensus, see Stanley Payne's review article, 'Historical fascism and the radical right', *Journal of Contemporary History*, 2000, Vol. 35, pp. 109–11.

9 See R. Griffin, 'Party time: Nazism as a temporal revolution', *History Today*, 1999, Vol. 49.

10 See particularly R. Griffin, *Fascism*, Oxford, Oxford University Press, 1995.

11 The only real exception to this generalization is the explosion of radical right groups both extra-systemic (some fascist) and others ostensibly democratic (ethnocratic), which took place in Russia in the 1990s. Though safely marginalized by the system, the sheer variety of them and the dramatic, though predictably short-lived, rise to international prominence of Zhirinovsky's Liberal Democratic Party underline the dependency on conditions of acute systemic crisis for radically palingenetic and ethnocratic forms of the right to achieve a popular resonance. Even in post-unification Germany and pre-democracy South Africa the radical right, though violent, remained safely marginalized, because in both cases populist palingenetic hopes for the rebirth of the country were projected onto liberal democracy/capitalism and channelled within the parliamentary system.

12 Kevin Coogan, *Dreamer of the Day*, New York, Autonomedia, 1999, pp. 317–24.

13 'Europe for the Europeans: the fascist vision of the new Europe', Humanities Research Centre Occasional Paper, No. 1, Oxford, Oxford Brookes University, 1994, available at <http://www.brookes.ac.uk/schools/humanities/staff/europ.txt>.

14 M.A. Ledeen, *Universal Fascism*, New York, Howard Fertig, 1972.

15 R.E. Herzstein, *When Nazi Dreams Come True*, London, Abacus, 1982.

16 Oswald Mosley, *The Alternative*, Wiltshire, Mosley Publications, 1947.

17 E.g., 'Sui presupposti spirituali e strutturali dell'unità europea', in *Europa Nazione*, January 1951, Vol. 1, No. 1. For a collection of Evola's highly influential essays on the

130   *Roger Griffin*

European empire, see Part One of J. Evola, *Saggi di Dottrina Politica*, Genoa, Dioscuri, 1989.
18 Maurice Bardèche, *Qu'est-ce que le fascisme?*, Paris, Les Sept Couleurs, 1961.
19 Francis Yockey, *Imperium*, n.p., Truth Seeker Press, 1962. See Coogan, *Dreamer of the Day*, which locates the book in its context of the fascist international and projects for a new Europe.
20 See Coogan, *Dreamer of the Day*, Chapters 30–36.
21 See ibid., Chapters 45–48. A highly influential expression of the ideology of Universal Nazism is *The Turner Diaries*, written (under a pseudonym) by William Pierce, leader of the neo-Nazi National Alliance; for a sample, see Griffin, *Fascism*, pp. 372–4.
22 See N. Lowles and Steve Silver (eds), *White Noise*, London, Searchlight, 1998.
23 The most famous example is the Christian Identity movement, which makes extensive use of the Internet. The characteristic blend of Christianity with a Universal Nazi ethos can also be sampled at the website of 'Kingdom Identity Ministries' at <http://www. kingidentity/com>.
24 See Jeffrey Kaplan, *Radical Religion in America*, New York, Syracuse University Press, 1997.
25 For a flavour of Third Positionist ideology and its sophisticated use of the Internet see the NRF's website at <www.nationalbolshevik.com/nrf/nrfindex.html>. Another Third Positionist *groupuscule* is Groupe Union Défense, whose ideology is discussed in R. Griffin, 'GUD reactions: the patterns of prejudice of a neo-fascist *groupuscule*', *Patterns of Prejudice*, April 1999, Vol. 33, No. 2. The tendency to extreme eclecticism so typical of fascist ideology is explored in R. Eatwell, 'Towards a new model of generic fascism', *Journal of Theoretical Politics*, 1992, Vol. 4, No. 2.
26 See Griffin, 'GUD reactions'.
27 Deborah Lipstadt, *Denying the Holocaust*, New York, Free Press, 1993.
28 E.g., Ernst Nolte, *Der europäische Bürgerkrieg*, Berlin, Proyläen Verlag, 1987; David Irving, *Hitler's War*, London, Hodder and Stoughton, 1977, the text at the centre of the libel case which Irving brought against Professor Lipstadt and lost so ignominiously in April 2000.
29 See Pierre-André Taguieff, *Sur la Nouvelle Droite*, Paris, Descartes & Cie, 1994; R. Griffin, 'Between metapolitics and *apoliteia*: the New Right's strategy for conserving the fascist vision in the "interregnum"', *Modern and Contemporary France*, 2000, Vol. 8, pp. 35–53; R. Griffin, 'Plus ça change! The fascist pedigree of the Nouvelle Droite', in Edward Arnold (ed.), *The Development of the Radical Right in France, 1890–1995*, London, Routledge, 2000.
30 See the website of *The Scorpion* at <http://www.stormloader.com/thescorpion>.
31 Horacio Cagni, 'Assenza di Dio e vitalismo tragico nel facismo', *Trasgressioni*, January–August 1995, Vol. 20, pp. 3–29.
32 This would appear to be true of two intellectuals who in the past have worked tirelessly to establish the New Right as the major current of radical right thought in their respective countries: Alain de Benoist (France) and Marco Tarchi (Italy), even if they are still associated with publications which betray the persistence of a belief in the 'interregnum' and its eventual dissolution in a new age.
33 An outstanding example of the richness and diversity of New Right cultural production was provided by Italy in the 1970s and 1980s: see especially M. Revelli, 'La nuova destra', in F. Ferraresi (ed.), *La destra radicale*, Milan, Feltrinelli, 1984; and P. Bologna and E. Mana (eds), *Nuova destra e cultura reazionaria negli anni ottanta*, Notiziario dell'Istituto storico della Resistenza in Cuneo, No. 23, 1983.
34 See Coogan, *Dreamer of the Day*, for an impressively researched exploration of just one 'story' in the internationalization of post-war fascism, its extraordinary ideological diversity and earnestness, and the bizarre fantasy world which some fascists still inhabit while they wait for the 'interregnum' to close.

35 On Eliade's time as an ideologue of the Iron Guard, see Coogan, *Dreamer of the Day*, pp. 318–26.

36 E.g., Hans-George Betz, *Radical Right-Wing Populism in Western Europe*, London, Macmillan, 1994; Herbert Kitschelt, *The Radical Right in Western Europe*, Ann Arbor MI, University of Michigan Press, 1995.

37 For more on this concept, see R. Griffin, 'Last rights?', in S. Ramet (ed.), *The Radical Right in Central and Eastern Europe*, Pennsylvania PA, Pennsylvania State University Press, 1999.

38 An allusion to Julien Benda's classic study of the European intelligentsia's betrayal of the humanist tradition in the interwar period, *La Trahison des Clercs*, Paris, Grasset, published in 1927.

39 For an excellent essay which underlines the anti-liberal thrust of communitarian notions of culture, see Z. Bauman's introduction to the reprint of his *Culture as Practice*, London, Sage, 1999, pp. xxxiii–xlv.

40 See Ramet, *The Radical Right*.

41 See Griffin, *Fascism*, pp. 118–19.

42 Since writing, an impressive wave of international and national protest was unleashed by Jörg Haider's success in manoeuvering the (ethnocratic but not fascist) Austrian Freedom Party into power as part of a coalition government in February 2000.

43 Franz Kafka, 'Betrachtungen über Sünde, Leid, Hoffnung und den wahren Weg' (No. 40), in *Hochzeitsvorbereitungen auf dem Lande und andere Prosa aus dem Nachlass Betrachtungen*, Frankfurt am Main, Fischer Verlag, 1980, p. 33.

44 T.S. Eliot, Choruses from 'The Rock', *Selected Poems*, London, Faber and Faber, 1961, p. 109.

9 Power and vacuity
Nationalist ideology in the twentieth century

Andrew Vincent

Nationalist ideology has had a tortured and complex relationship with twentieth-century politics and still appears as a crucial driving force into the twenty-first century. However, in discussing it, in retrospective terms, at the dawn of a new century, it is important to realize that the legacy of nationalist ideology constitutes a continuous strained debate and practice from the early nineteenth century. The twentieth-century experience of nationalism is thus partly configured in the nineteenth century. In assessing nationalism, we ignore this longer-term history at our cost. Most of the nationalist controversies and political practices which have figured during the late twentieth century, have been echoes of those from the nineteenth century. Many contemporary nationalist movements have not outgrown the powerful myths and aspirations of the earlier nineteenth-century debates. The fierce nationalist myths, fantasies and aspirations – lovingly embodied in lexicography, historical writing, painting, poetry, literature and monuments during the nineteenth century – which then boiled over, in many cases, in the conflagration of the First World War, arose once again, phoenix-like, from the flames (literal flames in many cases) in the closing decades of the twentieth century. Old agendas were still very much the present realities of the 1980s and 1990s. Old national battles of the nineteenth and early twentieth century were being refought with rekindled hatreds.

The same point would hold for many anti- and postcolonial nationalisms of the twentieth century. The national renewal of postcolonial regimes in Africa or Asia during the twentieth century was, in part, also a recovery of national myths promulgated, or, in some cases, foisted onto earlier history. The language of national recovery, in postcolonial terms, was itself also partly adopted from the European political vocabularies of the colonial and imperial era. There is a sense in which nationalism always contains its own self-fulfilling historical prophecy, wherever it occurs. In effect, it commandeers history and tradition to establish its own existence and ineffable continuity with the past. All history therefore becomes literally the history of the nation.

During the twentieth century there have been two broad approaches to nationalism both within political and historical studies to date, as well as in the apprehensions of ordinary citizens of most states. One approach has been generally uneasy with nationalism. This sense of unease was profoundly affected in most European states (and in some Asian states like Japan) – on theoretical and practical levels – by the events surrounding the Second World War. Thus, for many, national socialism, fascism and extreme authoritarianism marked out early to mid-twentieth-century nationalism for specific abhorrence. Many commentators, from the 1930s period up to 1989, consequently saw nationalism as an unduly narrow, tribalist, potentially totalitarian, and inherently irrationalist and bellicose doctrine. Furthermore, liberal, Marxist and social democratic theories in this same period (particularly post-1945), self-consciously developed more internationalist or cosmopolitan stances. This was the era of the setting up of the significantly titled United Nations. The only exceptions to this anti-nationalist process, for some, were the various anti-colonial nationalisms, which had an emancipatory imprimatur.

The second approach to nationalism dates originally from the early nineteenth century and the first inception of the ideology. This sees a positive social, political and economic value in nationalism. In nineteenth-century writers such as Mazzini, Renan and J.S. Mill, amongst others, there was a strong sense of civic liberation attached to nationalism. Nationalism implied the emancipation of cultures from large-scale empires and oppressive political structures. Yet, the later nineteenth century, and particularly the early twentieth century, also saw the growth of authoritarian, conservative, extreme and radical right and later fascist forms of nationalism. This latter development, in many ways, delivered a body blow to the 'liberal' or simple-minded emancipatory civic patina of earlier nationalist ideology. Liberation and self-determination were still embedded in the argument, but the focus had shifted to something far more opaque and politically unpredictable.

However, two additional factors in recent years have highlighted the profile of nationalism in contemporary politics. Paradoxically, most current positive claims for nationalism now acknowledge that it embodies a cluster of perspectives. In this sense, it is accepted by most proponents of twentieth-century nationalism that there are ideological variations, both civic and liberal-minded as well as racist, insular and bellicose forms. These complex variants were not envisaged by the early- to mid-nineteenth-century ideologists of nationalism. Thus, nationalist ideology in the twentieth century appears as a much more varied and complex pattern of thought than previously imagined. Secondly, many have also seen a link between forms of nationalism and liberal ideological values like freedom, democracy and popular sovereignty. Consequently, since the collapse of the Berlin wall in 1989, and the changing political landscape of international and domestic politics, there has been once again a surge of theoretical and practical interest in nationalism in the Western academic environment. Not only are vast amounts being written about it, from both empirical and ideological perspectives, but it has once again become a central player in world politics. The fundamental flaw and problem in this post-1989 post-communist interest in nationalism is that very little of it has been civic or liberal in practice. If anything, the bulk of the nationalism seen, for example, in Europe in the last decade has been quite markedly insular and deeply xenophobic in character.

This historical practice thus runs totally contrary to much of the more optimistic liberal-minded academic writing about nationalism.

However, this is but one of a number of deep paradoxes running through nationalist ideology in the twentieth century. Historically, nationalism is a comparatively recent historical phenomenon. Conversely, one of its central substantive claims has been its longevity and antiquity. Further, nationalists often identify the roots of nationalism within nature. This arises out of the semantics of the word nation. Yet it is clear from even the most cursory study of the subject that nationalism is a comparatively modern artefact. In fact, for some, nationalism equates with modernity. It is largely a phenomenon of the late nineteenth and twentieth centuries. In addition, nationalism is in the peculiar position of claiming a universality for its ideas, yet the ideology only makes sense in terms of its particularity and localism. Finally, and most significantly, there is the problem of, on the one hand, the immense power of nationalism in this and the last century in the actual practice of politics, coupled with, on the other hand, nationalism's oft remarked theoretical naivety. These paradoxes appear throughout this essay.

Ideology and terminology

Any discussion of nationalism implies some form of identification or minimal definition about exactly what is being discussed. How else could one distinguish nationalist from other types of social movement. This is where we encounter the first major problem. From its inception in the European political vocabulary in the early nineteenth century, there has been little solid or consensual agreement as to what is being spoken about. Admittedly, virtually all political concepts are subject to some contestation, however, there is something more to nationalism's problem with conceptual identity which needs to be accounted for. There is, in fact, a constellation of interrelated problems here which hamper any discussion of nationalism. In the short span of this essay I will only note most of these in passing.

The first problem concerned the *semantics* of the word nation. The word nation derives from the Latin terms *nasci* (to be born) and *natio* (belonging together by birth or place of birth). The initial commonplace sense of *natio* is thus concerned with people related by birth or birthplace. One important connotation of this point is that such a birthplace provides the groundwork for a sense of a 'natural' form of human association. *Prima facie*, one can begin to appreciate immediately the difficulties of categorizing nations – as etymologically related to nature or natural – as human artefacts. The critic who considers that nations are political artefacts or fictions can be fighting on a number of fronts, not least semantics. The link between nation and nature is exemplified in the quasi-biological patina of some discussions of nationalism, particularly ethnic nationalism. Sociobiologists have not been slow to pick up this theme.[1] However, deep scepticism is expressed on this issue by other commentators. In fact, the oddity of this latter point can be brought out further with an often-used synonym for nation, namely, culture. Recent academic commentators who have focused on nationalist thought, such as Will Kymlicka, Joseph Raz, Avishai Margalit and Kai Nielsen, amongst others, all dwell upon nationalism as 'culture'. Indeed, for Kai Nielsen, 'all nationalisms are cultural nationalisms of one kind or another'.[2] Kymlicka also remarks that ' "a culture" [is] . . . synonymous with "a nation" '.[3] This use of culture, *qua* nation, is unusually narrow and stipulative. The notion of culture itself also remains profoundly unclear. However, minimally, culture is not usually directly linked to nature. In fact, it is usually regarded as a primary human artefact and separate from natural causation. In this sense, to make culture and nation synonymous completely undermines any link between *nation* and any *natural* sense of human association. For some, there is no problem here, for other nationalists it is of crucial significance.

The question concerning semantics and the naturalness of nationalism is closely linked to a second problem, concerning the *origin* of nationalist ideology which has been a matter of profound and ongoing argument during the twentieth century. Logically, if one accepts the supposition that the nation is natural in some way, then it follows that the origins will lie in the remote prehistory of humanity. Nation becomes a synonym for a remote tribe or kinship group. One does not have to look far into most nationalist assertions during the twentieth century to find this kind of claim being asserted time and again. The claims of certain national groups to specific territories, as part of their ancient spiritual heritage, is grist to the mill of twentieth-century nationalist conflict. The nation is thus seen as a concept of immemorial antiquity, virtually, in some cases, identifiable with a genetically-based social instinct in human beings.

The debate over origins is by no means resolved in this pre-historical thesis, since, ironically, a large majority of commentators on nationalist ideology, in fact, do not accept it. At most, some argue that nationalism is a premodern, rather than a pre-historical ideology. This in turn weakens the naturalistic claim. Thus, in an attempt to identify the origins of nationalism, some commentators have focused on medieval Europe, although usually only in terms of the etymology of the word nation.[4] Others see national identity developing in the fifteenth or sixteenth centuries in Britain.[5] One recent nationalist exponent has remarked that 'The distinctiveness of nations was, long before 1789, advanced as a reason why they ought to live under their own kings subject to their own laws'. Thus, it is 'quite irrelevant that the term "nationalism" as a term of art in political theory comes into general usage only in the nineteenth century'.[6] Hans Kohn, the doyen of post-1945 commentators on nationalism, focused on the early 1600s as the seedbed of nationalist ideas, although he saw this as a more unconscious form of national awareness.[7] The Enlightenment of the eighteenth century is another favoured interpretation.[8] Lord Acton favoured the 1772 partition of Poland as the groundwork for both Polish and European nationalism.[9] The more popular inception is the period leading up to and immediately after the French Revolution.[10] Others, like Elie Kedourie, have traced nationalism to the revolutions in eighteenth-century German philosophy, particularly thinkers such as Kant, Fichte, Schlegel, Schleiermacher and Arndt. Finally, some historians have argued that nationalism is very much a product of the early nineteenth century. Hobsbawm, for example, claims that the modern usage of nationalism, as distinct from ethnicity, is in fact comparatively recent. It probably only dates from the 1830s, although some aspects of its populist meanings were traceable to the American and French Revolutions. This latter point more or less corresponds with the thrust of Ernest Gellner's, and to some extent Benedict Anderson's, ground-breaking work, which also presents nationalism as a modern term corresponding with the growth and modernization of states in the nineteenth century.[11] Anthony Smith's work is a form of *via media* between premodernist and modernist claims, asserting, in short, that early ethnicity is subtly transformed into modern nationalism. Smith thus argues that ethnicity is an essential preliminary to full-blown modern nationalism. Nations drew out and developed the ways in which members of *ethnie* associated and communicated. Unlike Ernest Gellner's and Benedict Anderson's stress on the modernity of nationalism, Smith emphasizes its continuity with the past, although he recognizes that certain profound changes transform *ethnie* into nationalisms.[12] Overall there is little or no consensus over this historical origin.

A third issue focuses on the *coherence* of the terminology of nation and nationalism. For example, no one would deny the word nation, as a noun, appeared first in English and French in approximately the fourteenth century. Its usage was relatively commonplace in certain more literary circles, although what exactly it connoted remains uncertain. However, as most commentators note, the term, initially, had no immediate connection with what we might term political ideology. Thus, nationalism – denoting an ideology – is often kept distinct from nation. Nationalism, as ideology, seeped into the European vocabularies in the late eighteenth and early nineteenth centuries, often, although not always, in conjunction with the state.[13] Thus many insist on a clear separation between the 'idea of the nation' and the 'ideology of nationalism'. The term nation is taken as a less protean and more descriptive term than nationalism – a form of 'registered anthropological fact', rather than an explicit political ideology. A nation can therefore exist as an empirical human community, but not coincide with an explicit avowal of an ideology called nationalism. Nationalism, as an ideology, is, for some, however, an altogether messier more inchoate term referring to 'a *process*, a kind of *sentiment* or identity, *a form of political rhetoric*, . . . a *principle* or set of principles, a kind of *social or political movement*'.[14] This argument is not only advocated by academic interpreters of nationalism, but also by many ideological proponents of nationalism. It can, for example, potentially salvage and add greater lustre to the argument concerning the antiquity of the nation – as opposed to modern rationalizations of nationalism.[15] Others again repudiate the use of both nationalism and nation. Thus, in the 1990s, David Miller directly followed J.S. Mill in the 1860s in advocating the term *nationality* as distinct from the other terms. Nationality, for Miller, avoids much of the confusing ideological baggage of the other terms.[16]

This particular issue concerning the consistency of terminology is linked to a fourth point concerning *typologies* of nations and nationalisms. The issue can be introduced via the synonym point above. One amongst a number of possible synonyms for nation is ethnicity – implying kinship, familial, blood or biological ties. Ethnicity forms the basis of the *ius sanguinis* tradition of national citizenship, as in twentieth-century German citizenship law. Citizens are identified in ethnic or blood terms. However, many nationalists have been keen to distinguish nation and ethnicity. In citizenship terminology, the distinction forms the basis for the opposite *ius soli* civic or juridical conception of the citizen, which repudiates the ethnic argument. Historians, such as Hobsbawm and Anthony Smith, as noted, also draw the terms distinct. However, nationalist ideologists, in general, have also made full use of the distinction to identify their theoretical roots. This point introduces the theme of *types* of nationalism, an issue which became central for all ideological discussion of nationalism during the twentieth century. It was particularly crucial for writers in the post-1945 era to make explicit their difference from the more ethnically based fascist and national socialist ideologies. This kind of typology concentrates on distinctive ideas and modes of thought. Thus, it has now become a commonplace in the extensive twentieth-century ideological literature, to find distinctions between ethnicity and nationalism, ethnic and civic nationalism, liberal and ethnic, liberal and cultural, civic and cultural, or, more crudely, civic and bellicose or even good and bad nationalisms. Despite the interest, during the 1990s, in liberal and civic nationalism, for many others, the more racially-orientated ethnic nationalism has been the preferable option. This would include many of the 1990s expressions of Serbian, Croatian, Kosovar nationalisms (amongst many others), as well as the radical and extreme right expressions of nationalism during the same period. In many ways, on the political ground, this latter more insular, ethnic and racial view was the more popular variant of nationalism during the last decades of the twentieth century.

Of course, one does not have to distinguish nationalisms along the above lines. Typologies of nationalism can, for example, be premised on differential nationalist *strategies*. In this context, one could distinguish unificatory and secessionist nationalisms, although the theoretical complexion of, say, two secessionist nationalisms, might well be diametrically opposed. Alternatively, one could focus on *historical* phases in the growth of nationalism, as indicating different types, and so forth. Hobsbawm, for example, identifies three phases: initially 1830–80, which was dominated by liberal nationalism; then 1880–1914 which saw a sharp movement to the conservative nationalism. Finally, the apogee of nationalism is identified with the period 1918–50.[17] It would now be an approximate rule of thumb to conclude that recent ideological discussion tends to adopt the 'belief-based' typology, usually distinguishing between civic and other forms of nationalism. However, the close of the twentieth century saw little overall consensus on this typological issue.

A fifth issue concerns differing *methods* of nationalist writing. Writings on nationalism have mutated through three main phases over the last two centuries. In the early to mid-nineteenth century, writers such as J.S. Mill, Mazzini or

Renan, stressed the political and moral dimension of nationalist ideology.[18] This was the heyday of positive, emancipatory and more liberal expressions of the ideology. Severe doubts concerning the destructive social and political effects of nationalism began to arise during the late nineteenth and early twentieth century, particularly in the context of the First World War. Nationalism for some was equated with 'jingoism' and mass psychosis. However, the period 1920–45 saw initially a new surge of interest in nationalist thought. Those who promulgated strong ideological nationalisms tended to focus on authoritarian and fascist forms. This had – as mentioned – an alienating effect on many more reflective observers. Thus, much of the academic writing on nationalism became more historical and distanced in character, while still retaining a residual interest in the ideological content. The Second World War period, 1939–45, particularly affected the whole character of this kind of work. Historians such as Hans Kohn, Hugh Seton Watson, Carlton Hayes, Alfred Cobban and Louis Snyder dominated this period.

From the 1950s, American political science eclipsed previous historical work, and the central theme of the research was premised on a commitment to empirical investigation, seeking to understand the *causal* or *empirical patterns* underpinning nationalism, rather than any ideological or historical arguments. The key methods of investigation were modernization theory, functionalism, structural-functionalism and development theories. With some rare exceptions, variants of modernization theory have informed the bulk of research on nationalism until comparatively recently. The key writers, through the 1960s and early 1970s, were academics such as David Apter, Karl Deutsch, Lucien Pye and Clifford Geertz. This form of more empirically orientated research, focused on modernization, also informed the background to the work of more recent scholars, such as Ernest Gellner, Anthony Smith and Peter Alter. It also affected a great deal of the writings on decolonization *qua* nationalism. The explicit ideology of nationalism in this period became relatively insignificant; what was of greater interest was nationalism's social and economic function.

Finally, since the events of 1989, there has been a recrudescence of arguments for the ideology of nationalism. In this sense, there has been, on the one hand, a partial return, in the 1990s, to the positive, civic and emancipatory aspirations of the 1840s' liberal nationalists. For a number of academic commentators, the ideology of nationalism, in the last decades of the twentieth century, has been seen as something to be welcomed and embraced. On the other hand, the bulk of nationalist political practice, in these same closing decades, has focused on the more insular, irrationalist and xenophobic forms of the ideology, most notably in the Balkans and Eastern Europe. It is also noteworthy that from 1945 to the present, there has also been a continuous and vigorous undercurrent across Europe of radical and extreme right variants of racially or ethnically based ideological nationalisms. However, this undercurrent has not been a major political player. It has not attained anywhere near the political unity and popular appeal that it had in the 1920s.[19]

Ideology and ideological practice

There are two further issues connected to the identification of nations and nationalism in the twentieth century which need to be discussed. One is that ideological writing on nationalism has often been different from its actual operational practice. Praising ethnic or cultural purity in an ideological text is very different from the grubby and bloody business of actual pogrom, although the text might provide the practice with a moral imprimatur. It is also an oft-noted paradoxical point that nationalist ideology, over the last two centuries, has often been *theoretically* naïve, but, at the same time, immensely powerful in political *practice*. Thus, ideological incoherence can be combined with political power. There is possibly an ideological conceit lurking here, namely, that only sound, ideologically coherent positions can have political effect. The reverse might well be the case. The second, related point – which expands and explains the first – is that the nation and nationalism may not, in fact, be fully theorizable in ideological terms. This latter point encompasses issues concerning the irrationality of nationalist ideology. Ironically, twentieth-century ideologists of nationalism have made their own contribution to this latter account. For example, the roots of the 'untheorizable' idea of the nation lie in nineteenth- and early twentieth-century romantic, vitalist and intuitivist philosophies and psychologies. Conservative and radical-right ideologies still find sustenance in the same ideas. The purported untheorizable mystery of the *Volk* is not an isolated case in nationalist literature. Many ideologies have deployed similar mythic and unanalysable concepts.[20] There are, however, a complex range of issues implicit in this 'untheoretical' point when utilized by ideologists.

First, the idea that nationalism is basically untheoretical, can elicit two responses, one positive and the other negative. The *positive* response, by ideologists of nationalism, sees the iconic mystery of the nation as that much more inviting and fruitful because it eludes all definition. For example, the quasi-religious mystery of the Serb (or any other) nation is that much more delectable when it transcends our feeble attempts at rationalization. The nation is immemorial and time out of mind.[21] The only caveat to enter here is that untheoretical does not necessarily mean irrational, in the same sense that the nonrational may not be irrational. Something which is not easily theorizable or readily embodied in rational categories is not necessarily irrational. For Margaret Canovan, for example, 'nationhood is hard to define not because it is confused and nonsensical, but because it is extremely subtle, and moreover, because . . . an element of myth is essential to it'. Thus, she continues, 'a phenomenon as complex as this is extraordinarily hard to analyse'.[22] Clarity is therefore not enough and vagueness may be embraced within an ideology. All organizations, especially the state, require some kind of collective identity or social cement. Thus there is a kind of 'ghostly presence' behind much politics. Nations are seen as powerfully present, in fact, conditionally necessary for states, yet often conceptually invisible.[23] Nations are therefore indispensable, if hard to deal with conceptually. In fact, Canovan suggests that nationalist ideology may be a stage in the evolution of the nation itself; the presence of nationalism may even mean the absence of the nation *per se*. This view is *prima facie* surprising given that the untheoretical character of nationalism is taken by other nationalist ideologists as a serious flaw.

The second *negative* response has two possible dimensions, one *external* and the other *internal* to nationalism. The *external* judgement sees nationalism as simply premised on mindless passions and irrationalism, in contrast to ideologies like liberalism which are premised on reason. Liberal theorists, like Elie Kedourie, Friedrich Hayek and Karl Popper, amongst many others in the post-1945 period, subscribed to this view. In other words, nationalism was disapproved of as an irrational tribalism. Fascist, national socialist and authoritarian national-isms were very much to the forefront of their minds in making this judgement.

The *internal* reading is promulgated by nationalist ideologists themselves, who also feel distinctly ill-at-ease with the 'untheoretical' claim. This view denies the 'untheoretical' claim and asserts the need for a rational theory of nationalism. The recent 1990s liberal nationalist writer, Yael Tamir, for example, is quite insistent on this point.[24] For her, nationalism is and ought to be theorizable. Thus, a theory of nationalism for Tamir structures itself 'independently of all contingencies. Its basis must be a systematic view of human nature and of the world order, as well as a coherent set of universally applicable values.'[25] This latter judgement is not helped by the fact that there are *no* great theoreticians of nationalist ideology. There are honorary figures, such as J.G. Fichte, Gottfried Herder, Ernest Renan, Julien Benda, amongst others, but one would hesitate to call them wholly self-conscious nationalist thinkers. The nationalist label is more of a retrospective judgement. Despite this, Tamir's general position is shared by the majority of contemporary political theorists who are interested in nationalist ideology, such as Brian Barry, David Miller, Neil MacCormick and Kai Nielsen. Thus, even Barry's more lukewarm instrumental and subjectivist view of nation-alism, nonetheless sees it clearly rooted in a theoretical conception of common history and participation in a common way of life. Nationalism is taken to be important for a stable and democratic civic society, generating trust and com-mitment.[26] Miller and Tamir identify much stronger, more objective theoretical components to the nationalist ideology than Barry.

Before turning to a brief discussion of some of these theoretical components, one further point needs to be examined. This focuses on the question: can nationalism, by definition, offer a general or universal theory of twentieth-century politics? One of the central claims, internal to nationalist argument, is that all meaning and value are particular to the nation. This is a crucial assump-tion for nationalism to work. Thus, it follows, how can the ideology offer a general or universal theory from a baseline which is by definition wholly particu-lar? If all theory (unless it is the one exception to the nationalist theory of meaning and thus the one metatheoretical truth in the world) is particular, then no theory – even a theory of nationalism – can be logically exempt. In this sense, could nationalists even have a universal view of human nature? Such a theory could not logically exist. In practice this has hamstrung all strongly nationalist-orientated movements. Thus, for example, the attempts by some in 1935 to form a fascist international foundered rapidly on this very rock of particularity.

Everything depends here on our understanding of 'theory'. Sociological, economic or more traditional anthropological theories tended to search for the causal conditions of nationalism in practice. In this sense, there could be a universal theory of nationalism – but the operative point here is that it is a theory 'of' or 'about'. Nationalism is a *social object* to be explained via, say, its economic or social function. In this reading, nationalism can be universal, since, regardless of its empty internal rhetoric, in reality, it performs other universal functional roles in particularly developing societies. This approach to nationalism was very prevalent in much mid- to late-twentieth-century writing.

However, others have contended that nationalism is not a social object, but is rather a *social subject* which has an important constitutive role in characterizing political realities. In this latter case, nationalist ideology is a normatively-inspired perspective which not only gives a descriptive account of political realities, but also prescribes what we 'ought' or 'ought not' to do. In this sense, the ideology is a form of thought-behaviour which provides both an understanding of the empirical political world and a groundwork for political action. The problem of all such ideological theorizing is its level of abstraction. Raising the level of abstraction may increase logical rigour and widen the net of explanation, but it ignores the messier or untidier aspects of day-to-day politics. Yet, to over-concentrate on the untidy particular aspects is often to thin down the rigour and consistency of the ideology. Thus, to superimpose an abstract ideology over a political event may in fact generate a distortion. For example, there are many forms of social and collective existence within which individuals are situated. Why should nationalism take priority in any such explanation? It clearly does not figure predominantly in most people's lives, except in extreme situations like war or civil conflict. So what reason can be offered for a superimposition of nationalist ideology over something which is far more complex and nuanced? One reasoned answer, which we have already canvassed, is that nationalism's non-existence in our everyday consciousness may be a sign of successful or mature nationalism; namely, it is subliminal. Yet it is difficult to see how this could be known or proved. An appeal to intuitions, common sense or the unconscious is never a very successful strategy in any process of rational argument. However, to be overly committed to the minutiae of the particular can thin down the theoretical force of the ideology. Most writings by nationalists are usually replete with the particular empirical details of political events. In fact, nationalism is theoretically committed to the significance of the particular. It is a key prop in the whole ideology. Yet, the exact line between rigorous abstract ideology and particular empirical facts is often very difficult to locate. Political ideology, in general, has this endemic problem. But nationalists, being ontologically rooted in particularity, are more subject to this pressure than other ideologies, such as liberalism or Marxism. Nationalist ideology during the twentieth century has been continually dogged by this problem.

One further reflection on the issue of nationalist ideology as a 'social subject': if ideological beliefs constitute the nation in practice then it follows that shared national characteristics *cannot* be embedded. To be embedded is by definition not to be intentionally constituted. If nationalist ideology does act constitutively, then the populace would always be reliant upon ideologists to create and feed them their nationalist pap. Nationalism itself would always be pure artifice super-imposed on idiosyncratic political affairs, even when claiming to be natural. Nationalism, in this reading, is an abstract theory, but embedded within its abstractions is a false, if effective, claim about the importance of natural embedded particulars. In this sense, nationalist ideology, throughout the twentieth century, has been an elaborate, if profoundly successful, charade.

Alternatively, nationalist beliefs could be said to be already deeply embedded in the community, in which case an appeal to an ideology called nationalism would be utterly superfluous. This is indeed one strong argument underpinning the separation, referred to earlier, between *nation* and *nationalism*, as well as one of the forceful contentions concerning the purported untheoretical character of the nation. This latter view has been held by many conservatives and radical and extreme right ideologists during the twentieth century. It has also been put forward ironically by disinterested academic theorists.[27] The problem with this embedded view is precisely the problem of particularity, mentioned earlier. How can an untheorizable embedded particular become a universal theory? I am not personally convinced that nationalist ideologists, throughout the twentieth century, have ever got round this conundrum. They have tried to in such forms as liberal nationalism, or its kissing cousin 'rooted cosmopolitanism', but ultimately they have failed to provide an adequate account.

The ideology of nationalism?

Returning to the earlier point that nationalist ideology has a definite belief content – what are these beliefs? The formal or regulative beliefs which are usually articulated are: *first*, at the most general level possible, humanity is understood to be naturally fragmented into distinct cultural or ethnic groups, each with their own historical continuity, tradition and language. Such groups are valorized or seen as significant. In this context there is also a potential link to racial theory. *Second*, the idea of independent valorized groups connects up with a strong sense of identity. Each nation expresses itself (as one writer has put it) through the 'first person plural', or a 'we saying'.[28] *Third*, the nation is also often identified with a territory, place or *Heimat* with identifiable boundaries. *Fourth*, the nation is also sovereign over any other groups, and thus the ultimate ground of legitimacy and loyalty. This sovereignty may well be an unconscious power, but it is nonetheless fundamental and foundational. *Fifth*, human beings must identify with their national culture for a meaningful existence. Other values, like freedom or autonomy, only make sense in this cultural context. *Sixth*, nations must be self determining. This list could be modified, subtracted from or added to, however, it encompasses most of the basic ideological themes. It is very important to emphasize at this point that these themes are purely formal and empty. Any nationalist, from the most liberal to the most extreme fascist, could interpret these themes from within their own perspective. In other words, the nationalist beliefs outlined above only constitute an empty skeleton awaiting the arrival of some flesh. They provide a bare outline. This can be illustrated if we analyse these themes in terms of three twentieth-century ideologies which have utilized nationalism: liberalism, conservatism and fascism.

Focusing on the first two themes, namely, that humanity is understood to be fragmented into distinct units, each with their own historical continuity, tradition and language, which leads in turn to a strong sense of identity. The core of the nationalist point here is that we are socially contextual beings. Membership of nations lets individuals transcend the constraints of time and place. It also provides a conceptual framework which permits them to comprehend their own existence within a community. We cannot be prior to society. The caveat that I wish to pursue is that the above, once said, needs to be explicated further. The above formal themes contain numerous logical substantive paths.

Taking the question of identity first: it was important for most liberal nationalists that individualism, and other such liberal values, were *embedded* in national communities. Consequently, for liberals, a social or contextual individualism – as against an atomistic individualism – was advocated. Second, for liberals national communities existed through belief, not race or ethnicity. It was *not* crucial for them that these values were pre-political. Although some liberal nationalists had a residual sense that there must be something present, most accepted that there was an element of *artifice* in nationalist thought.[29] Third, the beliefs which were constitutive of identity ought to be liberal and democratic. Thus, national identities were liberal identities. In the context of common identity, it was liberal values which were crucial.

Common identity has also been immensely important in conservative theories of nationalism throughout the twentieth century. The nation stood for the continuity and destiny of a unique community. This argument has underpinned conservative unease with the European Union during the closing decades of the twentieth century. Piety to the established order was a necessary concomitant of realizing the importance of tradition. Tradition incorporated more wisdom than any individual, since it embodied a concrete manner of life over generations. National traditions could therefore be trusted, unlike abstract theories. The national community was premised on a belief in a pre-political objective natural order. It could not be invented or imposed. This sense of being pre-established and unavailable to 'reasoned alteration' has been central to traditional conservative ideology. Conservative ideologists have however read the nature of that order differently. The more religiously-minded have seen god as the author. For previous generations of conservatives, revolution was an offence against an objective divine order. The religious reading can still be found in some conservative interpretations into the twentieth century. The more prevalent argument during the twentieth century identified the secular national tradition as the meaningful order.

For many conservative theorists, national identity was also considered organically. The organic analogy conveyed the idea that society was a mutually dependent interrelation of parts. Change or reform had to be consonant with the slow complex pace of the whole organism. Each individual had a place in the organism. This implied, for most conservatives, a natural hierarchy and inequality of rank and status. Inequality was nothing to be ashamed of. The organic analogy also implied a strong inclusive and insular sense of community which looked outward fearfully and suspiciously. The contemporary conservative writer, Roger Scruton, put this point concisely, in arguing against modern communitarians. He insisted that 'none of them [are] prepared to accept the real price of community: which is sanctity, intolerance, exclusion, and a sense that life's meaning depends upon obedience, and also on vigilance against the enemy'.[30]

The conservative idea of the strong national community therefore implied an intolerant and insular identity. Roger Scruton, using the organic analogy, doubted that there could even be a state without this *natural* sense of national identity. He thus contended that national membership should only refer to pre-political beliefs. In consequence he constructed three moments of membership: attachment, patriotism and ideology. This applied the distinction, referred to earlier, between nation and nationalism. The ideology of nationalism is therefore described as a 'kind of emergency measure, a response to external threat . . . Ideologies can be used to conscript people to an artificial unity; but they are neither substitutes for, nor friends of, the loyalties on which they mediate.'[31] Genuine national attachment cannot be recovered once lost. In a move wholly characteristic of conservative writers, Scruton insisted that national feeling arose organically. The above argument utilized the implicit distinction between *nation* and *nationalism*, the nation being deeply embedded and not available to conceptual investigation, whereas the ideology was seen as more superficial and shallow.[32] In summary, the conservative view of common identity was pre-political. It was organic, inertial and insular, premised upon an unequal hierarchy and hostile to liberal individualism.

Common identity also formed a crucial motif in twentieth-century European fascist and national socialist ideology. The common features of fascist nationalism were, first, a focus on humans as foremost creatures of strong national communities. No humans, *per se*, exist, only Germans, Frenchmen or Italians, and so forth. In many ways, this more insular and xenophobic use of nationalism was already integral to some conservative theories. Second, as in conservatism, there was an insistence on inclusive communities. True identity was found in the community of the nation and the nation was prior to the individual and any rights they might possess. As the Italian fascist Charter of Labour stated, 'The Italian nation is an organic whole having life, purposes and means of action superior in power and duration to those of individuals . . . of which it is composed'.[33] Third, nationalism was used by fascists as a counterbalance to the Marxist conceptions of class struggle and the liberal conception of civil society. Fascist nationalism prepared the nation for heroism, self-sacrifice and ultimately war. The liberal perception undermined such ambitions and weakened human endeavours in materialistic longings and time-wasting parliamentary politics.

There were however some marked differences between the German and Italian variants of national identity. With Italian fascism, national identity was a more traditional xenophobic doctrine, not unlike an extreme variant of conservatism. In national socialism, the identity expressed the *Volk* spirit and was underpinned by a biological doctrine of racial purity. To be German was to be of a particular biological *racial* stock. One explanation for these differences is the idiosyncratic intellectual heritage behind national socialism. The most important intellectual elements of this were the racial theories of Arthur de Gobineau and Houston Stewart Chamberlain.[34] These racial ideas were linked by Nazi writers with the much older romantic *Volk* traditions. The national socialist writer, Alfred Rosenberg, particularly focused on the centrality of the *Volk*, as expressed in Nordic peoples in his *The Myth of the Twentieth Century* (1930).[35] The same racial history was used by Hitler to justify his *Lebensraum* doctrine.[36]

In summary, fascist and national socialist senses of common national identity were strongly organicist, inegalitarian, and, in the national socialist case, were racially-based. Both doctrines were also anti-liberal and anti-individualistic.

The third and fourth nationalist themes concern *sovereignty* and *territory*. I will assume here, for brevity's sake, that sovereignty and territorial space are coterminous. Sovereignty usually implies dominance over a particular space and population. For liberal nationalists sovereignty, however, did not necessarily follow from nationhood, trade-offs were possible; thus federal, confederal and consociational policies were possible. Sovereignty and territory should therefore not become fetishes. In fact, many late-twentieth-century liberal nationalists, like Yael Tamir and Neil MacCormick, fought shy of firm connections between nationalism and sovereignty. Further, international justice could place limits on national sovereignty. In addition, most liberal nationalists took for granted the essentially liberal belief of mutual respect between nations.[37] The argument was that nations make up a part of our identity. Identity was deserving of respect. The principle of respect obliged us to respect that which in others constituted part of their sense of their own identity. Thus there ought to be respect between nations.[38]

Conservative and fascist nationalisms also focused, for different reasons, on the self-determining sovereign nation. However, unlike liberal nationalism, fascism and national socialism were quite self-consciously imperialistic, illiberal, irrationalist, aggressive and militaristic and premised on the superiority of the particular nations. Territory, in this context, took on a sacrosanct quality. Little respect was shown, however, to other nations' territory or sovereignty. As the Italian fascist Papini noted, 'in order to love something deeply you need to hate something else', thus, the true nationalist could not possibly be internationalist in any sense of the term.[39] Nationalism, for fascists and conservatives, implied not respect, but suspicion, contempt or hatred. In other words, such nationalism was premised upon a hierarchical or unequal understanding of nations. The sovereignty and territorial integrity of the nation could not be compromised. If anything, in a crude social Darwinist sense, weaker nations should give way to the stronger.

A similar pattern of argument occurred over the question of the fifth theme of *culture*. Liberal nationalism asserted most of the core liberal values.[40] For liberal nationalists, individual autonomy did not conflict with nationalism. The liberal nation provided a freedom-enabling context for individuals. Self-determination by nations was linked to the self-determining individuals within them. However, in conservative and fascist thought, the preference for organic analogies and strong consensual readings of community led to a profound suspicion of liberal autonomy. The individual was part of an organic whole and could not be understood except through the whole. This theme figures continuously in the twentieth-century conservative writings of Charles Maurras, T.S. Eliot, Christopher Dawson, Russell Kirk and Roger Scruton. Scruton, for example, argued that 'the liberal state is . . . a solvent of unity and therefore contains the seeds of its own destruction'. He suggested that liberalism provided only simple-minded asocial foundations, such as individual autonomy, which in the final analysis, undermined national order. He thus commented that 'as prejudice dwindles, tolerance is left unguarded . . . and falls prey to the ever-vigilant schemes of the fanatic'.[41] Thus, conservative theorists tended to exhibit a disdain for liberal individualism and its correlative, individual autonomy, as against the virtues of a more traditional community and hierarchical order.

The kind of national community envisaged by conservatives, despite its homogeneity, was also deeply unequal. Conservative theorists saw the nation as an ordered hierarchy of leaders and subjects, emphatically not a body of equal citizens. Leadership and political judgement were skills limited to the few and should be linked to the responsibilities of property ownership. Respect for an established order meant respecting the existing natural hierarchy and inequality. National order always entailed authority, authority entailed inequality and natural élites. Whereas previous generations of conservatives, like Edmund Burke and Maistre, focused on a more fixed hereditary and landed aristocracy, twentieth-century conservatives thought in terms of a broader élite – incorporating a cultural intelligentsia. For fascists, freedom also coincided with the nation. Freedom was never individualistic, and could never conflict with the ends of the nation. The stronger the national unity the richer the freedom. Freedom was therefore seen as a 'spiritual' idea, usually contrasted to the false 'grubby materialism' of liberal freedom. True freedom was an inner condition of the agent, willing the higher ends of the group. The Nazi ideologist Rosenberg was quite explicit on this point, focusing on the racial theme within German nationalism: freedom, he commented, literally meant 'fellowship of race'.[42]

Taking up the sixth theme: liberal nationalism was also focused on very specific political arrangements. National communities should provide the political conditions conducive to the secure and free development of individual citizens. Once the liberal nation had valorized the rights and freedoms of the individual, this logically entailed democratic constitutional arrangements. Nationalism thus implied liberal democracy. This could be said to have followed from the principle of self-determination. Formally, each nationality should have its own state, but it must be one embodying constitutional government, democracy and the rights of the individual. Liberal nationalism basically assumed that each nationality, large enough to survive, should be independent, but with a free constitutional demo-cratic government. The high point of this original expression of liberal national-ism could be seen at the Treaty of Versailles (1918) and more particularly in President Wilson's contemporaneous Fourteen Points. However, it was also a continuous motif amongst liberal nationalists throughout the century.

For the late-twentieth-century liberal nationalist, David Miller, national self-determination was therefore particularly significant because it corresponded to the idea of nations as active communities. Self-determination followed from the earlier identity-based argument. If people shared substantive beliefs, which were reflected in their acting representatives, then the nation could be said to act and determine itself. Nationalism and democracy were therefore linked.[43] The state was therefore 'likely to be better able to achieve its goals where its subjects form an encompassing community and conversely national communities are better able to preserve their culture and fulfil their aspirations where they have control of the political machinery in the relevant area'.[44]

However the connections between nationalism and democracy, and demo-cracy and self-determination, during the twentieth century were, to say the least, tenuous. The emphasis on hierarchy and leadership led most conser-vatives and radical-right ideologies, despite being focused on nationalism *qua* self-determination, to a deep suspicion of democracy. A nation in conservative and radical-right ideology could be self-determining and yet undemocratic. For conservatives, characteristically, perfect democracy implied perfect despotism. Ironically, fear of the mass mediocrity of democracy was also present in the liberal writings of Alexis de Tocqueville, J.S. Mill and Friedrich Hayek, as well as in a wide spectrum of European writers, such as Jacob Burkhardt, Friedrich Nietzsche, and probably most notably, Ortega y Gasset, in his *The Revolt of the Masses* (1930). Thus, the link that some have made between nationalism and democracy during the twentieth century has to be severely qualified. For conservatives, humans could not govern themselves, they needed wise guidance from national prejudice and governing elites. Freedom was not acquired through democracy. Authority and hierarchy were incompatible with popular rule. Democracy and individual self-determination implied rampant self-interest and consumerism, a destruction of the national community into an alienated atomized mass and the end of authority and civilization.[45] This would also be the root to a similar unease with multiculturalism at the end of the century.

In the early twentieth century, conservative nationalists such as Charles Maurras in France, Christopher Dawson and T.S. Eliot in Britain and Carl Schmitt in Germany were led by the same logic to criticize even limited representative parliamentary democracy. In the 1920s and 1930s, this was also a path followed by most conservatives in Germany and Italy, although it had very different consequences to France and Britain. Fascists and national socialists also ex-pressed deep contempt for liberal democracy. Nationalism was, however, used by them to bestow legitimacy on certain more oblique senses of democracy and socialism. These were often referred to in fascist writings as the 'nobler democracy' and 'nobler socialism' (*qua* national socialism). Socialism and democracy, when devoted to the primacy of the integral nation or *Volk*, were seen as superior to liberal democracy. The worst of all worlds, for the fascist, was the mutual contamination of socialism and liberal democracy.

In conclusion, therefore, the idea, which was promulgated by liberal nationalists throughout the twentieth century, that there was a substantive connection between individual self-determination, democracy and national self-determination is demonstrably false. Although liberal nationalists promulgated it, it makes little or no sense to other contemporaneous ideologies.

The above discussion only represents a snapshot of nationalist argument over the century. The analysis could have been considerably extended and illustrated much more fully. However, one important conclusion about nationalism in the twentieth century can be drawn from the above analysis. The formal themes which have been used as thematic devices to analyse twentieth-century nationalist ideology are in themselves vacuous. What makes them significant and pointed is the entry of other thicker ideologies, which carry the argument forward. Thus, in examining any of the above claims, one looks in vain for something distinctive about nationalism *in itself.* Another way of putting this is that nationalism, from its nineteenth-century inception in the European political vocabulary up to the present time, has been parasitic on other host ideologies to make any sense or headway. Nationalism, *per se*, has had no answers to any substantive political problems. It is not, in fact, equipped to answer them. It is other forms of thought (conservatism, liberalism and fascism) which have provided answers or ways of being and acting in the world. Liberalism at the close of the twentieth century was able to make considerable headway with nationalist discourse, partly because it was itself hegemonic. But this was little more than a contingent connection with nationalism; it was not an ontological connection. Nationalism is therefore in a dilemma in terms of its role in the next century. If it feels discomforted by its intellectual vacuity it can appeal to the 'untheoretical' claim – which is demonstrably theoretically weak and politically unpredictable. Alternatively, it can appeal to a rational theoretical content; yet, this content turns out to have no necessary connection with nationalism, only a contingent one.

Conclusion

Even the most casual observer of the twentieth century will have noted that nationalism has been an immensely powerful force. Yet, in spite of the surge of often anti- and post-colonial nationalisms in post-1945 Asia, Africa, India and the Middle East, some still considered, during the 1945 to 1989 period, that nationalism had had its day. This mid-century period definitely inhibited nationalist ideology and movements. The historical association of nationalism with fascism and national socialism dampened the efforts of all but the most determined enthusiasts, particularly in Europe. Post-war liberal democracy and communism presented an unholy internationalist alliance in the face of nationalism. Liberal democracies also tended to slow (and continue to do so) the effects of nationalism, through their emphasis on pluralism, tolerance and diversity within civil society. Further, the Cold War military, economic and political confrontation between the USA and USSR curtailed nationalist activity within their respective spheres of influence. Finally, the comparative material and economic prosperity of many liberal democratic regimes in the post-war era blunted the appeal of nationalism as a vehicle of protest.

However, the events of post-1989 in Europe and elsewhere have not exactly borne out the hopes of those who looked for the demise of nationalism. Many of the early-twentieth-century fears, criticisms and doubts about nationalism appear all of a sudden to be relevant again. Nationalism looks, in many East European contexts, like a rediscovered tribalism, which raises once again the horrible spectres of extreme racism, pogrom and military adventurism. Yet, paradoxically, unlike all the other twentieth-century ideologies, nationalism is still most lacking in any substantive doctrine. It tends to absorb the ethos around it. It is the ideological Janus *par excellence*. It can both be liberal and tolerant and insular and xenophobic in different idea environments.

The role of nationalism in twenty-first-century politics remains uncertain. There are two key pressures which will determine the shape and character of nationalist ideology into the next century. These are the pressures of globalism and localism. In terms of globalism, the rapid post-1960s growth of international trade and international trade treaties (like GATT); international financial organizations (as in the IMF and World Bank); international legal, political and military organizations (like the United Nations, human rights conventions, the International Court of Human Rights, and NATO); the vast increases in international travel and migration; the growth of international electronic communication, in terms of the Internet and e-mail; and the enormous increases in intergovernmental and non-governmental agencies, have all subtly changed the character of the national state.[16] In Europe, the growth of European institutions, legal, military, monetary and trade processes, and so forth, have also been part of this process.

Nationalism can move in two directions in the face of these globalizing developments. Firstly, it is an ideal vehicle for expressing anxiety. Recent nationalist growth in industrialized and developing countries could well be more a result of factors like a sense of displacement in the face of swift global socio-economic change. In other words, nationalism could still function as a reactive attitude, which expresses feelings of unease with disruptive economic and social change, which states appear unable to fully control. The second direction could be for nationalism to become an increasingly irrelevant, anachronistic and inappropriate vehicle of such expression. This latter possibility might well be fuelled by the second, more localized, pressure of multiculturalism and new social movements.

Both multiculturalism and new social movements, particularly the former, present the most awkward problem for nationalism, partly because they arise internally out of the same generic structure of thought as nationalism itself. The same logic which drives nationalism, in all its shapes, also drives movements like multiculturalism. There is an assumption, within nationalism, of the need and crucial role of a common culture, language and/or sense of identity. Despite the importance of this claim, its coherence, *qua* multiculturalism and multinationalism is implicitly undermined from within. Thus, the very existence and recognition of secession movements within nation-states, and the simple fact of multinational and polyethnic states across the globe, shakes the singular consensual nationalist argument at its foundations. It is a fact that within virtually all world states there are many cultural groups and subnationalities, which could be said to have some form of group right, based on language or culture. Even within such subnational or ethnic groups themselves there are further minorities, which might again demand – by the same logic – group rights, protection, tolerance and even a right of exit. This point extends to new social movements. We can see the seeds here of further fragmentation, although, again, it is important to realize that the logic of the argument for social and cultural implosion derives from within nationalism. Nationalism has few resources to deal with this argument, because these very resources are the same as those of multiculturalism. In this context nationalism looks profoundly vulnerable.

Notes and references

1 See J.G. Kellas, *Politics of Nationalism and Ethnicity*, New York, St Martin's Press, 1991.
2 Kai Nielsen, 'Cultural nationalism, neither ethnic nor civic', in R. Beiner (ed.), *Theorizing Nationalism*, Albany NY, State University of New York Press, 1999, p. 127.
3 Consequently, a society is multicultural if and only if 'its members either belong to different nations (a multination state), or have emigrated from different nations (a polyethnic state), and if this fact is an important aspect of personal identity and political life', see W. Kymlicka, *Multicultural Citizenship: A Liberal Theory of Minority Rights*, Oxford, Clarendon Press, 1995, p. 18.
4 The Faculty of Arts of many medieval universities was divided administratively into 'nations' for voting purposes, according to place of birth, see Louis Snyder, *Meaning of Nationalism*, New Brunswick NJ, Rutgers University Press, 1954, p. 29; Boyd Shafer, *Faces of Nationalism: New Realities Old Myths*, New York, Harcourt Brace Jovanovich, 1972, p. 14; Anthony Black, *Political Thought in Europe 1250–1450*, Cambridge, Cambridge University Press, 1993, p. 91.
5 Liah Greenfeld in an immensely detailed and scholarly book focuses on nationalism as an élite phenomenon which arose in England in the early sixteenth century in the reign of Henry VIII. In France, Russia, and Germany it also predated industrialization and modernization, see Liah Greenfeld, *Nationalism: Five Roads to Modernity*, Cambridge MA, Harvard University Press, 1992.
6 Neil MacCormick, *Legal Rights and Social Democracy: Essays in Legal and Political Philosophy*, Oxford, Clarendon Press, 1982, pp. 256 and 260.
7 Hans Kohn, *The Idea of Nationalism: A Study in its Origins and Background*, New York, Macmillan, 1945, p. 4.
8 See Andrzej Walicki, *Enlightenment and the Birth of Modern Nationhood*, Notre Dame, Indiana, University of Notre Dame Press, 1989.
9 See Lord Acton, 'Nationality', in J.E.E.D. Acton, *History of Freedom and Other Essays* London, Macmillan, 1907.

10 See Anthony Smith, *Nationalism in the Twentieth Century*, Canberra, Australian National University, 1979, p. 1; Kohn, *The Idea of Nationalism*, p. 3, although Kohn does see strong elements of what he calls an 'unconscious nationalism', predating the French Revolution; Snyder, *Meaning of Nationalism*, p. 29; Kedourie also places a strong emphasis on the French Revolution in conjunction with certain crucial philosophical ideas, in Elie Kedourie, *Nationalism*, second edition, London, Hutchinson, 1974, p. 12; J. Mayall, *Nationalism and International Society*, Cambridge, Cambridge University Press, 1990, p. 43; E. Kamenka, introduction to *Nationalism: The Nature and Evolution of an Idea*, London, Edward Arnold, 1976, p. 4; I. Berlin, *The Crooked Timber of Humanity*, London, John Murray, 1990, p. 244.

11 E. Hobsbawm, *Nations and Nationalism since 1780: Programme, Myth and Reality*, Cambridge, Cambridge University Press, 1992; Ernest Gellner, *Nations and Nationalism*, Oxford, Blackwell, 1983.

12 See B. Anderson, *Imagined Communities: Reflections on the Origin and Spread of Nationalism*, London, Verso, 1983; Gellner, *Nations and Nationalism*, and Anthony Smith, *The Ethnic Origins of Nationalism*, Oxford, Blackwell, 1986.

13 Nationalism, from this period, suggested that there was such a thing as a form of collective consciousness embedded in a community of people, which was formed through cultural or linguistic (and later ethnic) identity. This collective consciousness was linked by some with the state, although, as mentioned, in early seminal writers like Herder, it had no such linkage.

14 See Wayne Norman, 'Theorizing nationalism (normatively): first steps', in Beiner (ed.) *Theorizing Nationalism*, p. 56.

15 This for example would be a favoured argument in many conservative writers who would not want to emphasize the rational or ideological nature of nationalism.

16 David Miller, *On Nationality*, Oxford, Clarendon Press, 1995.

17 Hobsbawm, *Nations and Nationalism since 1780*.

18 The only partial exceptions to this were Karl Marx and Friedrich Engels and the tradition which derived from them. The Marxist interest in nationalism was primarily driven by concerns in political economy. Nationalism was seen as a contingent phenomenon appearing at a particular stage of economic development. However, the paradox in the twentieth century is that many apparently Marxist and anti-colonial movements – like those in Vietnam – were really nationalist movements in all but name, something that was never really resolved in the Cold War Marxist mind.

19 See the chapter by Roger Griffin 'Interregnum or endgame? The radical right in the "post-fascist" era' in this volume.

20 For example, the 'general strike' in syndicalism or 'immemorial tradition' in conservatism.

21 See for example, Tim Judah, *The Serbs*, New Haven CT, Yale University Press, 1997, pp. 43–7.

22 See Margaret Canovan, 'The skeleton in the cupboard: nationhood, patriotism and limited loyalties', in Beiner (ed.) *Theorizing Nationalism*.

23 M. Canovan, *Nationalism and Political Theory*, Cheltenham, Edward Elgar, 1996, p. 68. For Canovan, for liberal justice and distribution to flourish, boundaries, powers and jurisdictions must be presupposed. John Rawls's whole theory is thus seen to be shot through with tacit assumptions.

24 Yael Tamir, 'Theoretical difficulties in the study of nationalism', in Beiner (ed.) *Theorizing Nationalism*, p. 67.

25 Yael Tamir, *Liberal Nationalism*, Princeton NJ, Princeton University Press, 1993, p. 82.

26 See Brian Barry, 'Self-government revisited' in David Miller and Larry Seidentop (eds) *The Nature of Political Theory*, Oxford, Clarendon Press, 1983, pp. 121–54.

27 See M. Canovan, 'Is there an Arendtian case for the nation state?' in *Contemporary Politics*, 1999, Vol. 5, No. 2, pp. 103ff.

28 See Roger Scruton, 'First person plural' in Beiner (ed.) *Theorizing Nationalism*, pp. 279–94.

29 However, for David Miller, there has to be some shared substantive beliefs for nationalism to exist and it is not something which can be simply conjured out of thin air. Thus, Miller still sees a pre-political element to nationalism, which forms a precondition to politics. Yet, he also contends that national values can be deliberately fostered through public education. This can shape cultural identities in the direction of common citizenship.

30 Roger Scruton, 'In defence of the nation' in R. Scruton, *The Philosopher on Dover Beach*, London, Carcanet Press, 1990, p. 310.

31 Ibid., p. 318.

32 This argument was discussed earlier in the essay.

33 'Charter of Labour' in Michael Oakeshott (ed.), *The Social and Political Doctrines of Contemporary Europe*, New York and Cambridge, Cambridge University Press, 1953, p. 184.

34 Gobineau saw three basic racial units arranged in a hierarchy, each with specific characteristics, see *Gobineau: Selected Writings*, edited by M. Biddiss, London, Jonathan Cape, 1970. As Marx and Engels had seen the motor of history in class struggle, Gobineau and Houston Stewart Chamberlain saw the motor in racial struggle. Gobineau's *Essay on the Inequality of the Human Races* (1853–5), was a direct assault upon liberalism. For Gobineau, human equality came up against the apparently immovable scientific fact of unequal races. Gobineau's message was not just one of racial typology. A great tragedy had befallen the human race, namely, the mixture or miscegenation of races. This meant decay and entropy in civilization. Little note was taken of Gobineau till the end of his life when he was befriended by the composer Richard Wagner in 1876. After both their deaths in 1882, Wagner's widow Cosima, set up the Gobineau Society in 1894. A noted member of this group was Houston Stewart Chamberlain whose *Foundation of the Nineteenth Century* (1899) carried on the theme of racial inequality. Drawing upon Gobineau, he noted the central role of race in nationality. Unlike Gobineau, however, anti-semitism appeared as the dominant motif, combined with the superiority of the Aryan. Again unlike Gobineau, Chamberlain looked more optimistically to the role of the Germans in maintaining purity and preventing miscegenation or *Volk*-chaos in Europe. Chamberlain joined the Nazi party shortly before his death in 1927. Both Hitler and the national socialist ideologist Alfred Rosenberg remained admirers of his work.

35 Deeply suspect history, classical studies, anthropology, phrenology, philology, the religious mysticism of Meister Eckhart, and even the mythology of the Nibelung and *Edda*, were all summarily roped in to support the case of the Nordic *Herrenvolk* (master race).

36 This racial and *Volkisch* reading of nationalism led to doctrines of racial cleanliness and the espousal of eugenics. National socialism set its face against mixed marriage. Medical science was also devoted to the same racial goals. One of the systematic Nazi writers on this theme was a trained agronomist. Richard Walter Darré, in works such as *The Peasantry as the Life-Source of the Nordic Race* (1928) and *A New Aristocracy out of the Blood and Soil* (1930), proposed a comprehensive eugenics programme in Germany comparable to animal husbandry, one of his academic specialisms. The peasantry were seen as the ideal eugenic breeding-stock for sustaining the *Volk*. The racial *Volk* perspective also idolized the peasantry and farming communities. Urban life was seen to be dominated by the liberals and Jews. The true *Volk* was rural. This led the national socialists to preferential policies being adopted towards the farming communities, providing tax incentives and subsidies, see G.L. Mosse, *The Crisis of German Ideology*, London, Weidenfeld and Nicolson, 1966, p. 19ff.

37 David Miller, 'The nation-state: a modest defence' in C. Brown (ed.), *Political Restructuring in Europe*, London, Routledge, 1994, p. 145.

38 Thus, as one recent liberal nationalist writer concludes, 'I assert it as a principle that there ought to be respect for national differences, and that there ought to be an adoption of forms of government appropriate to such differences', see MacCormick, *Legal Rights and Social Democracy*, pp. 261–2; also Tamir, *Liberal Nationalism*, pp. 73–4.

39 Giovanni Papini in A. Lyttelton (ed.), *Italian Fascisms: From Pareto to Gentile*, London, Jonathan Cape, 1973, pp. 101–3.

40 In many ways, President Wilson's Fourteen Points, promulgated after the First World War, represent, if only symbolically, the high point of liberal nationalism, in so far as they stressed the sovereignty of the national state, but sought to limit the implications of this principle by stressing individual rights and liberties.

41 Scruton, 'In defence of the nation', p. 312.

42 See *Rosenberg: Selected Writings*, edited by Robert Pois, London, Jonathan Cape, 1971, p. 98.

43 Miller, 'The nation-state', p. 144.

44 Ibid., p. 145.

45 A detailed and wry examination of this can be found in John Carey's *The Intellectuals and the Masses: Pride and Prejudice among the Literary Intelligentsia 1880–1939*, London, Faber and Faber, 1992.

46 'The number of *intergovernmental* international organizations grew from 123 in 1951 through 280 in 1972 to 365 in 1984; the number of *international non-governmental* organizations from 832 through 2,173 in 1972, more than doubling to 4,615 in the next twelve years', Hobsbawm, *Nations and Nationalism*, p. 181.

10 Threads and plaits or an unfinished project?

Feminism(s) through the twentieth century

Diana Coole

Like many of the twentieth-century's major political movements, feminism's origins reside in the broad social changes associated with modernity. Although women's subordination (along with that of many categories of men, too) had been fairly uniform across traditional cultures, it had appeared to be naturally or divinely sanctioned and was rarely questioned. A transformation of social, productive and familial relations which was becoming apparent in Britain by the seventeenth century, coupled with the more individualistic and self-reflective culture associated with it, however, laid the basis for women to begin identifying themselves as an unjustly oppressed category of persons. Feminism as a discursive response to this recognition was indebted to the eighteenth-century Enlightenment, but its emergence as a mass movement was a nineteenth-century phenomenon. It is helpful then to think of its entry into the twentieth century in terms of two intimately yet contingently related components: as a women's movement equipped with a feminist ideology. The role of the ideology was to present women's case for emancipation. In liberal cultures ostensibly dedicated to reason, justice and social utility, arguments revealing the unwarranted discrimination women suffer should carry considerable weight. It was nevertheless obvious that reasoned argument alone would be insufficient for gaining sexual equality where established patriarchal interests were at stake, and women were accordingly motivated to organize politically in pursuit of their goals. Despite the many changes the twentieth century would bring to their politics, to their identity as women and to their aspirations, feminists' primary aim has remained one of abolishing discrimination or exclusion on the basis of gender.

The history of the women's movement's successes and setbacks in pursuit of this goal has been often and lovingly reconstructed, particularly in its British and American contexts.[1] Indeed this is part of feminism's ideological arsenal, its own mythology of origins and victories in the face of adversity, which grants it continuity and identity over time. It is a history that an overview such as this one must surely re-present. Yet it is a history that cannot be presented innocently or straightforwardly from the beginning of the twenty-first century, because of the way representations of the past inevitably pass through the concerns of the present. Now one must ask who speaks and from what perspective, as well as acknowledging the political implications for feminism's future that any particular account of its history will bear.

Among ideological movements, feminism has been unusually self-critical in reflecting on its own foundations and values since it must constantly elicit, criticize and deconstruct unexpurgated patriarchal or phallocentric assumptions there. Accordingly it interrogates itself as rigorously as it does the male-dominated culture and society in which it operates. At the same time feminism has been atypically open to the influence of changing intellectual paradigms, using them to deepen its own analyses of gender power while evaluating their implications for women. It has critically assimilated both major ideologies – liberalism, socialism and Marxism in particular; to a lesser extent anarchism, environmentalism, even liberation theology – and fashionable methodologies, such as dialectics, existentialist phenomenology, structuralism, post-structuralism, deconstruction, empiricism, critical realism and analytical philosophy. Moreover its political interests have drawn it into profound philosophical questions regarding ontology (what does it mean to become a woman or to be gendered?), epistemology (is there a distinctly feminine way of knowing? Is reason itself gendered?) and ethics (what does it mean to relate to others and to oneself as a woman or as a gendered subject?).[2]

As a result of this promiscuity the perspective feminism brings to bear on its own past is quite different from the one embedded in that past as it was experienced at the time. Where feminists previously saw themselves participating in modernity's progressive unfolding, pursuing its promises of personal autonomy and liberty on all women's behalf, both this project and its self-perception have subsequently been subjected to widespread criticism. This has arisen as part of a more general antipathy towards the Enlightenment with its rationalist and universalist orientations. Despite their own indebtedness to the Enlightenment, feminists have come to recognize the masculinist assumptions embedded in its conception of rational individuals and its aspirations for equality.[3] This has affected their understanding of their own history. The women's movement's lived and willing participation in modernity's rationalist project, subsequently recounted in grand narrative terms (as a single story of progress and continuity in pursuit of a specific emancipatory goal), begins to look problematic. Its familiar history might unwittingly sustain deeper structures of oppression while its monolithic recounting might perpetuate an exclusionary logic.

Conventional accounts of the women's movement further suggest a rather pessimistic, even paralysing, political prognosis for contemporary feminism and its future inasmuch as they privilege the model of a mass movement predicated on a shared identity and collective goals, where participants' level of solidarity, organization and commitment grants them the efficacy needed to bring about significant political and material change. Judged against such criteria the contemporary women's movement looks virtually non-existent. In so far as vestiges do remain they seem scarcely related to theoretical developments within feminism, so the crucial relationship between theory and practice embodied in the collectivist paradigm appears fatally sundered.[4] While feminism as the study of gender-related issues has certainly burgeoned as an academic field of enquiry, its political import here generally looks hazy and indirect. Even where feminism has remained explicitly political, its emphases on diversity and deconstruction seem to rule out the very unity which political efficacy requires.

One outcome of such developments has been frequent reference to a *post-feminist* era, where feminism would have gone the way of other ideologies and mass movements whose goals have (allegedly) been met or rejected. Most feminists remain nevertheless more circumspect in their response. A typical Anglo-American reaction has been to lament the loss of a recognizable women's movement but to encourage diverse women, together with others among the excluded and oppressed, to forge shifting alliances where mutual interests emerge (and disintegrate). According to this sort of modernist pragmatism, collective action might yet be simulated under the more evanescent conditions associated with late- or post-modernity, while women are exhorted for political reasons to emphasize their shared identity despite recognizing its fragility.[5] Inevitably there have been considerable doubts as to the feasibility, desirability or efficacy of such a politics.[6] Accordingly others – even while they might eschew the feminist label due to its identitarian and universalizing implications – have embraced postmodern sociology and post-structuralist approaches more enthusiastically, insisting that a radically new kind of politics is now appropriate and that if it is to remain efficacious and relevant, 'feminism' must avoid nostalgia for its earlier more totalizing discourses and models of collective action in favour of qualitatively different modes of political intervention.[7] From this latter perspective it would be important not to view contemporary feminisms as falling short of some earlier, exemplary model since politics always involves experimental, creative strategies which change with context.

It is with such concerns in mind that I have structured my reflections on twentieth-century feminism in this chapter. They invite a rather hazardous strategy which involves both recounting and contesting the way its history has been commonly presented. Now that the century has ended it is surely important to remind ourselves of, indeed to celebrate, the enormous political gains won through women's struggles; to remember their sacrifices and strategies. But at the same time it is unhelpful to present these as stages in a single, unfolding itinerary against whose criteria contemporary feminisms fall short. Accordingly I will argue that the kind of interventions made at each stage were those appropriate to the specific situation they engaged, rather than phases of one continuous project. This means that the historical force field, a particular way of understanding politics, the sites of contestation deemed relevant, the kind of acts and agency that are summoned, the identity and identification of participants: all these form a *constellation* that is historically specific and which must not be reified as a model for whose loss we feel nostalgic (or indeed relieved) and against which contemporary feminism would perhaps be judged lacking (or indeed superior).

This brings me to the chapter's title and the alternative it poses between two ways of thinking about feminism's history. On the one hand there is the idea, congenial to the way feminists have most often presented their past, of the women's movement as an unfinished emancipatory project. It is from this perspective that a now-familiar story can be recounted and feminism presented as (part of) a grand narrative of modernity. But it is also this approach which courts the triple dangers of nostalgia, reification and political pessimism mentioned above. It is to indicate a rather different approach that the title refers to 'threads and plaits'. This attributes a more pluralistic, heterogeneous and contingent history to feminism, emphasizing the discontinuities between its different phases or constellations as well as a more genealogical understanding of the shifting permutations of power in relation to gender. The crucial question posed here, then, is this: is feminism an unfinished (and perhaps incompletable) emancipatory project or was it always a plethora of loosely-related demands, innovations, perspectives, alliances, resistances that have had a (perhaps dubious) narrative imposed upon them but which nevertheless continue unabated?

Grand narrative accounts of feminism as an unfinished emancipatory project

The typical way in which the women's movement has understood itself accords, I suggest, with a certain narrative tradition famously summarized by Lyotard in terms of grand narratives and dismissed by him as having lost credibility. Lyotard himself had identified two grand narratives of modernity: a liberal, emancipatory one associated with Kant; a speculative one originating with Hegel. In each case a self-legitimizing story is told of history's progress towards reason and freedom through the accumulated knowledge and self-consciousness of rational subjects.[8] Feminism has been tempted by both these grand narratives.

First it has perceived itself, and often indeed continues to do so, as part of the emancipatory narrative. Sexual equality (which may or may not entail recognition of women's difference) becomes here one dimension in the development of a rational, just society. This is why feminists have been able to draw on the same liberal and socialist discourses as other groups contesting authority or distribution patterns indefensible before the courts of reason and justice. It is in this light that feminism is often categorized in terms of two waves: a first, liberal wave that ebbed around 1930 and a second, more socialist and radical wave which crested between the late 1960s and early 1980s, whence material, cultural and psycho-sexual as well as political obstacles to gender equality were tackled. This trajectory accords nicely with T.H. Marshall's definition of citizenship as granting civil, political and social rights to individuals, especially if more recent concerns about social inclusion are added.[9]

True, this makes it difficult to privilege the women's movement once other social groups in turn demand the rights, resources and recognition they have won (where, for example, race or ethnicity are equally sources of discrimination). It has even led some contemporary feminists to concede that gender can no longer be privileged as the main source of (even some women's) exclusion, with all the attendant difficulties this raises for a feminist politics (although one could still argue that this anti-discriminatory openness is typical of a feminist ethics). But others have insisted that gender oppression remains the most universal, ubiquitous and profound one since it is Woman who is quintessentially Other. Simone de Beauvoir's classic study of the second sex, as well as psychoanalytic emphases on unconscious and corporeal sexual difference and most radical feminisms, can be situated here, along with the problems of essentialism and the advantages for a women's politics that such a position entails.[10]

It was in this context, and in the now-classic guise of 1970s Radical Feminism, that feminism came to look more like the speculative version of a grand narrative, with the history of women's oppression and liberation becoming a meta-narrative in its own right rather than simply a strand of modern progress. Modelled on a dialectical philosophy of history, the task here was to establish the origins of sexual oppression, usually located in pre-historical, quasi-biological relations; to re-conceptualize history itself as so many forms of sexual oppression and to identify, then galvanize, the material forces and strategies which would force a rupture with the entire patriarchal past. It was such claims that underlay the solidarity and militancy characteristic of the Women's Liberation Movement, when universal sisterhood was opposed to an equally universal patriarchy. Shulamith Firestone's *The Dialectic of Sex* exemplified such an approach:

> the assumption that . . . feminists are talking about changing a fundamental biological condition – is an honest one. That so profound a change cannot be easily fitted into traditional categories of thought, e.g., 'political', is not because these categories do not apply but because they are not big enough: radical feminism bursts through them. If there were another word more all-embracing than *revolution* we would use it.

She went on to identify developments in reproductive technology as a key material condition of liberation and called on women to 'resensitize a fractured consciousness' in pursuit of solidarity and an analysis of ever-deeper layers of sex discrimination. Such a process, she added, 'presents problems far worse than the black militant's new awareness of racism: feminists have to question, not just all of *Western* culture, but the organization of culture itself, and further, even the very organization of nature'. To this end she commended using a Marxian methodology but in order 'to develop a materialist view of history based on sex itself'.[11] Feminism had now emerged as the grandest narrative of all, substituting women for the proletariat as the primary and collective agency of historical transformation. Such totalizing meta-histories were subsequently attacked by post-structuralists, while the sheer variety and complexity of oppressions has rendered them untenable. Few feminists at the beginning of this century would subscribe to this kind of grand narrative.

However, the liberal grand narrative still remains powerful in many accounts of feminism's history and continuing project. Grand narrative claims that women's subjection is merely a legacy of pre-modern customs were exemplified in the nineteenth century by J.S. Mill. He referred to 'the primitive state of slavery lasting on' and predicted that as modernity progresses, 'command and obedience become exceptional facts of life, equal association its general rule'. Yet because of the strong feelings aroused by sexual relations, 'we may not wonder to find them as yet less undermined and loosened than any of the rest by the progress of the great modern spiritual and social transition'.[12] Rather than recognizing the many ways in which sexual inequality and difference are reproduced in modernity, women's subjection was simply an index of historical inertia.

It is this faith in modern progress that has underlain the familiar story of two centuries of women's politics. This typically begins with feminism's late-eighteenth-century foremothers, Mary Wollstonecraft in particular; it notes women's struggle for citizenship rights throughout the nineteenth century and its victory in winning the vote, followed by feminism's eclipse between the wars and its rebirth in more radical form during the 1960s. Here then are its two waves, but after this the story unravels. As a result of deepening its critical analyses, especially where these turned on emancipatory, egalitarian values and reason themselves, feminism has found itself obliged to confront the related spectres of relativism and nihilism. At the same time the women's political movement was being thrown into crisis by the late 1970s by an insistence on differential identities – first concerning race, class and sexual orientation, then involving a plethora of additional distinctions and commitments – which split the sisterhood and troubled its faith in either of modernity's grand narratives. After this feminism's history is difficult to construct because it seems to lead in so many directions, but it does retrospectively problematize the narration of its antecedents, inasmuch as this looks like the story of a particular group of – essentially middle-class, white, Anglophone – women whom it now privileges a second time.

One response has been to encourage the sort of small, local narratives commended by Lyotard, where women have many different tales to tell about their oppression and resistances and whose heterogeneity defies subsumption under any totalizing account. Numerous recent feminist anthologies testify to this proliferation of micro-histories written by women from a huge variety of situations, and this grants twentieth-century feminism a far richer, denser appearance than the schematism of two or three waves. At the same time it is nevertheless important to recognize that many of these stories, as well as the sort of piecemeal grassroots and everyday women's politics that take place across the globe, do still involve struggles for equality and rights. There is a difficult negotiation to be made here between recognizing the specificity of different women's struggles and locating points of identity or synthesis that sustain a recognizably feminist process.[13]

Confronted by such questions of difference, many feminists have endorsed the sort of procedures associated with deliberative democracy or discourse ethics.[14] However this Habermasian solution is itself a version of the liberal, emancipatory project even if in this more recent guise it has more successfully accommodated both diversity and some criticisms of rational subjectivity, by introducing a paradigm of intersubjective communication. It is from its perspective that modernity, including feminism, still looks like an unfinished emancipatory project.

It is from this point of view that concerns about feminism's commitment to such a project, as well as its ability to execute it in light of postmodern relativism, have engendered a certain *fin de siècle* anxiety.

But there are also some difficult questions posed by discourse ethics for a feminist politics.[15] Is a more militant politics only typical of insufficiently modernized societies where women are demanding access to the public sphere, and should feminists thenceforth reconcile themselves to solely rational, discursive procedures? Given that no actually-existing political system lives up to the rational, egalitarian practices idealized in communicative action and an ideal speech situation, might (especially marginalized) women not also need more militant strategies to instantiate them, especially in light of the sort of patriarchal, juridical, capitalist and bureaucratic incursions that limit democratic power anyway? Was it not after all their recognition of the limits of rational discourse and criticism that prompted earlier generations of women to organize and sometimes to deploy alternative strategies? But, on the other hand, is it perhaps simply anachronistic to fantasize about the sort of direct action that typified women's politics earlier in the previous century? Even if it is, are these the only alternatives? When feminists identify deeper, more non-rational levels of gender power, do these not remain untouched by deliberation and summon different kinds of intervention: perhaps the more aesthetic and performative strategies associated with postmodernism?

Threads and plaits: feminisms and the genealogy of gender

The title of this section relates to what is sometimes portrayed as a third, postmodern, wave of feminism. This implies a further stage in its development, another chapter in its narrative which is identified, in late- or postmodern cultures especially, with the closing decades of the twentieth century. There are indeed grounds for emphasizing such continuity. Despite their attacks on the Enlightenment as founded on ideals of rational, masculine subjectivity, postmodernists do continue the feminist tradition of critical interrogation, tracing the ephemera and tentacles of gender power beyond their visible social supports and into the recesses of desire and fantasy, gestures and bodies, language and logic, knowledge and reason.

In other ways, however, and precisely as a result of such interrogations, an apparently oxymoronic postmodern feminism represents a break with, even a rejection of, what had gone before. Indeed it could be argued that feminism is an intrinsically modern movement; that since it is by definition concerned with women's emancipation or liberation the rejection of these notions, along with those of the rational, autonomous subject who would be set free, marks the end of a recognizably feminist project. Moreover, the deconstruction of woman's identity, coupled with the postmodern disintegration of women's solidarity, robs feminism of individual or collective agency such that the connection between criticism and social transformation, which has always lain at the heart of feminism, becomes hard to discern. In short, judged by modernist criteria of political action and purpose, postmodernism and feminism are a contradiction in terms.

It must be acknowledged both that many feminists would agree with this judgement and that postmodernists freely acknowledge the conundra their position entails. Inasmuch as it is postmodernizing social factors and the logic of critique that have engendered postmodern paradoxes, however (and, as we have seen, it is the women's movement's own internal fragmentation and the logic of feminists' own criticisms of reason's gendering which have pushed it in this postmodern direction), it can plausibly be argued that the challenge for twenty-first-century feminism is to adjust to this new social and discursive context, continuing its task of exploring the convolutions of gender power and inventing new political strategies for intervening effectively. To this extent this 'third wave' marks both continuity *and* rupture with the past. How could this be thought? I suggest a helpful beginning would be to think afresh about feminism's own history – which I alluded to several times in the preceding section as a continuous emancipatory project – in more genealogical terms. To explain what this entails it will be useful to look briefly at some comments by Foucault (whose influence on feminism has been substantial).[16]

There are a number of ways in which the history of the women's movement can be accommodated in remarks Foucault made. First, he did suggest a certain chronology to modern struggles as consecutively opposing domination, exploitation and the management and production of subjectivity.[17] Liberal, Marxist and radical/postmodern feminisms would fit quite neatly into this typology, where it is the latter that explore and contest the nature of feminine subjectivity, although it might be more useful to think of all three as also operating concurrently (as Kristeva did in her discussion of three generations of feminism).[18] Second, Foucault also distinguished between situations of domination and of power; applied to women's situation this would suggest a somewhat different historical periodization. In states of domination, asymmetrical relations are relatively immobile. What

> makes the domination of a group, a caste, or a class, together with the resistance and revolts which that domination comes up against, a central phenomenon in the history of societies is that they manifest a massive and universalizing form, at the level of the whole social body, the locking together of power relations with relations of strategy and the results proceeding from their interaction.[19]

In such cases, Foucault concedes, actors would rightly aspire to a more totalizing politics of liberation. However this is naïve and dangerous if protagonists believe they pursue an impossible transcendence of power (of for example patriarchy). At best they gain access to a situation of power which, unlike domination, opens up a mobile and 'very complex field' where power, freedom and resistance circulate and incite one another. From this perspective one might view first- and even some second-wave feminists as fighting patriarchal domination: not (as was often claimed at the time) in order to become free (asexual, ungendered or androgynous) human subjects in some absolute yet abstract sense, but in order to enter the agonistic game of power as such. Arguably this is then what citizenship rights and more general routes of access to a public sphere gained for women. Later twentieth-century feminism can then be understood as something qualitatively different from its predecessors: as participation in a dense fabric of shifting gender relations that involve piecemeal, contingent and multiple resistances coupled with a more affirmative experimentation with (differently-gendered) 'practices of liberty'.[20]

This latter activity is again consonant with a politics of subjectivity while it also accords with a more general post-structuralist insistence that subjectivities, identities, political agency (Woman, embodied women or feminine psychologies, political constituencies, rational individuals, etc.), are not natural or ontological givens awaiting mobilization or liberation but are constituted discursively, incessantly (re)produced in varying forms. If traditional or modern feminine identities have been produced and maintained through discipline and normalization, it is by entering into this complex discursive field that they are contested and recreated. From this perspective 'postmodern' feminisms are not apolitical but participate in a politics and on a terrain that is simply different from those relevant to struggles against domination or exploitation. Women ask: who are we? How have we been constituted as gendered subjects and how might we be different? This cannot be all of politics but without it, women are always in danger of reproducing identities and pursuing interests that are already effects of phallic power.

Yet historical inquiry must still 'put itself to the test of reality, of contemporary reality, both to grasp the points where change is possible and desirable, and to determine the precise form this change should take'.[21] It demands, according to Foucault, no global project but attention to specific, partial, local transformations which are always ongoing rather than definitive. It is not a question of liberal voluntarism and unconstrained choice but again, of engaging with the shifting, dense mesh of forces that produce and subvert, perform and transgress, gender. The kind of historical inquiry Foucault summons here is accordingly both genealogical and archaeological. The genealogist would not think of women's history as a continuous narrative or project, but as a matrix of many interventions – threads and plaits, power and resistance – which may be quite heterogeneous. 'The isolation of different points of emergence does not conform to the successive configurations of an ideal meaning; rather, they result from substitutions, displacements, disguised conquests, and systematic reversals.'[22] The emphasis is on discontinuities and contingencies, where historical structures emerge out of many random and disconnected details and events as well as from larger processes of colonization and multiple strategies of power. This does not mean that history is without enduring forms. The genealogist must avoid reifying them or assuming they always have the same meaning; she seeks what Nietzsche refers to as their 'whole, long, hard-to-decipher script'.[23] But more archaeologically she also recognizes the discursive regimes, or constellations, that circumscribe and facilitate historical acts, determining what can or cannot be said or done.

For example: the public/private opposition is a conceptual index that has been almost definitional of feminism, both as a source of theoretical criticism and as an explanation of women's exclusion.[24] In its massive binary form it carries immense political weight. Yet at the same time it is important not to reify it: public and private, as well as their relationship and boundaries, involve a variety of meanings and practices reliant on a host of discourses (such as classical, liberal, capitalist). The implications and historical manifestations of this division are accordingly many and complex, sliding over time and within diverse contexts. It is therefore necessary to trace the shifting senses of public and private genealogically in order to respond effectively and pluralistically within the dynamics of gendered space, acknowledging too the ways women have themselves been constituted as well as excluded within it. There is then no one massive public/private divide to be emancipated from, but a political region of multiple contestation where in some contexts (for example freedom to make decisions regarding one's own reproductive choices) women might actually want to defend the distinction. A similar argument could be made regarding the equality/difference dualism. This has been used to distinguish between different feminisms and theoretical positions, where the three historical waves have also respectively been identified with equality, difference, and diversity. But in fact there is a more complex genealogy at work; one calling again for a more pluralistic analysis and response.[25] In looking back over particular, perhaps privileged, moments of women's politics it is advisable to be aware of the particular configuration(s) of such indices, since they form part of the complex force field they acted in.

The history of the women's movement

It would be impossible in the remaining space to honour all the methodological imperatives sketched above; in particular, it is necessary to focus on some particular history and I will concentrate here on the British one. It is important to acknowledge its specificity as well as its increasing linkage with other national feminisms. But there are some grounds for privileging the British or American stories inasmuch as key developments in feminism occurred in these societies in the vanguard of modernization. If feminism would subsequently emerge in, or be exported to, other cultures, it would necessarily manifest itself there in different ways so its first appearances should not be seen as offering some exemplary model of which it might be said to other cultures, as Marx had, 'De te fabula narratur!'. But the first feminisms did open a discursive field whose ideological and strategic inventions would influence and provide resources (as well as limits) for subsequent feminisms.

The struggle for rights

British feminism has always been composed of many feminisms. Its different phases and aspects have occupied distinct constellations or fields of forces to which political strategies, sites of contestation and agency are specific. Nevertheless it is during the opening two decades of the twentieth century that the label of an emancipatory project is surely most accurately appended to the women's movement. According to the Foucauldian schema this marks its struggle against domination. Once women had won access to the public sphere, they would enjoy more freedom to participate in a greater variety of strategies revolving around questions of gender power.

The early years of the twentieth century saw mounting agitation on behalf of the unfinished business which had galvanized women during the nineteenth century. The struggle for civil rights had encompassed a range of activities and goals, motivated in part by demands for a literal liberation from the stultifying confines of the bourgeois household. Access to educational and employment opportunities, as well as protection against domestic violence and recognition under the law, were all aspects of a demand for entry into the public sphere, but by the turn of the century the battle for enfranchisement had become its most visible aspect.

Gaining the vote had powerful *symbolic* worth for women in terms of their recognition as equal citizens, as well as a vital *instrumental* value inasmuch as political representation was deemed necessary to advance other rights claims. The more reluctant governments were to grant female suffrage, the more women were incited to identify themselves as an oppressed class sharing common interests. If most activists were bourgeois, universal suffrage was also the goal of socialist parties and proletarian women, although they of course had other agendas too. Despite the varying nature and degree of their political allegiances, hundreds of thousands of women were motivated by a common cause because they shared a common situation of disfranchisement and second-class citizenship. Their identification did not arise from some shared ontological status, experiential homogeneity or essentialist belief that all women are the same, but from the fact that the law defined them as an excluded, inferior category regardless of their differences. As a consequence a specific feminist identity was constituted in the course of this particular struggle. If equality and a shared goal were pursued, this was not because women already existed as a latently political group with definite interests merely awaiting a voice. Their unity, interests and egalitarianism sprang from a specific political context. Their becoming political actors was encouraged by a liberal sense of agency whereby it is rational individuals who make history, but tactically it was inflected through socialist lessons that the powerless acquire efficacy by becoming a collective agent.

The sense of the political held by these early feminists was the one appropriate to liberalism: that politics involves activities associated with government and the state. It was this understanding that dictated which feminist activities and goals were politically appropriate, both definitionally and strategically. Women's activities can be divided into two categories here. First there were discursive interventions.[26] At one end of the spectrum these involved a powerful propaganda machine, developed to win hearts and minds. At the other, there was a sophisticated engagement with political theory, which provided both a vocabulary for contesting women's subjection as unjust *and* grounds for its legitimation which their opponents wielded. This sort of discursive activity was consonant with the emphasis in enlightened cultures on rational argument, although it rarely approached an ideal speech situation of ideologically undistorted communication.

In addition there was a second kind of more activist strategy. A number of points are germane here. First, the type of activity pursued was also both incited by, and appropriate to, the understanding of politics early liberal feminists held. Second, these acts had two sides: both the sort of legitimate activities which the liberal state encourages and, since it did not recognize the legitimacy of *women* participating in them, a more militant strategy centring on civil disobedience, which the failure of conventional practices incited. Third, I want to emphasize these more militant acts since there is today a tendency to present first-wave feminism as a rather tame and polite affair; but fourth, inasmuch as such activities might be romanticized as ideal models of collective political action, it is important to see them as responses to a particular configuration of political forces and a specific, rather narrow, understanding of the political.[27]

The two types of political action distinguished here were exemplified during the franchise struggles in Britain by the split between the law-abiding, reformist suffragists (who formed the National Union of Women's Suffrage Societies) and the more militant suffragettes. Both sides engaged in typically liberal political practices: they addressed meetings, raised funds, organized election campaigns, sold newspapers, went from door to door with their message. There were 'meetings which multiplied in halls and drawing rooms, in schools and chapels, at street corners, and on village greens' and which 'did not seem like the dull and solemn stuff of politics'.[28] There were massive public demonstrations and marches with banners and bands, whose female entourages were themselves a source of scandal. For even these legal activities exhibited a more subversive dimension since in the context of Victorian culture they looked intrinsically transgressive. Indeed they were, inasmuch as mainstream conventions of femininity as passive, submissive, were being challenged. Simply by becoming active in public, women were reconstituting their identities and challenging performatively what had looked like a natural feminine modesty. As a consequence they incited acts of counter-resistance: participants were frequently heckled, pelted with rotten fruit, ridiculed in the press and even assaulted. In a way this helped since the first tasks were to make women's cause visible in order to put their demands on the political agenda, while politicizing women themselves. Reminiscing in 1928, Ray Strachey offered a clear picture of the suffragettes' particular success here.

> Day after day, as the militants provided fresh headlines for the newspapers, the breakfast tables of England resounded with the debate, and the comments flowed out from the domestic hearth to railway trains, smoking rooms, clubs, and public houses, and wherever men gathered together.[29]

Such activities were effective, then, in an age which still boasted something like a lively, critical public sphere[30] – although one into which women were obliged to force their way. At the same time they represented an invention of political strategies designed to counter the limits of liberal political culture and the intransigence of its governments. These acts were not merely instrumental: in an age when women's public defiance was itself offensive to customary sensibilities, their very performance bore a significance scarcely imaginable today.

Other suffragette exploits looked – and were indeed designed to be – even more shocking. Some of the theatrical, spectacular, carnivalesque dimensions of their performances already anticipated the situationist and avant-garde street politics of later decades, while their resort to direct action was more redolent of socialist and anarchist strategies. Their motto was 'deeds, not words'. They proclaimed moral violence, which spilled over into violence against property; they harassed cabinet ministers and were charged with obstruction, battled with police, chained themselves to railings and made raids on Parliament. They threw stones, smashed windows in public buildings, poured acid in pillar boxes, wrecked golf courses, slashed pictures in galleries, burnt houses and cut telegraph wires.[31] Such civil disobedience during the early years of the previous century was in response to successive government betrayals over the vote, and in return the agitators were arrested, jailed, force fed. They were reconstituted as criminals, victims. Intransigence and coercion by the state, and direct action by (a minority of) feminists, thus incited one another in a ferment of political extemporization. The cycle would be broken not by the logic of collective action or debate but by the exigencies of the Great War. After 1914 women threw themselves into the war effort, which undoubtedly wrought greater and more far-reaching changes in gender relations (regarding for example women's access to public life, their identities and roles, their dress and general comportment) than the political activities themselves. Even so, it would take a further decade of peace for British women to gain enfranchisement on the same terms as men.[32]

Strachey's conclusion to her history of *The Cause* is worth quoting here since, written contemporaneously with this victory, it is symptomatic of the grand narrative, emancipatory optimism of the early part of the twentieth century. While acknowledging, prophetically, the limits of legal change and the moral and economic problems that would continue to motivate feminist struggle, she insists nevertheless that

> the main fight is over, and the main victory won. With education, enfranchisement, and legal equality all conceded, the future of women lies in their own hands; and it has been a fundamental belief in the Women's Movement that in those hands it is safe.[33]

In other words, women had won the right to become players in the agonistic field of power relations. In many other societies of course the struggle for political equality had not even begun, while it would clearly be quite wrong to suggest that emancipation from domination or accession to full equality had been won in Britain by 1930. Indeed the following decades would be characterized by a period of reaction, while the next generation of feminists would insist that patri-archal oppression remained omnipresent. But subsequent struggles would occur within quite a different configuration of forces.

The battles over civil society, personal life and gendered subjectivity

When a women's movement re-emerged in the late 1960s it was tempting to see it as continuing but deepening the earlier egalitarian project. Of course such continuities did exist but the new emphasis on liberation, rather than emancipa-tion, already signalled a far more ambitious idea of social transformation. The sense of the political had already expanded to incorporate relationships in civil society. Whereas previously Marxists had flirted with 'the woman question' but generally retained a critical distance from it, now there was a lively – although ultimately fruitless – attempt at some synthesis of Marxism and feminism.[34] The focus on material rather than legal or political equality here could be identified with Foucault's schematic shift towards struggles against exploitation. But it was always clear that women's inequality could not be reduced to exploitation inas-much as it occurs in the productive realm. Their very access to employment, as well as their experiences once there and the latter's articulation with the ideology and power structures of the family, were also at stake.

Accordingly a new focus on sexual relations, in particular regarding the sexual division of labour and the economy of desire, came to the fore. This was encour-aged by a variety of developments, some of which were: new opportunities for working women that post-war capitalism was opening up (with all their attendant tensions regarding traditional sex roles); the influences of the 1960s' counter-culture and its demands for sexual liberation; the availability of reliable contraception; the corrosive effects on traditional family structures of factors such as the war, greater affluence and mobility, and the gains previously won by women themselves.

To begin with, the new feminism did remain a primarily white, middle-class passion. Sketching in feminism's history from the vantage point of 1971, and utilizing the sort of structuralist analysis that was then becoming fashionable, Juliet Mitchell nevertheless implied that feminism's association with advanced industrial societies and middle-class women was neither a western bias nor a false universalism. Rather it was a response to the particular conditions of capi-talism whose ideological battles and contradictions foregrounded the struggles of bourgeois women. 'The economic changes that thrust into revolutionary promin-ence the new "educated", youthful middle class, that provoked radical attacks on the ideological institutions, caused the rise of the Women's Liberation Move-ment.'[35] Yet such women's concerns already overflowed their limited aims and social base, Mitchell insisted, encouraging them to forge alliances with other oppressed groups on whose ideological resources they also drew. She accordingly located the re-emergence of feminism in the broader context of the counter-culture: civil rights and Black Power movements, student militancy, anarchism and terrorism, sectarianism, the labour movement and the anti-psychiatry politics of experience.

In this context ideas about liberation were interwoven with anti-capitalist sentiments as well as with overcoming patriarchy. The speculative grand narrative structure mentioned earlier was common to both Marxist and radical feminists during the 1970s and much of the creative tension between them arose from the difficulties of reconciling two totalizing versions, one privileging class and production, the other sex and reproduction. It is in fact useful to distinguish in this second wave between a more Marxian, materialist and egalitarian orientation (which in retrospect looks rather closer to liberalism in terms of its basic assumptions) and the stronger emphasis on psycho-culture and difference associated with radical feminisms, which already operated on the terrain of the politics of subjectivity identified by Foucault. While Marxists and liberals disagreed on important political and economic questions, they shared broadly modernist, Enlightenment aims, especially regarding the importance of equality and rationality. While radical and postmodernist feminists shared a certain scepticism regarding the latter, they nevertheless disagreed about questions of perspective and identity. Radical feminism sought woman-centred concepts and methodologies as well as identifying women as a distinct social group in opposition to men, male interests and masculine identities. Mostly its exponents emphasized difference rather than equality. Postmodernists have deconstructed such oppositions, whether male/female (or masculine/feminine) or equality/difference, emphasizing instead the fluid instabilities and diversities of gendered identities.

The last four decades or so of feminism in fact exhibit far too many threads to be brought under one project and if they remain susceptible to the feminist label it is only in so far as they all participate in the complex genealogy of gender. The ways in which politics and political agency have been understood, and consequently the way political strategies have evolved, have all shifted markedly during this period and it is on such factors that I will focus here.

As far as politics is concerned, there has been a marked shift away from definitions and practices revolving around government, so the state has generally occupied a diminished place within post-war feminism.[36] For Marxists the state was always considered somewhat epiphenomenal since determining changes would occur in the economy. Although structuralist versions would grant it a relative autonomy, feminists have tended to perceive it in a similar way: as a patriarchal institution that mirrors and supports broader structures of patriarchy which are more effectively tackled elsewhere. Since winning the vote, women have certainly campaigned for particular laws (such as legalized abortion) and policies (in particular concerning welfare and equal opportunities) while organizing to shift agendas and gain greater representation for themselves. But women have often found the masculine ethos of parliamentary politics uncongenial while feminists have always seen themselves as far more than just a pressure group. Postmodernists, meanwhile, have argued that women's interests are already an *effect* of state policies, while doubts about women's common identity have raised perplexing questions about political representation.[37] Feminist conceptions of politics have anyway tended to focus elsewhere. One of their most enduring claims here has been that the personal is political, since even the most intimate relationships are dependent on public structures of patriarchy.[38] As the capillaries of gender power have been traced to ever-deeper structures, so consequently the horizons of the political have expanded and the sites of political contestation multiplied.

Such developments have profoundly affected feminists' understanding of political agency. During the 1970s women still aspired to collective action and the emphasis on sisterhood was conducive to an ethos of solidarity. It was during this decade that a mass politics was incarnated in the Women's Liberation Movement and a strong connection between theory and practice persisted. As the Movement fragmented and attention shifted to more personal and cultural politics, such collective agency began to seem neither possible nor perhaps necessary. In personal life it was up to individual women to contest the sexual and domestic roles male partners expected, while relatively small groups might initiate subversive cultural experiments that would open spaces others could exploit. Structuralists and post-structuralists anyway cast doubt on individualist, voluntarist notions of agency, as well as suggesting that identities are too unstable to support any enduring mass politics. Although such doubts have troubled feminist theorists, however, and while it is difficult currently to imagine any resurrection of a mass movement, this has not prevented huge numbers of women individually and collectively from acting politically on a more piecemeal basis in response to the various exigencies of their situations.

Finally, then, what sort of political strategies have typified late- and postmodern feminism? These vary, of course, according to the way politics and agency are understood and the sites of contestation as defined by current discourses and configurations of power. Where Marxism was influential, feminists adapted dialectical and structuralist analyses in order to read the historical situation and the confluence of forces wherein women might act efficaciously. The aim was to generate theory out of women's own experiences rather than imposing it from outside. Through consciousness-raising groups, women would share experiences and realize that their apparently individual suffering was part of a more general syndrome, and this in turn would motivate them to intervene on a political rather than a simply personal level. At the same time, theoreticians would relate these indices of patriarchy to yet broader structural contradictions in order to grasp at what point women might most effectively target the system. The process of understanding their subjection together, too, would instil among women the requisite solidarity for an effective praxis.

Like the suffragettes, the Women's Liberation Movement had a certain penchant for direct action and mass politics. Huge marches and demonstrations, symbolic and theatrical acts, civil disobedience are probably the most memorable tactics of the 1970s. These were paralleled in other arenas of the New Left – civil rights, anti-Vietnam war, CND and so on – and indicative of a revolutionary faith that fundamental change might yet be possible. There was also a more utopian emphasis on prefigurative politics. Some radical feminists, in particular, despaired of overthrowing patriarchy but concluded nevertheless that there remained sufficient space in its interstices for a separatist politics. This had the advantages of forging women-only organizations; its predisposition towards political lesbianism entailed both a direct rejection of heterosexuality and a demonstration of its contingency, and the ethos of women-only groups was to be exemplary of a different kind of ethic from the dominant masculine one. Other women experimented with a variety of domestic arrangements which were similarly designed to reveal the suppressed possibilities of creative child-rearing. Like utopian socialists a century earlier they hoped by their examples to demonstrate the potential for alternative lifestyles, now centred on woman-friendly communities.

To some extent these instrumentalist and prefigurative strategies have been combined in the patient work of the considerable numbers of women who have organized on a grassroots or local level. Their mode of organization, too (anti-hierarchical and non-bureaucratic, co-operative rather than confrontational, etc.), is intended to demonstrate a more sisterly way of practising politics (thereby complementing theoretical interests in insinuating an ethic of care into public life). Help lines, rape crisis centres and so on can all be understood as innovative responses to the exigencies of patriarchal power in its many manifestations as well as attempts at empowering women themselves.

As attention focused more on cultural issues during the 1980s, new symbolic strategies of contestation, experimentation and resistance also emerged. Women protested against exhibitions or films that conveyed degrading images of them; they boycotted products advertised by gender-stereotypes; they broadcast novel and affirmative images of themselves; they demonstrated the instability and contingency of gendered identities. In many ways postmodernists have continued this symbolic politics, but they have focused more radically on deconstructing gender and identity as such, promoting aesthetic and performative strategies that disclose all identity as a masquerade. Insisting that both sexed bodies and gendered subjects are effects of power, where it is the repetition of performances as well as a host of microscopic normalizing and disciplining techniques that maintain such effects, they have engaged in transgressive acts which confuse boundaries and render what looked like unassailable distinctions undecidable, untenable.[39] Such strategies are partly a response to the realization that gender and sexuality are crucially produced and sustained by non-rational processes such as unconscious desire, corporeal acts or rhetoric. Any rational, deliberative politics must at least therefore be supplemented by non-rational strategies that work on this level.

Conclusion

In the foregoing reflections on feminism in the twentieth century I have noted how the intimate connection between feminist theory and a women's movement, with which that century began, became much weaker at its end. In part this is simply a response to the differential rhythms of political and theoretical progress, where enduring blockages and interests in material or institutional life mean lengthy, repetitious struggles for equality which simply look boring and unoriginal if they are repeated too often in theory. But feminists have also come to see the relation between theory and practice rather differently, while they have shared in a more general drift towards emphases on theoretical practice and away from collectivist politics. At the same time, feminist strategies and identities have both fractured and proliferated. Although all this looks problematic from a mass-movement, grand-narrative, perspective however, I have suggested that a focus on the genealogy of gender would note the way feminisms have always arisen in response to the particularities of context and that changing political tactics or agents have been generally appropriate to the field of forces in which women intervene. From this point of view I suggested that perhaps the most significant distinction to be made in looking back over women's struggles is that between their fight against domination – typified by the language of emancipation and demands for access to the public sphere – and their participation in the agonistic spaces of gender power thereby opened. If the latter has summoned a variety of novel and experimental interventions, then these are still justified by and part of an ongoing enlightenment process of critical interrogation, even if the strategies it commends are not always themselves rational ones. From this perspective feminism, perhaps uniquely among the great ideologies of modernity, finds itself in a healthy position to confront the challenges of the millennium.

Notes and references

1 See for example R. Strachey, *The Cause: A Short History of the Women's Movement in Great Britain*, London, Virago, 1978, first edition 1928; J. Mitchell, *Woman's Estate*, Harmondsworth, Penguin, 1971; V. Bryson, *Feminist Political Theory: An Introduction*, London, Macmillan, 1992; S. Rowbotham, *Women in Movement: Feminism and Social Action*, London, Routledge, 1992. Other national histories have also of course been recounted. See among many examples R. Stites, *The Women's Liberation Movement in Russia*, Princeton NJ, Princeton University Press, 1978; C. Corrin, *Magyar Women: Hungarian Women's Lives, 1960s–1990s*, London, Macmillan, 1994. Less familiar histories of British women have also been presented. See for example B. Bryan, S. Dadzie and S. Scafe, *The Heart of the Race: Black Women's Lives in Britain*, London, Virago, 1985.
2 See for example C. Battersby, *The Phenomenal Woman: Feminist Metaphysics and the Patterns of Identity*, Cambridge, Polity Press, 1998; S. Harding and M. Hintikka (eds), *Discovering Reality: Feminist Perspectives on Epistemology, Metaphysics, Methodology and Philosophy of Science*, Dordrecht, Reidal, 1983; L. Alcoff and E. Potter (eds), *Feminist Epistemologies*, New York, Routledge, 1993; C. Gilligan, *In a Different Voice: Psychological Theory and Women's Development*, Cambridge MA, Harvard University Press, 1982. Judith Squires has recently offered an excellent summary and analysis of conceptual and methodological debates within feminism in her *Gender in Political Theory*, Cambridge, Polity Press, 2000.
3 See for example G. Lloyd, *The Man of Reason: 'Male' and 'Female' in Western Philosophy*, London: Methuen, 1984; D. Coole, *Women in Political Theory*, Brighton, Harvester-Wheatsheaf, 1988, 1993; L. Irigiray, *Speculum of the Other Woman*, Ithaca NY, Cornell University Press, 1985.
4 This rupture between theory and practice formed the theme for the *Radical Philosophy* conference in 1996, which was entitled 'Torn Halves: Theory and Politics in Contemporary Feminism'. For explicit responses to this theme in a historical and primarily

British perspective, see L. Segal, 'Generations of feminism', and D. Coole, 'Feminism without nostalgia', *Radical Philosophy*, May/June 1997, pp. 6–16 and 17–24.

5 See for example N. Fraser and L. Nicholson, 'Social criticism without philosophy', in L. Nicholson (ed.), *Feminism/Postmodernism*, London and New York, Routledge, 1990, pp. 19–38.

6 Judith Butler notes the challenges that arise here: 'What's needed is a dynamic and more diffuse conception of power, one which is committed to the difficulty of cultural translation as well as the need to rearticulate "universality" in non-imperialist directions. This is difficult work and it's no longer viable to seek recourse to simple and paralysing models of structural oppression . . . there can be no pure opposition to power, only a recrafting of its terms from resources invariably impure.' 'Gender as performance', an interview with P. Osborne and L. Segal, in P. Osborne (ed.), *A Critical Sense*, London and New York, Routledge, 1996, p. 125.

7 See for example the various contributions to J. Dean (ed.), *Feminism and the New Democracy: Resiting the Political*, London, Sage, 1997 and A. Yeatman, *Postmodern Revisionings of the Political*, London and New York, Routledge, 1994.

8 J.-F. Lyotard, *The Postmodern Condition*, Manchester, Manchester University Press, 1984. The debate about grand narratives and an emancipatory project has specifically engendered a polemic between Lyotard and Habermas, but feminists have also commented extensively on the idea of grand narratives and their alleged decline in relation to feminism. See for example S. Benhabib, *Situating the Self. Gender, Community and Postmodernism in Contemporary Ethics*, Cambridge, Polity Press, 1992, Chapter 7; N. Fraser and L. Nicholson, 'Social criticism without philosophy', see note 5; D. Coole, 'Master narratives and feminist subversions', in J. Good and I. Velody (eds), *The Politics of Postmodernity*, Cambridge, Cambridge University Press, 1998, pp. 107–25.

9 T.H. Marshall, *Citizenship and Social Class*, Cambridge, Cambridge University Press, 1950.

10 S. de Beauvoir, *The Second Sex*, Harmondsworth, Penguin, 1972. Feminists influenced by Lacan, especially, also speak about woman as Other.

11 S. Firestone, *The Dialectic of Sex*, London, The Women's Press, 1979, pp. 11–16.

12 J.S. Mill, *The Subjection of Women*, London, Everyman, 1929, pp. 259ff., 219.

13 See for example C. Corrin, *Feminist Perspectives on Politics*, London and New York, Longman, 1999, p. 7.

14 See for example Benhabib, *Situating the Self*; I. Young, *Justice and the Politics of Difference*, Princeton NJ, Princeton University Press, 1990.

15 There have been many feminist criticisms of Habermas, even among his sympathizers. See for example N. Fraser, *Unruly Practices: Power, Discourse and Gender in Contemporary Social Theory*, Minneapolis, University of Minneapolis Press, 1989; M. Fleming, *Emancipation and Illusion: Rationality and Gender in Habermas's Theory of Modernity*, Pennsylvania, Pennsylvania State University Press, 1997; I. Young, 'Communication and the Other: beyond deliberative democracy', in S. Benhabib (ed.), *Democracy and Difference: Contesting the Boundaries of the Political*, Princeton NJ, Princeton University Press, 1996; D. Coole, 'Habermas and the question of alterity', in M.P. D'Entrèves and S. Benhabib (eds), *Habermas and the Unfinished Project of Modernity*, Cambridge, Polity Press, 1996, pp. 221–44.

16 See for example L. McNay, *Foucault and Feminism: Power, Gender and the Self*, Cambridge, Polity Press, 1992. Many additional citations of feminists engaging directly with Foucault's work could be offered but additionally there are many others who write under the influence of a broadly Foucauldian perspective – most famously, perhaps, Judith Butler.

17 M. Foucault, 'The subject and power', afterword in H. Dreyfus and P. Rabinow, *Michel Foucault: Beyond Structuralism and Hermeneutics*, Brighton, Harvester Press, 1982, p. 212.

18 J. Kristeva, 'Women's time', in T. Moi (ed.), *The Kristeva Reader*, Oxford, Blackwell, 1986.

19 Foucault, 'The subject and power', p. 226.

20 M. Foucault, 'The ethic of care of the self as a practice of freedom', *Philosophy and Social Criticism*, Spring 1987, Vol. 12, No. 1, pp. 113ff.

21 M. Foucault, 'What is Enlightenment?', in P. Rabinow (ed.), *The Foucault Reader*, Harmondsworth, Penguin, 1984, p. 46.

22 M. Foucault, 'Nietzsche, genealogy, history', in *Language, Counter-Memory, Practice*, Ithaca NY, Cornell University Press, 1977, p. 151.

23 F. Nietzsche, *The Genealogy of Morality*, Cambridge, Cambridge University Press, 1994, p. 9.

24 For explicit insistence on the public/private opposition's centrality to feminism, see for example A. Phillips, 'Universal pretensions in political thought', in A. Phillips and M. Barrett (eds), *Destabilizing Theory: Contemporary Feminist Debates*, Cambridge, Cambridge University Press, 1992, p. 17. For my own genealogical reading of the public/ private relationship see D. Coole, 'Cartographic convulsions: public and private reconsidered', *Political Theory*, 2000, Vol. 28, pp. 337–54.

25 See for example A. Phillips (ed.), *Feminism and Equality*, Oxford, Blackwell, 1987; G. Bock and S. James (eds), *Beyond Equality and Difference: Citizenship, Feminist Politics and Female Subjectivity*, London and New York, Routledge, 1992; Squires, *Gender in Political Theory*, Chapter 4.

26 Unfortunately the terms discourse and discursive have become quite ambiguous in feminist theory and it is important to keep in mind a distinction between a more Habermasian sense (the one used in this particular context), where discourse refers to rational, linguistic, communicative acts, and the broader Foucauldian sense of discursive fields or regimes which encompass material structures, acts and norms, as well as language, and which are inevitably interwoven with power.

27 Sheila Rowbotham's history of feminism's revolutionary legacy is interesting in this context. See her *Women, Resistance and Revolution*, Harmondsworth, Penguin, 1972.

28 Strachey, *The Cause*, p. 305.

29 Ibid., p. 303.

30 J. Habermas, *The Social Transformation of the Public Sphere*, Cambridge, Polity Press, 1989.

31 Strachey, *The Cause*, pp. 309–30. Juliet Mitchell was nevertheless eager to distinguish this radical politics from that of the 1960s: 'The slogans of feminists today may seem no more radical than those of spokeswomen in the past, but the context alters the meaning'. In particular, she insisted that the 'predominantly middle-class membership of the earlier feminist struggles *did* limit them: among other things, it directed them (despite the acute awareness by some members of working-class and/or Black problems) towards focusing on largely bourgeois issues'. Mitchell, *Woman's Estate*, pp. 20, 36.

32 The table reproduced by Corrin, *Feminist Perspectives on Politics*, pp. 231–3, shows how global struggles for women's enfranchisement have continued throughout the twentieth century.

33 Strachey, *The Cause*, p. 385.

34 See for example M. Barrett, *Women's Oppression Today*, London, Verso, 1988, first edition 1980.

35 Mitchell, *Woman's Estate*, pp. 38ff.

36 Although Squires has noted a recent return to a more state-related politics and suggests that feminists have perhaps become disillusioned with alternative strategies: Squires, *Gender in Political Theory*, p. 199.

37 On postmodernist doubts, see R. Pringle and S. Watson, 'Women's interests and the poststructuralist state', in Barrett and Phillips (eds), *Destabilizing Theory*; on the puzzles of representation, see A. Phillips, *The Politics of Presence*, Oxford, Clarendon Press, 1995.

38 K. Millett, *Sexual Politics*, London, Virago, 1977, Chapter 2.
39 The most celebrated example of this analysis and politics surely remains Judith Butler's *Gender Trouble: Feminism and the Subversion of Identity*, New York, Routledge, 1990, with its exploration of gender as performative and its strategy of drag.

11 Green political perspectives at the dawn of the twenty-first century

James Meadowcroft

As a well-defined ideological current, the green perspective is comparatively new. For most of the twentieth century, variants of liberalism, socialism and conservatism (combined with admixtures of nationalism), and for a brief period fascism, occupied the centre of the political stage. Momentous developments of the last hundred years – including the world wars, the ending of the colonial era, the rise and fall of the Soviet experiment, the genesis of the welfare state, and the punctuated diffusion of democratic mechanisms – have been closely associated with conflict, but also with cross-fertilization and hybridization, among these major traditions. Compared with feminism, or even with such manifestations of late-twentieth-century ideological creativity as the new right, religious fundamentalisms and emergent nationalisms, the immediate impact of the greens may appear modest. Yet in the few decades of its existence the green perspective has made an initial mark, and it seems likely that it will assume a more significant role in the future.

The green perspective

Like other ideological trends, greens are characterized by diversity; and the green perspective is more a family of related approaches than a single integrated viewpoint. Contributions to this emergent tradition of political argument – which offers a biting critique of modern society, particularly with respect to the damage industrial civilization is inflicting upon the planetary ecosphere – have been made by environmental campaigners, anti-nuclear and animal-rights activists, political organizers and radical journalists, environmental philosophers and academic theorists.[1] Ministers in the German coalition government, 'monkey-wrenchers' fighting to preserve the American wilderness, and advocates of alternative technologies and lifestyles can all claim to identify with the green political project. And 'social ecology', 'eco-socialism', 'bio-regionalism', 'eco-feminism', and 'deep ecology' are just some of the variants and hybrids associated with green politics.[2] Yet despite the diversity, there are some things greens share.[3]

At the heart of the green perspective lies a profound preoccupation with the relationship between human beings and the natural world. Pollution of air, water and land, the profligate consumption of resources, the destruction of natural habitats and wilderness, the decline of biodiversity and the dangers of climate change are routinely decried. But for greens environmental issues are not merely a series of discrete concerns that can be managed through specific remedial technologies. Rather they are symptomatic of fundamental flaws in contemporary civilization. They result from a value system which treats nature as material to be harnessed to human ambition, a world-view which ignores the complex inter-dependence of ecological processes, an economic system addicted to expansion, waste, and inequality, and a political system manipulated by those who gain most from existing practices. What distinguishes this view from the perspective of others who worry about environmental destruction is that for greens the socio-ecological problematic provides *the privileged terrain* for defining political identity and orienting political action. In other words, the ills of contemporary society are such that the political division between those who advocate a radical break with current practices and those who defend the existing industrial order is paramount. Thus while greens (implicitly or explicitly) accept insights culled from established political perspectives, they affirm the need to build a distinctly 'green' political movement.

Four elements are typically present in green critiques of the ecological delinquency of contemporary society. First, there is an affirmation of *the fundamental value of nature*, natural processes, and the environment. According to greens industrial society devalues the natural world, neglects the extent to which humans are dependent on natural systems, and denies the independent worth of non-human natural entities. Yet nature provides the bounty on which human society depends – not only in material terms, but also in an aesthetic, psychological and spiritual sense. Moreover, nature should be understood as possessing a value that is independent of human purposes. Natural entities deserve respect and consideration, and should not be approached merely from the standpoint of their potential utility. Instrumental and non-instrumental reasons for valuing nature receive varying patterns of emphasis in different green approaches: some insist that recognition of intrinsic values in nature is the hallmark of true greens; others emphasize the importance of nature for human flourishing; while still others privilege the lived experiential bond between humans and the non-human natural world. Among philosophically-inclined greens arguments about the sorts of natural entities that possess value, the relationship between moral agency and moral considerability, egalitarian or hierarchical approaches to ordering conflicting claims, and whether value exists independently of valuers, abound. But any perspective that can reasonably be called green draws on some of these elements, arguing that we must reassess the way we look at the natural world.

Second there is an idea of *the reality of natural limits* – that the ecosphere is finite, that physical and biological systems are bounded, and that a society which continuously expands (its economy, population, resource inputs, or waste outputs) will eventually come to grief. In a finite world, exponential growth cannot go on for ever. According to greens industrial societies are already transgressing these limits, consuming resources and dumping wastes at unsustainable rates. And if this profligate way of living were to be extended around the world, the strain upon the global ecosphere would prove intolerable. Although the predictions made in the early 1970s of imminent ecological collapse proved premature, the notion of natural limits remains a central theme of green argument. The exhaustion of renewable resource systems (the depletion of fish stocks, for example), the congestion of cities, roads and airways, the continuing destruction of natural habitats, and impending climate change – serve as icons for pervasive ecological limits. Ignoring such limits not only guarantees the continuing destruction of nature, but also spells potential disaster for human society.

Third, there is a *repudiation of the overall development trajectory of contemporary industrial civilization*. Greens argue that the pattern of development adopted by modern society is desperately wrong. Humans have built a civilization predicated upon the ongoing pillage of natural systems. Progress has been mistakenly identified with ceaseless growth, and the quest for material satisfactions. While greens differ over the diagnosis of the underlying causes of this malaise (Enlightenment thinking, hierarchy, capitalism and so on) and over the relative acceptability of specific technologies or patterns of economic and social activity, they all believe that society has taken a wrong turning. What is required to set this to rights is a radical re-orientation of social development towards a 'sustainable' society – one which lives in harmony with natural systems, imposes no burdens which the ecosphere cannot bear, and leaves ample place for the flourishing of non-human nature.

Finally, there is what may be described as *the emancipatory impulse* of the green vision. It is not just that natural limits ultimately will prevent us from continuing our profligate life-style, but also that the green alternative promises us a much better world than the one we know today. And this in two senses. On the one hand, in a green society the burden imposed upon the environment will be lessened dramatically: humans will once again 'walk lightly upon the earth'. Nature will, in a sense, be set free from humanity's ruthless quest for absolute dominion. And, on the other hand, the advent of a green society will also set humans free. Relieved of the pressures of commercial civilization, we will enjoy lives that are happier and healthier, that are more meaningful, and that are more closely attuned to nature. While greens may disagree about the precise description of the society that is to come, they all promise that a green future will be a bright future.

Taken together, these four points frame an indictment of the ecological sins of contemporary society: but they also suggest that the green perspective embodies a multi-stranded critique, and a set of positive values and prescriptions, which are not directly deducible from 'environmental' postulates. Social and economic inequalities, centralization and bureaucratization, the erosion of local control, militarism, and the oppression of women are all denounced by greens. In contrast, they affirm the centrality to their social vision of equity, participation, grassroots democracy, local control, vibrant communities and women's rights. These elements are cashed out in very diverse ways in different green perspectives – but all are staples of green argument. They are interwoven with the environmental critique, but their significance is not exhausted by the environmental dimension. Militarism, for example, leads to environmental destruction; but it is also condemned for the direct harm it inflicts on human societies. A re-localization of economic and social life would reduce environmental loadings, but it would also revive bonds of community. The interaction of environmental preoccupations with these critical foci and positive values gives green discourse its distinctive flavour: the arguments of green anti-militarism resonate differently from those of earlier pacifist movements, while the life in imagined green communities is not quite that presented in other communitarian visions.

Although the four ideas cited above – 'natural values', 'natural limits', a rejection of the prevailing 'development trajectory', and 'green emancipation' – were presented in relation to the environmental dimension, they potentially tie together many strands of green belief. Valuing nature, for example, can be interpreted also as an injunction to 'learn from nature' – to accept what nature can teach us about the ways of the world. Thus principles held to characterize natural systems can be commended as norms to orient human practice. 'Mutual-dependence', 'diversity', and 'equality' are often cited in this regard: the interdependence of species in ecosystems suggests the importance of co-operation and community among humans; the variety of living forms typical of mature and healthy ecosystems is taken to endorse diversity within human societies; while the absence of stable hierarchies in nature is invoked to justify egalitarian social organization.

The notion of limits can be applied not only to denote 'external' constraints which a finite ecosphere imposes on human projects, but also to imply that human capacities are bounded, and/or to refer to controls which we (should) choose to impose upon our behaviour. Many greens denounce the reductionist stance of modern science, and the arrogant assumptions of technological civilization: so much of the history of industrial society is a history of miscalculation and unintended consequences. They suggest that it is impossible for us to fully comprehend complex, unique and continuously evolving natural systems. Instead, we should acknowledge limits to human understanding and be cautious in our interference with natural processes. In parallel to this idea of human fallibility, greens may also argue (somewhat paradoxically) that one capacity humans *do* have is the ability to reflect on their conduct and modify their behaviour. We can say 'this is enough', and choose to limit the demands we place upon nature, to accept a more modest share of the earth's resources, and to enjoy a less wasteful way of life. In other words, self-imposed limits can contain our behaviour within bounds proscribed by prudence and/or morality.

The notion of a pathological development trajectory can be related not only to what humans have done to nature, but also to what we are doing to each other. The unjustified extremes of poverty and affluence, the exploitation and oppression of one group by another, the brutal conflicts which rage in many corners of the world, are attributed to a distorted pattern of development which puts power and profit before ethics and the general welfare. And so the 'emancipatory impulse' is linked to various struggles to oppose injustice and to defend the vulnerable against oppression. The plight of the poor, of people in developing countries, of women, of working people, of pensioners, of indigenous peoples, and of many others can be presented as further indictments of the existing system. In some cases even producer groups – such as farmers, fishermen, and loggers (who are directly responsible for environmentally destructive behaviour), can be presented as victims of a system which offers them little alternative. Emancipation for each constituency can be seen as congruent with the overall objective of dismantling modern industrialism in favour of an environment-friendly, people-friendly, 'green' society.

An idea like that of 'appropriate scale' which plays an important role in green argument also relates to these four elements. Most obviously, scale engages with limits – for a limit is a boundary beyond which rules that hold at one scale no longer apply. If the scale of disruption to a given ecosystem passes certain limits, the system will collapse; if the scale of the human economy trespasses beyond environmental limits, the result will be catastrophe. But scale also relates to natural values: for nature can be taken to 'suggest' appropriate scales for many activities. Communities should be grounded in ecological scales, and natural features and processes (mountains, river catchments, and so on) may suggest suitable political boundaries. The pathological development trajectory has led us toward a cult of the 'mega' and the 'global', while institutions based in the local scales (where humans function most comfortably) are being undermined. Emancipation therefore depends upon rescaling the human world, in harmony with natural and human need.

Analytical controversies

To develop this account I would like briefly to turn to four issues which have troubled students of the green perspective: first, determining the point at which it gelled into an independent ideological approach; second, understanding how greens relate to the traditional left/right political continuum; third, assessing the place of the environmental critique within the green world-view; and fourth considering diversity within the family of green approaches.

Although it is possible to trace back to antiquity ideas or dispositions associated with today's green thinkers (such as reverence for nature, concern for the welfare of animals, voluntary simplicity and so on), it is generally accepted that as a coherent alternative the green perspective is a comparatively modern creation. Two views predominate in the literature: one locates the origins of a current which is typically referred to as 'political ecology' in the late nineteenth and early twentieth centuries; the other associates the genesis of green perspectives with the turbulent decade of the 1970s.

The first approach emphasizes philosophical foundations: that 'ecologism' emerged in the last third of the nineteenth century, as part of the intellectual response to the Darwinian challenge to traditional belief. It combined scientific, evolutionary and materialist ideas with organicist, holistic, naturalistic and vitalist cosmologies which invested nature with deep spiritual meaning.[4] The dualism between man and nature (and between the sciences of man and the sciences of nature) was overcome as humans acquired a place within nature, and both were understood to be subject to the same evolutionary process. Faith in traditional religion was displaced by a veneration of nature and the natural. 'Holistic biology', and the ideas of 'energy economists' preoccupied with resource scarcities, helped focus a diffuse unease with the modern world and a longing for a simpler rural existence.[5] The names of thinkers such as Peter Kropotkin, Ernst Haeckel (who coined the word 'ecology'), Konrad Lorenz, Patrick Geddes, Lewis Mumford, and Frederick Snoddy feature in this sort of account. From nineteenth-century beginnings ecological thought is seen to ramify through the twentieth century, its exponents linked to currents as diverse as the 'Back To The Land' campaigns, town planning, the scouts, and organic farming. Particularly during the 1920s and 1930s there was a strong link with conservative, nationalist, and fascist movements. On this reading, late-twentieth-century green perspectives appear as the most recent incarnation of ideas that have been with us for at least a century.

Although this approach casts some light on connections among diverse eddies of nineteenth- and twentieth-century belief, it contributes little to an understanding of the greens as a political phenomenon. Despite a welter of historical detail, the absence of attention to the specific contexts within which ideas emerged, and to the articulation of these ideas within the visions of individual thinkers and movements, means that this approach remains profoundly ahistorical. Similar organicist or evolutionary vocabularies, shared metaphysical assumptions, and endorsement of similar projects or technologies are confused with evidence of substantive political ideological affiliation.

The alternative account sets politics at centre stage. It sees the 1970s as the formative moment when the green perspective coalesced as a new ideological current, which self-consciously proclaimed its distinct identity and demonstrated a capacity to organize independently. Ideologies are, after all, phenomena of the era of mass politics; they are not just theories, but ideational constructs bound to political practice. To borrow Freeden's idiom, they require not only creators but also consumers.[6] And the tension between ideas and political practice propels their evolution. It was during the 1970s that a host of new environmental (as opposed to conservationist) movements were born and the first green parties took shape. Political thinkers and publicists articulated a distinctive vision in parallel with such movements; and it was at this point that the label 'green' was appropriated to characterize the emergent perspective. This ideological creation was original, not because no one had suggested similar thoughts or advocated like causes before, but because here the ideas were drawn together – acquiring a political focus, critical mass, and practical embodiment – which gave birth to a new ideological tradition.

Much has been written about factors that explain the flowering of modern environmental consciousness during the 1960s and 1970s. Attention has been drawn to rapid technological and industrial development during the second half of the twentieth century which dramatically increased the scale of the human impact on the ecosphere. Changes in class and social structure leading to a 'post-industrial society', shifts in values and beliefs with the growth of 'post-material' concerns, and the transformation of risk profiles have been highlighted.[7] Whatever the relative weight accorded to such factors, it is clear that a radical change in the political salience of environmental issues did occur. This can be chronicled in media coverage and survey data;[8] but it was also manifest in significant institutional change: between the late sixties and the end of the 1970s new environmental agencies and ministries were established and new pollution-control laws were introduced by governments across the OECD states.[9] Environmental movements generated pressure for reform, but they also benefited enormously from this legitimization of environmental concern. Greens took as their starting point that the new administrative response to the environmental challenge was inadequate, that a more radical form of social reconstruction was necessary, and that the campaign for such a transformation should form the basis for a new political identity. But the consolidation of the green alternative was paradoxically dependent upon this simultaneous 'mainstreaming' of environmental concern. The green alternative emerged in an epoch when environmental worries had become part of the dominant social discourse.

Other political developments which conditioned the context for the emergence of the greens included the heritage of the 'counter-culture' and 'new left' protest movements of the 1960s, and the anti-nuclear and 'new social movement' campaigns of the 1970s. The oil price shocks and a period of high inflation and economic instability strengthened the perception of the vulnerability of the existing system to crisis. Public faith in big science, big business and big government had been weakened. And, among those inclined to be critical of the *status quo*, there was disillusionment with the orthodox Marxist and social democratic variants of the socialist project, and frustration with the rigidity of the East/West ideological fissure.

Consider the famous slogan 'think globally, act locally'. This notion is only fully intelligible in an era when the 'global' has already achieved mass cultural resonance: in an era of satellites and inter-continental ballistic missiles, of transnational corporations and live television feeds covering events around the world. Much the same can be said for another slogan which played a role in carving out the initial space for green parties: 'neither left nor right, but moving forward'. The idea of transcending established ideological opposition is not new, but it achieved a particular bearing towards the close of a century during which national and international politics had been marked by a continuing left/right fissure. And it served to define a particular political space which could not have been marked out in that way in the 1940s, 1950s or 1960s.

This points to another important conundrum: the left/right orientation of green politics. Although some greens continue to insist that their political perspective cannot be located on the left/right continuum, most observers (and many greens) now agree that the centre of gravity of contemporary green politics is actually towards the left. Greens tend to support the cause of disadvantaged social groups, and advocate greater social equity. They criticize the existing distribution of economic and political power and advocate grassroots participation. Of course, this identification is far from complete: there are some greens with more traditionalist orientations; many greens support specific policies generally associated with the right (stringent controls on immigration, for example); and the caution which all greens display when it comes to disturbing nature and embracing new technologies (and associated patterns of life) gives their perspective a somewhat conservative tenor which is alien to the confident rationalism which long characterized the left. And yet, for the most part, greens find themselves allied with left-of-centre political formations and advocating policies that historically have had more appeal on the left.

This 'left bias' of green politics is hardly accidental, and it seems likely to continue for the foreseeable future. Its grounding is intellectual and practical. The modern green movement drew its ideas and activists primarily from oppositional movements of the left. At the time the perspective 'gelled' into a distinctive political current, resistance to established economic and political practices came largely from the left. The historical project of the extreme right was discredited in the eyes of the generation which gave birth to the greens, and the conservative projects for restructuring the regulatory/welfare state which were beginning to take shape offered little appeal. Moreover, the forces which greens continue to see arrayed against them – especially the powerful economic interests (the agro-industrial, construction, transport and military complexes) whose existence is predicated on the continuing pillage of nature and the perpetuation of social inequality – are more closely associated with the right. The greens want change, change which will inevitably disturb existing rights and entitlements and established distributions of power. In the context of the current disposition of political and ideological forces, the left seems more sympathetic to this project than do conservative parties. To put this another way, environmental issues are quintessentially distributional issues, and this establishes a certain affinity with the left. This is not to say that green parties might not find themselves in coalition with conservatives, or that some greens might not tilt in a rightward direction, but it is to argue that the centre of gravity of green perspectives is likely to remain on the left for the foreseeable future.

Also problematic is the inter-relation between the environmental and political values embodied in the green creed. Broadly speaking, green philosophers and political theorists emphasize the primacy of the ecological element – that this is the core of green thought, the central impulse from which attitudes to other issues (naturally) flow.[10] In contrast, green politicians and activists often present a more polyvalent account, where social justice and equality, democracy and participation, women's emancipation and opposition to militarism bulk large. No doubt a professional bias comes into play here, as theorists strive for foundational rigour and logical consistency, while politicians are more conscious of rallying diverse constituencies to the cause. Yet an underlying tension does seem to be operative: for if the environmental strand is accorded the role of prime mover, what is the status of the political conclusions that are held to follow? And if the environment is reduced to just one issue among many, how can the green perspective avoid being reduced to an eclectic mishmash of oppositional postures?

One approach to this issue is represented by Robert Goodin who proposed a reconstruction of green theory based around a 'green theory of value'.[11] He suggests that at the core of every ideology is a theory of the good which defines the moral vision which gives the perspective coherence. Goodin argues that greens should give pride of place to their value theory – which, roughly speaking, holds that things are valuable in proportion to their 'naturalness', and that the presence of a world beyond the human-made allows individuals to set their lives in a wider context. Green views on other issues, particularly 'agency' (including attitudes to democracy, decentralization, participation, and so on), and lifestyle change, should be rigorously subordinated to their theory of value. In this way, greens will remain focused on their core environmental concern, avoid distractions which might deter potential supporters, and expose the incoherence of attempts by other parties to co-opt elements of the green programme.

Goodin's account functions as both a description of green theory (what greens would believe if they were entirely consistent with the logic of their own principles) and as an explicit attempt to recast the ideology into a more potent configuration. On the first count, the problem is that the vast majority of greens would not recognize themselves in Goodin's portrayal. Setting aside the contentious presentation of 'the green theory of value', his understanding of the relationship between environmental and political elements in the green programme would not go down well. For example, Goodin adopts an essentially instrumental approach to democracy, emphasizing a means/ends distinction. He explains, 'to advocate democracy is to advocate procedures, to advocate environmentalism is to advocate substantive outcomes'; and he asks 'what guarantee can we have that the former procedures will yield the latter sorts of outcomes?'.[12] In contrast, most greens do not approach politics in this way. They consider democracy and participation as foundational political values; and much the same could be said for decentralization and egalitarianism. These are judged to be important not only because they secure a specified environmental outcome, but also because they represent the right way for humans to live. In other words they are important in their own right, and help to secure other instrumental, essential and expressivist values. Even if one could show that in a specific situation democracy or participation would lead to unfavourable environmental outcomes, the faith of most greens in these values would remain unshaken. For they are convinced that if people had an appropriate value set, and a suitable institutional context, then democracy *would* work, and correct (environmentally sensitive) decisions *would* be forthcoming.

On the second count (strengthening the green case), Goodin thinks that the potency of an ideology depends upon its articulation of a unique value theory, and the building of tight logical links between this moral principle and a political programme. In fact, ideologies have complex cores: liberalism is associated not just with liberty, but with equality and rationality, and each of these may be interpreted and inter-related in diverse ways in different liberal variants. Links between moral perspectives and policy prescriptions are typically loose, multiple and historically – as much as logically – determined. Indeed, the capacity of an ideology to survive changing intellectual fashions and political circumstances is directly related to its internal complexity, and the plurality of sources from which it can draw. In the evolution of ideologies, ambiguity and redundancy may defeat parsimony and faultless logic. Thus, far from strengthening the green edifice, Goodin's reduction of its foundation to a single moral pillar could render the green tradition more vulnerable to assault.

A very different way of understanding the unity of green ideology has been proposed by Gayil Talshir.[13] Surveying different approaches to the greens, she rejects the suggestions that greens have no ideology, that green thought is just a neo-Marxist variant, that it should be considered a 'new politics' ideology, or that it constitutes an 'ecological' or 'environmental' ideology. Like Freeden and many other analysts, Talshir insists that concern with nature cannot in and of itself found a coherent political world-view. The environment represents a complex of problems, not a political solution. But while Freeden[14] links this with a suggestion that green ideology has an undeveloped core, Talshir takes it as evidence of the free-standing significance to greens of the political values they typically articulate. She insists 'toleration, stability, democracy, equality, tradition and feminism . . . are independent core concepts of an emerging green ideology, not derivable from ecological perceptions'.[15] But Talshir also argues that the greens are peculiar in the extent to which different perspectives – which develop their critiques of the growth economy and of the uni-dimensionality of contemporary society on different terrains – exist within a single ideological formation. She argues that while 'ecologism' is a family of ideologies, it is but one ideological family 'coexisting within the group known as "Green Ideology" together with a family of feminisms, a range of minority-rights organizations and varied radical conceptions'.[16]

Talshir's emphasis on the independent grounding of important green political values and on the multi-dimensional character of the green critique is perceptive, but we do not necessarily need to postulate a new type of 'modular' ideology to account for the diverse perspectives present within parties such as the German Greens. Considerable ideological diversity, hybridization and tension are typically manifest in political parties of most ideological complexions; but differences of vision and emphasis co-exist with a certain perception of shared identity and common purpose. Different sorts of conservatism have, for example, always co-existed within the British Conservative Party, although such diversity has not always been celebrated by the party leadership. There are greens who emphasize feminism or anti-militarism, but if their political perspective is to be designated 'green', as opposed to simply feminist or anti-militarist, it is because there is substantial affinity with the perspectives of other greens, both within and without the ranks of a given party.

To return to the more general issue of the role the environmental critique plays in green ideology, it is most accurate to regard it not as the sole animating impulse, but rather as an ineliminable denominator. In other words, a perspective which did not place environmental protection and the revaluation of nature at the core of its political concerns would not qualify as 'green'. In contrast, one which failed to cite grassroots democracy (or decentralization, or egalitarianism, or feminism, or anti-militarism) as a core political concern would not necessarily be 'ruled out' in the same way. Indeed, an approach might have virtually nothing to say about any one of these elements and still reasonably be considered 'green'. And yet a perspective which did not include *any* of these elements among its core values would also not properly be termed 'green'. It is not that this cluster of concepts is logically entailed by environmental concern, but that historically and practically they have become associated with the political perspective we term 'green'. In other words, the ecological component of green thought is 'special', not in the sense that it logically determines the physiognomy of the creed, but because without it the ideological manifestation in question would not be recognizable as green.

Finally, there is the problem of the range of perspectives manifest within the green ideological family. It is conventional to approach this diversity in terms of basic dichotomies, between 'dark' and 'light' green views, between 'radical' and 'reformist' greens, between 'deep' and 'shallow' ecology, between 'fundamentalism' and 'realism', between 'ecocentrism' and 'anthropocentrism', and between 'ecologism' and 'environmentalism'. As discussion in the literature has established, however, these terms capture different (though partially overlapping) oppositions which are of varied importance for characterizing different green currents. Most of the terms have their origins in efforts by one segment of the green movement to differentiate its positions from those of its rivals; but no single opposition does more than hint at the complexity of contending currents. For instance, the 'ecocentrism' versus 'anthropocentrism' polarity which Robyn Eckersley posits as the fundamental divide in her valuable work on green political theory[17] is primarily a philosophical and ethical distinction; it is not necessarily useful for teasing out political divisions, the more so since (as Dobson[18] and others have noted) in their public pronouncements most greens emphasize instrumental arguments for environmental protection. The 'fundamentalist' versus 'realist' fissure is more explicitly political, relating to the extent to which greens should adopt conventional political forms in order to advance their agenda through electoral politics; but it relates only loosely to other divisions. Dobson's emphasis on 'ecologism' versus 'environmentalism' turns on the extent to which a perspective advocates a *radical* break with the 'existing mode of social and political life'. Indeed, for Dobson 'environmentalism' (although qualifying for inclusion in a discussion of 'green political thinking') is not actually part of green *ideology*, because it lacks substantive content, can be reconciled with other existing ideological perspectives (you can have liberal environmentalists), and advocates a 'managerial approach to environmental problems secure in the belief that they can be solved without fundamental changes in present values or patterns of production and consumption'.[19] This, of course, takes us back to our earlier discussion of what makes green perspectives 'green'; and the problem is that Dobson emphasizes the degree of hoped-for change, rather than the definition of political allegiance in terms of green identity. But 'degree of radicalness' is hard to specify: on some readings OECD governments already go beyond Dobson's 'environmentalism' (for they explicitly state that value changes and major shifts to patterns of production and consumption are required to address the environmental challenge); while leaders of some European green parties would fail to qualify as 'ecologists' for they do not embrace the 'ecocentric', 'holistic' values Dobson associates with true 'ecologism'.

Green views vary on more than one dimension, and divisions which appear acute from the position of someone outside the movement may not be those perceived as most significant to those within the movement. As a start, one needs to distinguish variation on three terrains: one related to valuation of the natural world (which entities deserve moral consideration? for what sorts of reason?); one related to the critique of existing social institutions (what are the sources of the current crisis? what kinds of institutions should replace today's flawed structures?); and one related to the strategy for generating change (what organizations and actions are most likely to effect change?). And on each of these terrains variation is multi-dimensional.

A future for the greens?

During the brief span of their existence greens have had some influence on political life in industrialized states. In some countries green parties have scored considerable electoral success, and (usually in coalition with other political forces) have participated in local, regional or national governments. More generally, the greens have articulated a perspective to which established political currents have had to respond. Certainly the green message is reaching a larger audience than ever before.

Four developments stand out in particular. First there is the geographic spread of the movement. Green politics has now gained adherents across the developed world, and in Europe during the 1990s green parties increasingly appeared in countries to the south and east. Where such parties have not been established, or have proved electorally unsuccessful, there has nevertheless been a growth in groups which identify with the green project. Even in the United States the green presence has expanded locally and, whatever else it achieved, Ralph Nader's presidential campaign raised the movement's profile nationally. Second, there has been a marked strengthening of the institutional supports for green advocacy. Ideologies require a material infrastructure; they need resources and organization if they are to prosper and survive. Labour unions traditionally provided an under-girding for socialist movements, and in the late twentieth century, liberalism relied on bases within the academy when the electoral fortunes of parties bearing the liberal name declined. For the greens, the increased strength of green parties and movements (which in many European countries receive state funding) are of obvious significance. But so, too, is the growth of a 'green civil society' – networks of co-operatives, professionals, and businesses associated with environmental and other green themes. Third, there is now a more widespread and complex interaction between green advocates and established power structures. Most obviously greens have been elected to political office and occupied posts in government; but more generally green movements have worked more closely with government officials and agencies, with business leaders and organizations. Rather than just protesting from 'the outside', environmental groups and green politicians have sometimes engaged in a more positive politics of co-operation to design practical solutions to immediate problems. This is not to say that green activists have been welcomed into chancelleries and board rooms. It is to suggest that some greens have moved in from the fringe. While there are analysts who see this as a sign of weakness and co-optation, on balance it appears to represent a widening of green influence. Finally, there has been a modest increase in the theoretical sophistication of green argument. Typically, green perspectives have been contrasted unfavourably with the theoretical depth of traditions such as liberalism or feminism. Of course, theoretical sophistication is not everything; but it can provide an intellectual foundation and resources to revitalize an ideology. Over the past two decades green philosophical perspectives have developed markedly, and in terms of political theory there have been interesting discussions of green democracy, sustainable development, justice and the environment, and of the structure of green thought more generally.[20]

In terms of the various strands of the movement, it is the reform-oriented, 'mainstream' greens – who have focused on greening existing institutions and accepted the norms of current political competition – who have developed the largest following. In electoral terms, the more fundamentalist 'anti-party party' orientations have proven self-defeating; while groups which made much of their ecocentric purity have also failed to find favour with voters. Greens active in the major campaign organizations (environmental non-governmental organizations, ENGOs) can take some comfort from the fact that on specific issues (animal welfare, genetically-modified foods, and so on) public consciousness has been raised. Away from the mainstream, there has been a continuous 'bubbling up' of protest groups and direct action networks, whose existence has been facilitated by the mobile phone and the Internet. But whether the work of either current has advanced the overall project of green social transformation remains unclear. The daring social visions of the more radical green theorists – those who call for the utter remaking of the world as we know it – have provided inspiration to many activists, and have kept alive a tradition of imagining alternative futures. But their relative disconnection from existing patterns of economics and politics, and their lack of substantive engagement with the vast body of theoretical findings and accumulated practical experience which casts doubt on the viability of small-scale, communistic and anarchistic social projects, means that the current political salience of their approaches is strictly limited. Indeed it is unclear whether, in the longer term, currents such as eco-communalism, bio-regionalism or eco-feminism will remain more than intellectual curiosities.

More generally, greens of all persuasions have grounds to be anxious about the future. At the dawn of the twenty-first century political and economic trends are running strongly against the greens. Despite endless governmental initiatives, the really big environmental issues such as global warming and biodiversity loss are hardly being addressed. 'Globalization' not localization is the order of the day. The pace of technological development (particularly in the life sciences) appears to be accelerating. And economic worries, re-emergent nationalisms and international tensions routinely eclipse the sorts of issues green wish to promote. If greens are content to do no more than articulate a continuously evolving social critique, then all may be well – for there is nothing more appealing than a clear target. But if they actually want to change the course of social development then current trends must be worrying; for the prevailing development model is spreading to every corner of the globe, economies and polities are being bound ever more tightly together, and with each year that goes by there is less 'nature' that remains to preserve. Now greens may hope that the excesses of the current orientation (the social, economic and environmental impacts of unbridled free trade, the indecent rush to cash in on genetic manipulation, and so on) will lead to crisis and backlash. But even if this proves to be the case, it is unclear that the greens would be the main political beneficiaries.

Underlying this is the issue of how broad an audience greens can hope to attract. Support for green currents varies across the developed world, but in some countries they have obtained up to 10% of the votes in national elections. Although there is wider public sympathy for the green stand on particular issues (opposition to genetically-modified foods or nuclear power, for example), the proportion of electors who buy into the project as a whole remains small. And while some may be content to see the greens as a junior coalition partner – upholding certain values and keeping an eye on the dominant parties – few would be prepared to trust their economic and political future entirely to the greens. And this is in the countries where they have been most successful. Elsewhere the greens remain more marginal, and nowhere is this more true than in developing countries. Indeed, the failure of greens to develop ideological variants which address the concerns of the three-quarters of the human population living in the poorer regions of the globe must count as a signal weakness of the movement. If the green project is to have coherence, it cannot remain as a luxury with appeal only to those who enjoy the rich fruits of industrialism.

Green ideology provides a multi-stranded critique of contemporary social practices and a promise that things need not be as they are. While the critique is detailed and concrete, the images of the alternative future lack precision or are often implausible. They posit either too facile a reconciliation of all good things, or too draconian a rupture with existing patterns of life. To some extent this problem is faced by any ideology radically at odds with the existing pattern of societal organization: the social critique gains purchase in the world of the here and now, but the social vision depends upon conjuring up a future that just might be.

A more serious weakness in the structure of existing green variants relates to the absence of convincing accounts which bridge the gap between the (rejected) present and the desired (but indistinct) future. In other words, they lack adequate theories of directed social change. Too often greens do not advance beyond the aspirational level, their vision running something like this: 'we know what we don't like about contemporary society, and when we convince people of the validity of our perspective (by running election campaigns, distributing leaflets, confronting polluters, and so on) we will implement the green agenda'. Despite complaints about corporate power and state bureaucracy, scant attention has been paid to examining the structural possibilities for radical change. The point is not to elaborate a grand theory of 'green social agency', but to suggest concrete pathways through which change can be achieved over short-, medium- and longer-term horizons. More adequate green theories of social change would need to engage with issues such as the material and ideational factors that support existing social practices, the potentialities and limits of 'social steering', and priorities, stages and potential alliances. Take the ecological issue: greens need to establish which practices are most pernicious, which social forces are most deeply attached to such practices, how such attachments can be weakened, and what sorts of political alliances might isolate die-hards. The idea of 'gate-key' reforms is also important – initiating processes which open the path to further change, rather than stimulating countervailing forces which preclude further advance.

In a closely related vein, greens could do with more sophisticated accounts of the state. So far green views are largely parasitic on established social democratic, anarchist and Marxist theories, and have only begun to consider the potential (and limits) of the state's role in a green society. Moreover, states stand at the juncture between the local politics which greens so enthusiastically endorse, and the transnational politics which appears necessary to mediate an international response to global problems.

Another difficulty lies in the green response to scientific and technological innovation. Although greens criticize the scientific and technological establishment and the hegemony of instrumental reason, they are not necessarily technophobes. Greens often invoke new scientific findings to challenge official claims, and they readily embrace certain types of technology (renewable energy, for example) – particularly when this appears compatible with 'sustainable' living and local control. Yet greens systematically reject 'technicist' solutions – proposals that appear to offer a technological way out of the contemporary environmental dilemma. For greens, social and lifestyle change remains essential. Moreover, there are many within their ranks who are happy to tap into emotive and anti-rationalist impulses, and the widespread fear of change in general, to gather public support for green campaigns. But does all this amount to a viable approach to the ceaseless rhythm of technological advance?

Like other political forces, greens are presented with a constant stream of technological innovation and potentialities, championed by powerful economic actors, to which they must react. But for the greens this is no peripheral issue, and responding to such developments (other than as 'nay-sayers', sitting on the sidelines) represents a real challenge. For example, environmental campaigners have had some success in stimulating public resistance to genetically-modified (GM) foods: they have exposed the commercial lobbies behind the drive to introduce GM technology, shown up conflicts of interest (where those who stand to gain from the new processes serve on the government safety panels), and revealed significant flaws in existing regulatory frameworks. Proposals for labelling GM foods have found widespread support, but (as reports of cross contamination of GM and non-GM seed confirm) it is already too late to prevent environmental impacts arising from this technology. The threshold for the rapid development of genetic manipulation (including conscious manipulation of the human genome) has already been breached, and the point at which 'blanket bans' might have been viable has long passed. In the next century the economic, social, political and military consequences of this technology will be enormous – certainly it has the potential to bring more positive, but also more negative, consequences (both deliberate and unintended) than we can imagine today. But what sort of response can the greens deploy? The simplest position is to reject such meddling with nature out of hand; but to stick to such a position may be to condemn one's perspective to irrelevance, as the technology penetrates daily living and transforms the natural and social world. Or will greens suggest a more nuanced view, in the hope of influencing the conditions under which the emergent technology is absorbed? Similar sorts of dilemma face greens in relation to other technologies and other problems, such as climate change politics.

Accelerating international economic and political integration – 'globalization' – poses yet another difficulty for greens. Again, they are not alone, for issues relating to free trade and international governance have regularly perturbed established ideological traditions for more than a century and a half. But the green preference for local action and their focus on environmental consequences introduce new elements into the controversy. Again, it is far from clear what response – other than carping from the sidelines and wishing for another world – the greens can deploy.

Looking forward to the politics of this new century, it seems likely that environmental issues will occupy an increasingly important role in political deliberation and conflict. Further growth in the rich countries, continued industrialization in the poorer regions of the globe, and the intensive deployment of exotic technologies (particularly in the bio-sciences) will aggravate existing environmental burdens and generate new problems. In principle this should provide fertile ground for the further development of the greens: after all this is a perspective which has set the human/nature interaction at the core of its concerns. Certainly there will be no shortage of ethical and political dilemmas to pre-occupy green theorists; and the more practically engaged elements of the movement are unlikely to experience difficulties identifying targets for their campaigns. Reformist greens will provoke some adjustment in the behaviour of dominant political and economic actors; and their more radical brethren will continue to float dreams of alternative futures, suggesting ideas no respectable politician would dare to voice. As a whole, the green movement will maintain a standing critique of the environmental and human consequences of the path being marked out by the advance of our civilization. Yet whether the greens will be able to do more than act as permanent critics, mounting a forlorn rearguard action, remains an open question.

Notes and references

1 For representative contributions consider: R. Bahro, *Building the Green Movement*, London, Heretic, 1986; H. Wiesenthal, *Realism in Green Politics: Social Movements and Ecological Reform in Germany*, New York, St Martin's Press, 1993; J. Porritt, *Seeing Green: The Politics of Ecology Explained*, Oxford, Blackwell, 1984; P. Kemp and D. Wall, *A Green Manifesto for the 1990s*, London, Penguin Books, 1990; L. Johnson, *A Morally Deep World*, Cambridge, Cambridge University Press, 1991; and L. Martell, *Ecology and Society*, Cambridge, Polity Press, 1994.

2 On 'social ecology' see M. Bookchin, *The Philosophy of Deep Ecology: Essays on Dialectical Naturalism*, Montreal, Black Rose, 1990; on 'eco-socialism' consider D. Pepper, *Eco-Socialism: From Deep Ecology to Social Justice*, London, Routledge, 1993; on 'bioregionalism' see K. Sale, 'Bioregionalism: a new way to treat the land', *The Ecologist*, 1984, Vol. 14, pp. 167–73; on 'eco-feminism' consider A. Collard and J. Contrucci, *Rape of the Wild*, London, The Women's Press, 1988; on 'deep ecology' see A. Naess, 'The shallow and the deep, long-range ecology movement: a summary', *Inquiry*, 1973, Vol. 16, pp. 95–100.

3 For varied accounts of green ideology see: J. Barry, 'The limits of the shallow and the deep: green politics, philosophy and praxis', *Environmental Politics*, 1994, Vol. 3, pp. 369–94; B. Baxter, *Ecologism*, Edinburgh, Edinburgh University Press, 1999; M. Clark, 'Environmentalism', in R. Bellamy (ed.), *Theories and Concepts of Politics*, Manchester, Manchester University Press, 1993; M. Kenny, 'Ecologism', in E. Eccleshall, V. Geoghegan, R. Jay, M. Kenny, Ian MacKenzie and R. Wilford (eds), *Political Ideologies*, London and New York, Routledge, second edition, 1994; M. Smith, *Ecologism: Towards Ecological Citizenship*, Buckingham, Open University Press, 1999; Y. Stavrakakis, 'Green ideology: a discursive reading', *Journal of Political Ideologies*, 1997, Vol. 2, pp. 259–79; M. Wissenburg, 'A taxonomy of green ideas', *Journal of Political Ideologies*, 1997, Vol. 2, pp. 29–50; S. Young, 'The different dimensions of green politics', *Environmental Politics*, 1992, Vol. 1, pp. 9–44.

4 The classic statement of this approach is to be found in A. Bramwell, *Ecology in the Twentieth Century: A History*, New Haven CT and London, Yale University Press, 1989. For a more nuanced account consider A. Vincent, 'The character of ecology', *Environmental Politics*, 1993, Vol. 2, pp. 248–76.

5 Bramwell, *Ecology in the Twentieth Century*.

6 M. Freeden, *Ideologies and Political Theory: A Conceptual Approach*, Oxford, Clarendon Press, 1996.

7 See, for example: D. Bell, *The Coming of Post-industrial Society*, New York, Basic Books, 1973; R. Ingelhart, *The Silent Revolution: Changing Values and Political Styles Among Western Publics*, Princeton NJ, Princeton University Press, 1977; U. Beck, *Ecological Politics in an Age of Risk*, translated by A. Weisz, Cambridge, Polity Press, 1995.

8 R. Dunlap, 'Public Opinion and Environmental Policy', in J. Lester (ed.), *Environmental Politics and Policy: Theories and Evidence*, second edition, Durham NC and London, Duke University Press, 1995.

9 M. Janicke and H. Weidner (eds), *National Environmental Policies*, Berlin, Springer, 1997; and K. Hanf and A. Jansen (eds), *Governance and Environment in Western Europe: Politics, Policy and Administration*, Harlow, Longman, 1998.

10 For example, R. Goodin, *Green Political Theory*, Cambridge, Polity Press, 1992; or A. Dobson, *Green Political Thought*, London, Routledge, second edition, 1995.

11 Goodin, *Green Political Theory*.

12 Ibid., p. 168.

13 G. Talshir, 'Modular ideology: the implications of green theory for a reconceptualization of "ideology"', *Journal of Political Ideologies*, 1998, Vol. 3, pp. 169–92.

14 Freeden, *Ideologies*, p. 545.

15 Talshir, 'Modular ideology', p. 182.

16 Ibid., p. 183.
17 R. Eckersley, *Environmentalism and Political Theory*, Albany NY, State University of New York Press, 1992.
18 Dobson, *Green Political Thought*.
19 Ibid., p. 1.
20 Consider, for example: B. Doherty and M. de Geus, *Democracy and Green Political Thought: Democracy, Rights and Citizenship*, London, Routledge, 1996; W. Lafferty and J. Meadowcroft, *Democracy and the Environment: Problems and Prospects*, Cheltenham, Edward Elgar, 1996; A. De-Shalit, *The Environment Between Theory and Practice*, Oxford, Oxford University Press, 2000; A. Dobson, *Justice and the Environment*, Oxford, Oxford University Press, 1998; D. Torgerson, *The Promise of Green Politics*, London, Duke University Press, 1999; J. Barry, *Rethinking Green Politics: Nature, Virtue and Progress*, London, Sage, 1999.

12 Conclusion

Ideology – balances and projections

Michael Freeden

Ideology and control

One of the most creative tensions in the assessment of ideologies over the past century has been that between their face-value study – an 'intentionalist' approach to ideologies as a narrative located in time and space, in which we are simply told what ideologies *want* to tell us – and a critical approach to ideologies, as telling us substantively more than they intend, or as raising issues that derive from the very act itself of telling a story. The seeds of doubt were laid by Marx, and more specifically by Engels, who believed that nothing of consequence could be imparted by a body of ideas that was a product of illusions generated by an alienated, dehumanized and partial material existence.[1] However, they threw out the baby of what was being said, while retaining the bath-water of how and why it was being said. That bath-water, cleansing though it was of previous platitudes, has by now been recycled rather too often. Ignoring the weight of such epistemological doubts, American behaviourists cemented the link between the study of ideologies and an account of what they voiced as a scholarly exercise in accurate description. This early- and mid-twentieth-century focus gave way to a re-emphasis on decoding ideologies and on their social construction, without many of the Marxist conclusions that could have followed. Diana Coole's chapter assists us in capturing that changed understanding. Feminism contributed to the new perspective by joining in the identification of the grand narrative as an organizing device rather than a representation of a reality. A different light could thus be shed on the nature of ideologies by presenting ideological families such as liberalism and socialism as a way of controlling narrative itself. Narrative became the dependent variable, one of the outputs of ideology, rather than the garb in which ideologies appeared. And because narratives were a noteworthy product of ideologies, the latter could be detached from the story they were telling. Feminism, often accused – together with other forms of postmodern thinking – of acts of intellectual vandalism committed on respectable overarching theories, was instead exposing (sometimes despite itself) the resourceful, malleable, pluralist nature of socio-political thought, yet still within the confines of a rationalist modernism. The discovery of ideational fragmentation turned out to be not a signal for the collapse of system and order but an affirmation of the microstructure and contingency of political thought. Once again, with this new knowledge at their disposal, human beings were offered the opportunity of being in control, rather than remaining the exploited subjects of an ideological strait-jacket from which escape was impossible. Rather than entailing a monotonous universality, rationality uncovered the differential tracing of order and purpose in word and deed.

Being in control over material conditions through the resurrection of human consciousness had of course been the early promise of Marxism. Contrast this with the Green aversion to control over nature and with its preaching of a biodiversity in which fragmentation is not a sign of social disintegration (or of the decline of interpretative paradigms that *assumed* the possibility of social cohesion) but a social policy indicative of an all-encompassing pluralism beyond even the imagination of liberals. Marxism, however, insisted on looking only at the macrostructure of ideology and in that sense removed the details of ideologies from serious examination. As Terrell Carver makes clear, the work ideology did for Marxism was to identify a social problematic, on both material and episte-mological levels, that required eradication in order for clear thinking and action to be possible. The concept of ideology was therefore negative not merely in applying a pejorative connotation to what it referred, but in its epistemological confidence in both the transitory and the contingent nature of ideology. In this dual-feature epistemology lies a crucial difference between – on the one hand – the post-Marxism that shares some affinities with postmodernism and with feminism, and – on the other hand – its Marxist ancestor. Post-Marxism has abandoned confidence in the *transience* of ideology, while retaining confidence in its *contingency*. In other words, ideology retains the spatial function of accounting for the world as a dissembled and segmented social construction, but has lost the temporal function of allowing for significant changes in how the world is accounted for. The result is a new impotence for one of the main conceptions of ideology. The radically transformative potential of ideology, forever associated with Marx's imperative against the detached interpretative role of philosophy, is abandoned. That abandonment arises out of a new epistemological despair based on the assurance that ideology screens an unfathomable abyss.[2] For post-Marxists, ideology conceals not truth or reality, but the strong probability, even certainty, that no conceptualizable social world is available to be represented in the first place. If that is the case, reality is unequivocally not amenable to radical, humanly-induced, change.

Fragments and forms

The resurgent anxiety concerning the nature of ideology contrasts both with the aura of crass yet unchallengeable political certitude exuded by totalitarian ideologies and with the quiet confidence in the fruits of considered argument, logic and moral certitude expressed by many mainstream political philosophers. As Coole observes, this kind of anxiety, with its collapse of world-views, has produced hesitancy about ideology's capacity to realize projects. But it has also invited greater experimentation with new forms, which may be assessed very differently. The new century is presented with globalism as a solution to the problem of fragmentation, and with multiculturalism as a disavowal of the problematic in the first place. One consequence is an urgent need to rethink the conceptual boundaries of the main ideological families themselves. Is globalism a new ideology, or is it no ideology at all but a narrower sub-set of ideas that fails to make the grade as a comprehensive system of political prescriptions? That both globalism and multiculturalism may find room under the umbrella of liberalism attests to the internal morphological flexibility of that belief system, a system in which sub-structures may occupy space without wreaking havoc on the complex overall structure. But it may also suggest that the ideological boundaries bequeathed by the twentieth century are themselves the product of an ideological view. For instance, as Donald Sassoon notes, class was not the major analytical category of socialism that it was made out to be by socialists and non-socialists alike. In other words, external perceptions of an ideology act as serious constraints on the options open to its supporters and on its possibilities of change and development.

The existence of hybrid ideologies then becomes one possibility – the location of late-twentieth-century libertarianism between liberalism and conservatism, with F.A. Hayek as a prime example of the genre,[3] comes again to mind. Ideologies not only overlap one another, but in many cases components of their conceptual repertory percolate into, or are deliberately adopted by, other ideologies. Certainly varieties of evolutionary socialism have assimilated features of liberalism as necessary though insufficient for attaining socialist ends.[4] Of course, the presence of identical features in different ideologies does not entail that those features do the same work in each ideology, or that their significance and interpretation is similar. Similar conceptual combinations and arguments may be central to one ideology and peripheral to another. At the same time, as is evident from both Gerald F. Gaus's and Sassoon's analyses, ideologies that perceive themselves to be in close ideational proximity tend to disparage each other. For example, as is well known in socialist discourse, socialists have often advanced a critical ideological portrayal of liberals as defending positions that liberalism has long abandoned. In turn, the detractors of socialism have created smoke-screens – such as an obsession with bureaucratic nationalization – that have alienated many variants of that ideology from the mainstream of progressive thinking of which, on closer inspection, they are an integral part.

Another kind of hybrid ideology, Christian democracy, is examined by Paolo Pombeni. It raises a further question of interest to students of ideology, namely, whether religious beliefs are ingredients of a political ideology. Here was a religious doctrine with heightened social concerns, whose promoters acted as a party-political organization would. The strength of Christian democracy – once an ideology of considerable force on the European mainland, and one that tends to be underestimated in accounts of centrist and left-of-centre ideologies – originally lay in the fluidity of its conceptual composition that cut across other ideological families in ways that both differentiated those families and pulled them together. Its subsequent failure as a political movement reminds us that the twentieth century is also a field of much ideological detritus. Ideological matter rarely dies out altogether, though, and more secular versions of Christian democracy took its place, once its mobilizing function of securing the construction of a new social order was no longer relevant.

Alternatively, new groupings such as welfarism redistribute the available ideological space. They cut across overbearing ideological families that have become inadequate categories in their inability to satisfy current comprehensions, that is to say newer re-readings, of the ideational and political achievements and failures of recent times. Welfarism, as a particular concatenation of understandings of human needs and health, of social rights, and mutual responsibilities, draws together portions of liberalism, socialism, social-democracy and even conservatism, while leaving out other important features of each of those traditional families.[5] Even before we need recourse to the spur of feminism in order to challenge the epistemological distinctions underlying political thinking as such, we should, more modestly perhaps, periodically examine the categories we have inherited from our ideological pasts and consider what a change of standpoint may accomplish. The twentieth century has in the past lent itself to categories of war and peace, of East and West, of dictatorship and democracy, of planning and markets. All these still retain considerable value, but they may have to share their space with other categorizations, the function of which is not to crowd out the earlier groupings, but to extend the multi-dimensionality of our political understanding. The fall of the Berlin wall has at the very least instigated such a re-categorization; but it may also have made us permanently suspicious – as Carver implies – of the fixity of traditional ideological categories. Lack of fixity is, however, far from tantamount to the end of ideology; it is the recognition that greater subtlety is necessary to tease ideologies out, and that the permutations they offer are boundless. All this furnishes proof of the continuing vitality of ideological conflict and variety in the face of assertions of a so-called 'post-ideological' age, a phrase that has replaced the 'end-of-ideology' as the mantra of sceptics, harmonizers, or anti-intellectuals.

Thoughts and emotions

Political theorists much prefer to discuss texts and utterances, inasmuch as ideas and rigour of argument are crucially verbal skills. For them, a study of language and logic in the form of conceptual maps, their provenance and structure, will always take precedence. Nonetheless, they will have to take on board that another aspect of twentieth-century ideologies has been an increasing resort to non-verbal imagery and iconography, whose communicability and instant impact have proved to be very effective.[6] No ideology has accomplished this more effectively than fascism. The very paucity of fascist argument will have contributed to the search for alternative means of communication, but so did two further factors. First, the need rapidly to appeal to popular support, outside the democratic process, bypassing the latter's constraints of time and education. Second, the growing appreciation of political passion both as a social-psychological need of group-behaviour in the public domain, and as a means of eliciting the backing of groups required to act in a manner that suspends political judgement. The study of ideology was now poised to distance itself from the philosophical analysis of theories of human nature and social purposes and to move instead into the cultural understanding of those texts, combined with a broader conception of the role of symbol in the consumption of political messages.[7] As Zeev Sternhell observes, although fascism was also an intellectual movement within some circles, it was a cultural force prior to becoming a political one; it was a revolt of feelings, instincts and primal forces; and it was, unusually, an ideology bereft of the active wooing of intellectuals. A different language had to be developed to register these timbres. The internal battles of fascism were fought, and temporarily won, in the films of Leni Riefenstahl and in the Nuremberg rallies as much as on the streets and through the death squads, nor has fascism produced any text that could remotely rival, in stature or in sophistication, the central works at the heart of other major ideologies.

Fascism also provides another lesson for students of ideology in general. Ideology has a salient emotional dimension precisely because it is a product and a manifestation of politics. Politics can never be reduced to a study of the good society or the rational elimination of conflict. It always and also includes the use of power and manipulation, the role of personality, the projection of a social imagination. That these can go badly out of control is acknowledged. Fascism, and many forms of nationalism, are not only arational but often deeply irrational in their failure to distinguish between myth or wishful thinking and reality, and in their abandonment of moderation and self-criticism. Unsurprisingly, there is considerable resistance to regarding emotion and imagination – in less extreme or repulsive forms – as normal features of ideologies. Hence the advent of fascism and nationalism both has been beneficial to the exploration of ideological thinking and – for another kind of emotional reason – has put students of ideology off the dispassionate examination of ideologies possessed of a large emotional content.

Failures and successes?

The fates of fascism and, to a lesser extent, communism invite speculation about the life-span of an ideology. Sternhell forcefully reminds us that deep historical analysis is necessary, not merely optional, in understanding current ideologies, and that many ideologies of the twentieth century had been maturing during the nineteenth. But some ripened and then declined with greater alacrity than others. The swift demise of fascism may lie in reasons diametrically opposed to its ascendance, namely, in the absence of serious intellectual reflection. That absence denied it enduring arguments that could survive contingencies and offer universal access. The survival power of ideologies lies either in their capture of political practices that exhibit stability across time or space – which is why some varieties of nationalism have proved more lasting – or in the production of texts that outgrow some of the purposes and intentions of their original formulators. Moreover, both fascism and communism lacked another important survival feature. They denied rival systems of thought even a limited right to plural existence. That set them on a collision course with other ideologies and made it virtually impossible for the totalitarian creeds to carve out an area in which they were sustainable in the long term. No wonder that extreme ideologies tend therefore to endure within pluralist political systems, though they then have to compete on the basis of their dubious merits and powers of persuasion. The mass politics that ensured the rise of doctrinaire-left and radical-right ideologies also secured their demise. Mill and Tocqueville already knew that the widening of the sphere of politics brought with it both danger and promise. Roger Griffin has observed that, in the West at least, mass ideologies were defeated after 1945. To that one must add that masses have learned to transform themselves into publics, with an emphasis not only on popular sovereignty but on a new-found diversity of social groups.

Is liberalism, then, the success story of the past century? Or has that once glorious ideology been dethroned, or cannibalized by its rivals? Gaus has rightly termed the twentieth century a surprisingly liberal one. How is it that an ideology low on symbolism and emotional potency has survived for so long in a century of extraordinary visual stimuli and manipulative messaging? And is liberalism still maturing, or are its days of glory in the past? And – as suggested above – which liberalism are we referring to: the one associated with a rampant, now global capitalism, or the one at the heart of the welfare state? One clue lies in Gaus's distinction between liberalism as a political philosophy and an ideology. As a political theory, he observes, liberalism is too severe and principled a doctrine to have wide political appeal. In other words, in that guise it focuses on a series of epistemological and conceptual issues, concerning agency, justice, subjectivity, and the nature of the self, which it disputes internally. But as a political ideology it has a range of aims concerning the primacy of individual liberty, autonomy, development and rationality, for the protection of which it preaches the constraint of power and the formation of enabling social and political institutions. With the exception of Marxism, no ideology has demonstrated such methodological bifurcation. This is not to be confused with a simple distinction between theory and practice; rather, there exist two conceptual approaches to liberalism that, despite considerable overlap, have produced dual bodies of political thought.

Towards the final third of the twentieth century, liberalism increasingly became, among political theorists, tantamount to the discursive site of Anglo-American political and moral philosophy. One way of putting this is to state the obvious to students of ideology but not to all philosophers, namely, that political philosophy itself occupies a domain of ideological decontestation, and that its philosophical disputes are also ideological ones. But the effect also pulled the other way. A high degree of intellectualization put liberalism outside the reach of ordinary citizens, yet it also accentuated some philosophical principles that combined modelling techniques with American interpretations of the nature of the political.

By transforming the precepts of liberalism into a quasi-universal theory of rule-bound justice, an ideal-type prescriptive approach to liberalism was combined with a preference for, first, a group- and community-averse autonomous individualism and, second, a faith in a fundamental constitutional fairness that could produce state neutrality. Alternatively, philosophical understandings of perfectionism rediscovered liberalism's irrevocable commitment to pluralist versions of the good life, but chose in 'perfectionism' a term that indicated an end-state. Canadian variants added the importance of groups, but restricted those groups in the main to cultural and ethnic ones, with a smattering of gender awareness. Social and economic groups, conversely, were perceived through traditional individualist spectacles that portrayed them as potentially illicit encumbrances on equality of access and opportunity. Remarkably, this philosophical version of liberalism spread across the Atlantic, while political liberalism in the US was on the decline internally and made little impact abroad. The power of American universities and publishing guaranteed export markets in universities, and indirectly in some arenas of high politics, across the Western world, even though the USA had been in the main a net importer of European liberal ideologies.

The diminished parallel resistance in Europe to that trend may be explained in a number of ways. First, the immense prestige of these variants of political philosophy has simply assimilated, if not monopolized, liberal intellectual argument, while many British and some continental philosophers have either gone with that flow or, especially on the continent, have developed professional interests in political theory nourished from outside the liberal tradition. Second, European liberalisms *qua* ideologies have failed to maintain the salient political identity from which liberalism benefited earlier in the twentieth century. In part, this is due to liberalism's success in penetrating both social democracy and moderate forms of conservatism in Western Europe. In part, it reflects a strong continental aversion to liberalism – as an ideology that manifestly failed to contain extremism in mid-century, or as an ideology that is still suffering from the aftermath of a vibrant Marxist and socialist critique that undermined its intellectual credibility. Because European intellectuals – France and Germany spring to mind – have maintained a high involvement in politics, the line between liberal philosophy and ideology is more blurred. The ostensible insignificance of liberalism has spilled over into a lack of interest in the Anglo-American focus on scholastic logical argument and its potential for universal rational appeal. Consequently European political philosophers, with a few notable exceptions such as Habermas, have not initiated an indigenous liberal debate.

The guises of liberal ideology

A broad overview of liberalism over the past century will however identify a series of features that differ markedly from the philosophical approach. The philosophical tendency has been towards social statics, attained through a quasi-legal conception of the right, through modelling devices that allow extra-social and extra-temporal individuals to emerge under veils of purported ignorance, and through the transcending of power relations. By contrast, liberal ideology was characterized by a profound belief in developmentalism and in its own vitality. Indeed, one of liberalism's strengths is to be found in conceptions of time and space, in the narrative it imparts and in the horizons it unfolds; a second lies in its moral and emotive appeal (a trait it bears in common with many other ideologies); and a third pertains to the flexibility of the ordering of its conceptual apparatus. The first feature was aptly acknowledged by L.T. Hobhouse, when he described liberalism as 'a movement of liberation, a clearance of obstructions . . . for the flow of free, vital, spontaneous activity'.[8] The evolutionary movement of liberalism was conceived by its intelligentsia as threefold: the development of individual faculties, the continuous progression of societies to increasing states of maturity, and the spatial expansion of liberalism across the globe, abetted by peace and free trade. This infectious nature of liberalism was carried by social feeling as much as by reason, and incorporated a plea to invest private energy in public co-operation, which in turn would provide private as well as social benefits. If philosophical liberalism aimed at converging on a fair set of procedures, liberalism as an ideology aimed at converging on a unified view of civilization and saw itself as the crowning achievement and expression of a civilized way of life. And if philosophical liberalism argued for an abstract universalism based on the given overlapping reasonableness of individuals seeking to moralize the political realm, liberalism as an ideology anticipated what might be termed a contingent, expanding universalism based on the attractive example of existing liberal societies and the growing persuasive force, both rational and emotional, of an already successful political order. In contrast, the distorted variant of universalism now in vogue, known as globalization, is no more than the capitalist shell of that drive to expansion, in which the qualitative civilizing force of liberalism, with all its blindness to some forms of social exclusion of women, non-white societies and the abjectly poor, is replaced with a reductive and quantitative economic individualism in which constitutional constraints are directed at maximizing a personal liberty that cashes out as entrepreneurship. The advent of that approach within the conservative New Right attests to its more comfortable classification as a form of conservatism, even though many of its themes feature in older versions of classical liberalism.[9]

A philosophical liberalism based on the chimera of state neutrality and on the premise of a foundational overlapping consensus, however, fails as a political doctrine that can be implemented. It offers an emaciated role to the state, one ill-suited to cope with the complexity of modern, and postmodern, politics – and it can only achieve that by politicizing the courts, that is, by shifting professedly impartial political decisions to another section of the polity. It cannot handle the inevitable zero-sum relationships between incompatible plural conceptions of the good, possibly even of the right, that cannot be settled privately but involve central policy decisions, such as those that arise out of clashing views on the sanctity of life, or on the linkage between politics and religion. As an ideology, however, liberalism is itself more usefully seen to contain non-negotiable beliefs – an ineliminable core – just as any other ideology, and it has to compete with other ideologies over the control of political language and political ends. The liberalism that succeeded in Britain for much of the twentieth century, and attempted to prevail in the US, was the one that adopted public welfare policies as a crucial complement to individual liberty. On the continent, for reasons mentioned above, it came in the guise of moderate social democracy or, as in France, solidarism, even if nominally unclaimed for the liberal cause. The decline of the welfare state allowed for the re-emergence of libertarian theories that became politically aligned to forms of conservatism. The tension identified by Gaus between philosophy and ideology has deposited on liberalism a set of burdens similar only to the one Marxism has experienced. The intellectual demands placed on both have required more consistency than either can deliver. But as political ideologies, neither can produce the formulations of best practice to which philosophers often aspire.

Yet although liberalism may no longer be doing very well in the realm of organized party politics, it has not quite lost its sting. Indeed, the inclusiveness and dominance of liberal ideology has been achieved, as Gaus argues, precisely because it has embraced inconsistencies. Put differently, an ideology – and this applies not only, but also, to liberalism – has to find a level of political language that can optimize its appeal, and a terminology that can gloss over inconsistencies through ambiguity. Non-totalitarian ideologies generally possess the capacity to assign to their key concepts more than one meaning. That feature is particularly noticeable in liberalism, for its internal morphological flexibility, or tolerance of multiple decontestations, allows for, say, diverse understandings of liberty to co-exist within its orbit. What Laclau has labelled equivalence[10] – the elision of the meaning of a concept as it journeys from word to word – performs a central obfuscating function, yet one that is necessary in order to address, as ideologies have to, large socio-political groups whose members will inevitably interpret, and want to interpret, the same phrases and ideas rather differently without breaking ideological ranks.

Times and spaces

The current wisdom among contemporary scholars is that ideology, in some of its recognized incarnations, is ubiquitous. That is to say, although not all political thinking is reducible to ideology, all prescriptive and interpretative political thinking has an ideological dimension. But how do ideologies themselves contemplate the conjecture of universality? Time and space are generally illuminating criteria by which to assess ideologies. For ideologies certainly are a device through which social time is organized. It is not only that the progressive ideologies of the past two hundred years have come up with plans for radical social change. The issue at hand revolves more generally around the ideological exploitation of time as a means of social control, deliberate or otherwise, through an enforced intimacy with a rewritten history and a projection of developmental trajectories. The control of time-as-narrative also contributes towards manufacturing the internal harmony that complex ideologies would otherwise lack. Moreover, the temporal dimension is fashioned in such a way that it offers optimal conditions for the realization of the central purposes of the ideology in question. Sassoon has astutely pointed out that for socialists, a view of history as culminating in a final but distant end-state was an important tactical move. Ideologies employ different methods for structuring time. It may be frozen, repetitive, accumulative, incremental, radically forward-looking, or imaginary (for which, broadly speaking, read, reactionary conservatism, traditionalism, enlightened conservatism, liberalism and social democracy, socialism, and utopianism). Every one of these solutions is crucial to the *political* domain, because politics concerns decision-making with consequences for public policy, and decisions always relate to the future. Marxism's dogmatism, for example, involved the rigorous controlling of time. This was initially to be accomplished through the attaining of epistemological truth underpinned by a revolution in the real material relations of production. Time as history would come to an end, though individual development would be unshackled. But in the distortions effected by the communist ideologies that acted in the name of Marxism, time was frozen through the imposition of worldly force on the meanings of words and ideas, undermining their essential plasticity. Liberalism was not, as some philosophers have it, perfectionist, but incorporated a theory of open-ended time, and this offered a range of futures that social democracy, as Sassoon notes, was also quick to adopt. Green ideology embraces an immediacy with respect to decision-making dictated by the urgency of environmental problems and the need for quick solutions. Long-term planning is not its *modus operandi*. While it is also in the forefront of theories concerning responsibility to future generations,[11] its conception of future time is unusually static, non-developmental and incapable of distinguishing between near and distant time. In other words, it disregards the possibility of a tapering temporal responsibility that would prioritize soon-to-be generations over remote ones, for similar reasons to those that cause societies to prioritize responsibility for those in immediate spatial proximity (the family or neighbourhood spring to mind) over the more distant in space. For an ideology that centres around natural processes, green preservationist impulses render it remarkably reluctant to factor in natural death and decay, of human beings and of ecosystems alike.

Then, as we have already seen, there is spatial universalism. Some ideologies, such as liberalism, socialism and communism, manifestly aspire to be adopted by all societies. But other ideologies make no direct claim for spatial or temporal universalism. Thus conservatism is not typically fired by a dynamic principle of change but by a recoil from uncontrollable change. It therefore forsakes one of the domains of politics – the transformative sphere. It retreats into specific space rather than aiming to inhabit general space. It has developed spontaneously but with little conscious connection between its various forms. Green ideology has a particular complex relationship to spatial universalism. It stipulates the absence of ecological boundaries and identifies a global ecosystem with profound effects on human societies. Yet it prefers on the whole to retreat into a localism based on sustainable communities; as James Meadowcroft puts it, to rescale the world according to natural values and needs. The response to the globalism of nature is to eschew human globalism as expressed in the slogan 'think globally, act locally'. The reasons for this lie mainly in a profound distrust of human initiative when harnessed to the industry and commerce that has been the staple of the economic activity of the modern world, a distrust incarnated in movements that have been termed post-materialist.

Nationalism, too, is not driven by an internal logic to a universalist stance, yet it may nonetheless signal a general solution to a specific political problem. As Andrew Vincent shows, nationalism exhibits the tension between universalism and particularism in another form. It is a particularist ideology that may either be reformist or conservative with reference to the extolling of the values, and desire for political independence, of a large social group claiming bonds of culture, language and territory. Historically, nationalism sought change as a response to issues of national and ethnic self-determination and, like the progressive ideologies of the time, was motivated by an active principle that created mutual inspiration and contagion. Its emergence on the European scene invoked a parallel though contingent universalism. Curiously, nationalism is now undergoing a dual process of reinvigoration and decline. While forms of internationalism and economic globalism threaten the nation-state and weaken its impact as a unit of political power, there are signs of cultural revolts against such forms of domination, often in the form of harnessing economic protest to active cultural and religious separatism.

As an ideology, nationalism is more blatantly linked to core political phenomena, such as the exercise of power in the shape of vigorous and focused persuasion, often physical force. It is here, as Vincent notes, that it may attain a deeper universalism in its functional role. But at the same time he characterizes it as theoretically naive. Indeed, nationalism is a narrow ideology, limited to periods of nation-building, the protection of national sovereignty or, in its extreme and unpalatable forms, the valorization of the nation in aggressive competition with others. It is hence better regarded as a 'thin-centred' ideology which does not contain the full or broad range of concepts and political positions normally to be found within the mainstream ideological families, but is parasitic on the host ideologies that harbour it, such as liberalism, conservatism or fascism.[12] The prevalence of a number of thin-centred ideologies is a feature of recent times, with feminism and green political thought displaying similar properties of dependence.

Modesty and maturity

The idea of thin-centred ideologies contends with post-Marxist views of ideological fragmentation. To begin with, it challenges the assumption of a post-ideological age that some post-Marxists have adopted, inviting us rather to descend from the Olympus of all-embracing *Weltanschauungen* and to recognize the less pretentious shapes in which ideologies appear. Its micro-structural focus contrasts with the traditional eschewal, by Marxists and post-Marxists alike, of the minutiae of ideological argument. These latter schools deem ideologies to be more important for what they do – producing a subjective social order masquerading as objective – than for what they are – cultural and logical decontestations of the political concepts they arrange, drawn from an indefinite pool of meanings those concepts can encompass. It also offers a clear notion of morphology, in which the unavoidable indeterminacy of the conceptual combinations that ideologies draw on is nevertheless configured into family resemblances of some duration.[13] That is to say, fragmentation – a term carrying a negative connotation – may equally be regarded as the normal multiplicity and pliability of essentially contested concepts that are drawn, for purposes of both interpreting the world and changing it, into specific patterns that become ideological families, sub-families, or, for that matter, mutants. Post-Marxism tends to regard such mosaics of form as far more plastic and short-lived, as less successful in creating a viable view of the social world, and as operating to a far greater degree at the level of unconscious and non-verbal solutions to problems of social disorder and individual identity. Given these new forms of ideological expression, perhaps the most significant distinction lies in diverging views on whether an ideology is always a *political* ideology, accessible through the analysis of its political concepts and views of society and public-policy formation; or whether an ideology is a broader amalgam of objects, symbols and identities.[14] The post-Marxist suspicion of paradigms challenges not only our understandings of social and individual reality but claims to reveal that 'reality' itself is shaky, fluid, and inconclusive, and held together only through discursive practices. Another effect of that understanding has been the drawing in of discourse analysis to the study of ideology.[15] Here patterns of ordinary conversation and speech are scrutinized for their ideological content, but this approach is inspired by behaviourism as much as by cultural and post-Marxist studies.

Must this then lead any educated observer of the multiple world of ideologies and sub-ideologies to an ineluctable relativism? Is this why moralists and philosophers need to reject the bland and indiscriminate casualness with which various ideologies manipulate human values in their entrenched temporal and spatial reserves? The choice, however, is not between moral absolutism – on many dimensions a frightening prospect in itself – and a moral relativism in which any ideological solution obtains validity, owing to the absence of an authoritative view from somewhere. Between the two lies an area of moral pluralism, an area where multiple moral positions, but not all, are legitimate. In parallel, major ideologies will create overlapping areas of rough consensus even while embracing sundry conceptual and value solutions to a range of human and social challenges, some of which escape the bounds of considered decency. Only an extreme moral relativism could be neutral among ideologies, social truths and ethical principles. Nevertheless, an interpretative leeway is itself part and parcel of a measured and critical morality. That leeway will be constrained through establishing some indisputable brute social facts, such as that torture and humiliation, suppression and silencing, corruption and discrimination, are all profoundly disturbing experiences for those who encounter them. But there are other, softer, facts – and even diverse tolerable responses to the hard ones – that do not allow unequivocal interpretations to be constructed on them and that justify and necessitate not only ideological pluralism but ideological experimentation and innovation.

The heart of the problem is that ideologists as political actors have the responsibility of producing good theory, as the raw matter they fabricate – in both senses of the word, occasionally – is deliberately designed to have impact at group, communal, state and international levels. That role of qualitative producers is one they share with moral philosophers, though not always to the satisfaction of the latter. The production of good theory is not, however, the task of *students* of ideology: here they part company with political philosophers. Ultimately, the investigation of ideologies has distinguished itself, as the contributions to this volume attest, by the need to put solid analysis before evaluation and judgement, the need to know what the contours of an ideological field are before expressing a view on our preferred position within or outside that field. Looking back on the past century, that development, and the emergence of scholars of ideology from under the life-giving yet occasionally smothering wing of political philosophers, have been significant signs of the maturity of the field of ideological studies. Not the least of these achievements has been a reconfiguration of the phenomenon of ideology, in its myriad forms, as an inventive and fertile form of political thought, and at the same time a typical and normal form.

Nature and transparency

There is yet another way of decoding ideologies which has been elided through the conventional distinction that separates theory and practice. But, as Robert Eccleshall observes, and as the study of conservatism teaches us, political practices themselves are decodable as constellations of ideological activity. Moreover, we may have to seek ideologies increasingly through visual sources which, although lacking in the relative precision language can provide, furnish symbols and representations of the ideas, preconceptions and aspirations that propel a society into this rather than that direction. The importance of political practices lies in their being a crystallization of norms, values and beliefs that recur over time and space; that is to say, a behavioural and institutional manifestation of a broader ideological complex of which the practices represent a part. Some ideologies are theory-averse. That is not to say that they have no conceptual apparatus. Far from it, they often possess intricate but unintended, even unconscious, patterns of thought, but their promoters prefer to interpret themselves as based on concrete experience, permitting existing human conduct to express itself through customs, rules and, as Oakeshott avowed, performances. Eccleshall sees conservatives as 'discreet decontestants', often resorting to words layered with multiple meanings for reasons of rhetoric or manipulation – incidentally, a feature evident also in totalitarian ideologies.

Eccleshall also importantly emphasizes the role of naturalism in conservative argument. In Plato's myth of the different metals that fashioned human beings, the Greek philosopher already knew something that ideologies ever since have been desperate to attain, namely, that whichever discourse colonizes the word 'natural' as its own is able to cast a cloak of non-transparency over its ideological assumptions and motives and to protect the existing order from criticism. Conservatism has always owed its greatest success to its epistemological claim to reflect reality in a 'self-evident' manner, to telling a story 'as it is'. True, Sternhell's analysis enables us to appreciate that fascism too was partially non-transparent in its reluctance to problematize economic relations, so that the transformation it called for was enshrined within a given capitalist ideology. Even philosophical liberalism has wrapped itself in an unassailable moral consensus, thus appearing as a super-ideology positioned beyond reasonable doubt. But for conservatism the plausibility of the present, emanating from an uncomplicated past, is bolstered by a universal fact of human socialization. If we are to accord proper weight to the findings of psychoanalysis, all human beings share the early political experience of being born into a world where their first perceptions of social relations involve hierarchy, authority and inequality. These conceptual cornerstones of mainstream conservative ideology constitute the ubiquitous first impressions of the conscious infant adjusting to the world of adults who tower over him or her, conveying instructions and pulling rank, however well-meaningly.

In that light progressive ideologies, such as liberalism or socialism, have the task of working against the grain, of re-socializing their members to a self-critical life in which opacity is occasionally exchanged for transparency, and in which what seems to be is not identical with what can be or even what is. The twentieth century has been saturated by ideological systems prepared to make the effort, take the risk, and persuade the state to undermine the traditional stabilities that have sustained it. Indeed, the presence of such conflict is an indicator of ideological health and a spur to constant ideational regeneration, while its absence may signal either atrophy or suppression. Of course, that alone is no guarantee of ideological triumph. In a pluralist world, and in a world where considered judgement and assessment are norms of public thinking, the justificatory function of ideologies is part of the process by which the decontestation and prioritizing of values takes place, whereas the legitimizing function of ideologies is part of their *successful* competition over the status of those decontestations. That is yet another reason why ideologies inhabit, and fuse, the ostensibly dual worlds of political theory and political practice. The test of ideologies has always been not merely in their intellectual and ideational persuasiveness, but in their efficiency in the cut-and-thrust of politics. Indeed, the fragmentation of many contemporary ideologies, as Griffin indicates, may contribute towards delegitimization and the lack of the directive power that ideologies require in their aspiration to capture the bastions of politics.

Durability and differentiation

The opportunities for understanding twenty-first century ideologies now open up. In future we may eschew some of the grand narratives in favour of ideologies that are more fragile, more subtle, but also far more elusive. One reason for that is that, in a world of open communication, the organizations that held ideologies together in a somewhat artificial amalgam – especially political parties – no longer exercise that dominant political role. The shrinkage of that function either mirrors a dissociation of parties from the production and implementation of exalted ideational blueprints, or the dissipation of the undemocratic monopoly of force that once imposed beliefs on populations. Combined with that, an under-standing of the unconscious, and historically contingent, formation of ideologies will necessarily play a greater role as their new fragility and fleetingness – itself partly a product of the increasing acceptance of human diversity, partly a product of the methodological pluralism evident in interpreting ideologies – renders them far less useful as mass-mobilizing forces offering alluring social visions.

The various chapters in this volume have also convincingly illustrated that the analysis of any one ideology cannot be contained within its imaginary bound-aries, but involves the consideration of patterns from other sustaining or reaction-provoking ideological groupings, as well as inter-ideological parallelisms and assimilation. We need to look more carefully at the product, rising above the artificial delimitations that are so frequently themselves the outcome of rash and unreliable ideological classifications. Furthermore, as the sources utilized by Griffin in his chapter demonstrate, the Internet is now providing outlets for the most slender, abstruse and eccentric variants within an ideological family. Never before did such variants extend out of the private domain, though they still are barely in a position to compete over public policy, and they far outstrip ideologies such as nationalism or conservatism in their particularistic provenance and narrowness. This new technology may have a profound effect not only on the formation of ideologies and their dissemination to centres of decision-making, but on the paradigms we use to identify, collate and organize them. Thin-centred ideologies may be here for a while, but even as we acknowledge their ephemerality, as do post-Marxists, we may want to examine them for what they tell us about ourselves and the political worlds we inhabit. It would of course be well to recall the capacity of societies to surprise themselves and us – their observers – and the (re-)emergence in future of an ideology in the grand-family format cannot be ruled out. But we now know two things that were obscured a century ago. First, the manifestations of ideologies are unavoidably multifarious and they may require detective work by their users and investigators alike. Second, underlying such disparities, the forms, functions and uses of ideology are identified yet again as permanent and pivotal ingredients of the political.

Notes and references

1 K. Marx and F. Engels, *The German Ideology*, edited by C.J. Arthur, London, Lawrence & Wishart, 1974.
2 See S. Žižek, 'Invisible ideology: political violence between fiction and fantasy', *Journal of Political Ideologies*, 1996, Vol. 1, pp. 15–32.
3 See especially F.A. Hayek, *The Constitution of Liberty*, London, Routledge & Kegan Paul, 1960.
4 See E. Bernstein, *The Preconditions of Socialism*, Cambridge, Cambridge University Press, 1993, pp. 147–59.

5 M. Freeden, 'The coming of the welfare state', in T. Ball and R. Bellamy (eds), *The Cambridge History of Twentieth-Century Political Thought*, Cambridge, Cambridge University Press, forthcoming.

6 See, for example, J. M. Balkin, *Cultural Software: A Theory of Ideology*, New Haven and London, Yale University Press, 1998, pp. 102–21.

7 See the path-breaking analysis of C. Geertz, 'Ideology as a cultural system', in D.A. Apter (ed.), *Ideology and Discontent*, New York, The Free Press, 1964, pp. 47–76.

8 L.T. Hobhouse, *Liberalism*, London, Williams & Norgate, 1911, p. 47.

9 Cf. A. Gamble, *The Free Economy and the Strong State*, London, Macmillan, 1988; K. Hoover and R. Plant, *Conservative Capitalism in Britain and the United States*, London, Routledge, 1989.

10 E. Laclau, 'The death and resurrection of the theory of ideology', *Journal of Political Ideologies*, 1996, Vol. 1, pp. 201–20.

11 See for example A. De-Shalit, *Why Posterity Matters: Environmental Policies and Future Generations*, London, Routledge, 1995.

12 See Chapter 1. 'Political ideologies in substance and method', pp. 10–11.

13 For a detailed exposition of this view see M. Freeden, *Ideologies and Political Theory: A Conceptual Approach*, Oxford, Clarendon Press, 1996.

14 For a lucid discussion of these differences, see A. Norval, 'The things we do with words – contemporary approaches to the analysis of ideology', *British Journal of Political Science*, 2000, Vol. 30, pp. 313–46.

15 See T.A. van Dijk, *Ideology: A Multidisciplinary Approach*, London, Sage, 1998.

Index